MW01633355

REPENTANCE AND FAITH

Bible quotations are from the King James Version of the Bible.

Translated by Yeong Kook Park, Joseph Park

Good News Publcations, Inc.:
http://www.goodnewsbook.co.kr

ISBN 89-85422-82-0
Printed in Korea

Repentance

And

Faith

Preface

Judas Iscariot sold Jesus. Afterwards, he realized what he had done and repented. He returned the thirty pieces of silver to the priests and elders and cried, "I have sinned in that I have betrayed innocent blood." But Judas Iscariot's repentance could not lead him to salvation.

For a very long time, like Judas Iscariot, I too regretted and repented of the sins I had committed. Everyday I said, "God, I lied. I stole. I hated someone," and I continually repeated such regret and repentance. However, I could not become freed from sin.

One day, by the grace of God, I saw the evil core of myself. I discovered that I was filthy, dirty, lustful, and deceitful from the very center of my heart. I came to realize that I had failed in spiritual life because of the wickedness found in the core of my heart. "Being an evil human is my nature. I cannot do any good. I am dirty." I realized that the root of me was filthier than the results of the sins I committed. I denied myself, distrusted myself, and threw my thoughts away from that point on. Then Jesus amazingly came upon my heart and my inner self was changed as my life became purified.

True repentance changes people's hearts. I began to testify of these words, and on a countless amount of times I saw how people who denied themselves lived changed and renewed lives.

I am thankful that the words preached at the Olympic Gymnasium have been made into this book. I hope that the Holy Spirit of God will work upon all those who read the words contained within and receive the grace of becoming born again and freed from sin.

February 7th, 2006

Ock Soo Park

Good News Mission Gangnam Church

Contents

1
Peter's Repentance

1.
Peter's Repentance

Hello everyone, we have held the IYF World Camp opening ceremony twice here at the Olympic Gymnasium. This will be our third event. Until now, we have held our conferences at Jamsil Gymnasium. I am thankful that I am able to share the Word of God with you for one week in such a nice place. There must have been many events held at this Olympic Gymnasium. I believe that the Lord will be pleased with us sharing these words of the gospel. Tonight, we will read the words in Matthew chapter 26. I will read from Matthew chapter 26, verse 69.

Now Peter sat without in the palace: and a damsel came unto him, saying, Thou also wast with Jesus of Galilee. But he denied before them all, saying, I know not what thou sayest. And when he was gone out into the porch, another maid saw him, and said unto them that were there, This fellow was also with Jesus of Nazareth. And again he denied with an oath, I do not know the man. And after a while came unto him they that stood by, and said to Peter, Surely thou also art one of them; for thy speech bewrayeth thee. Then began he to curse and to swear, saying, I know not the man. And immediately the cock crew. And Peter remembered the word of Jesus, which said unto him, Before the cock crow, thou shalt deny me thrice. And he went out, and wept bitterly.

I read up to the words of verse 75.

Repentance: the Exact Process of Change

This time, I will be preaching to you about the topics of repentance and faith. We train college students and send them all over the world as short term missionaries for one year. Most of these students are students who only live for themselves, but as I preach the Word of God to these students, the students change tremendously. And when I see this, I can't help but be thankful. This year, we have gathered and are currently training the students who will be going out in 2006. The students who are being trained attended our workshop a little while ago, and as they saw the students who went before them, they were very amazed and asked, "Pastor, after these four days of training at the workshop, how long is our next training session?"

"Three weeks."

"Can we change as they have in that short amount of time? Can we also become like them?"

This is what all the students ask. But last October 27th through the 30th, as we held the training session at our retreat center in Gimcheon, the students changed very much. Many of those students are here tonight. As we teachers saw the image of these students changing, we and all those who were involved were all very amazed. Last week, we had a conference at the KBS Hall in Ulsan. During that time, there was an event held for the IYF students. During the event, we watched a play based on a true story that presented a student's life and how she had received salvation at the workshop we held in October. Most of the people in attendance watching this cried. How could it be that a person's life could change so much? Everyone, among us there are people who have gone to church for ten years, twenty years, and thirty years. It would be nice if we could do well in our spiritual lives. You want to live by faith and you want to have your prayers answered. You want to be filled with the Holy Spirit. But no matter how hard you try, it just does not work out.

I have searched everywhere in the Bible about the process of how people have changed. Peter changed, Apostle Paul changed, and the Samaritan woman changed.... There was surely a process to all of these people changing. That process of change is precisely defined as repentance. Sadly, many churches in Korea today do not teach about repentance Biblically and precisely. They simply tell people to confess their sins. "God, I have committed such and such sin. Forgive me." This is how people live their spiritual life. They repent and they sin; they repent again and sin again. No matter how much they repent--even if they do it a hundred, a thousand, or ten thousand times--they are still unable to depart from sin.

I preached from Romans chapter three last spring at Jamsil Gymnasium. Before that, I preached about the tabernacle and Noah's flood. This time, I am going to be preaching about true repentance. If one goes through the true repentance the Bible speaks of, it is like the change a broken tool makes when melted in a furnace. It comes out of the furnace recast as a new tool. In the same way, a change will be brought about in your heart. The Bible calls the process that brings about true change repentance.

Beginning tonight, I will be speaking to you, step by step, about repentance. How did Peter repent and how did he change? How did Judas Iscariot repent so that he was unable to receive the grace of God? What kind of repentance did Apostle Paul have whereby he gained true faith? What kind of spiritual life did Cain have? What kind of repentance did he have? We will have time for reflecting those aspects upon our lives and distinguishing between them. If you do not do a single thing from now on and simply listen to the words I am preaching, I believe that faith will come into your hearts. I hope you will receive such grace.

You Must Play the Piano Relaxed

Soon after marrying my wife, we had a beautiful daughter. I don't know whether anyone else may say so, but to me, I can't believe how such a beautiful daughter could exist in this world. When she was young, I took her traveling with me on many occasions. One time when my daughter was four or five years old, we were riding on an express bus and a black man sat next to me. I hadn't noticed and sat down, but when my daughter stared at the black man's face for a long time, she shouted and began to cry. I felt so sorry and I apologized to that black gentleman. I told him that my daughter was like that because she had never seen a different world yet. He smiled and said that it was okay. Some people who sat nearby switched seats with us and gave my daughter chocolate as we continued our travel.

When I was single, I thought to myself that if I marry and have a daughter, I would have her learn to play the piano. I would imagine, "Ah, when I am tired, I will tell my daughter to play the piano and I will listen to the piano being played." But after getting married and my daughter and son were born, our circumstances as they were growing up were very difficult. Nowadays, they say that if you are not close to Benjamin Franklin, it is difficult to live. At that time, not just Benjamin Franklin, but it was difficult for me to see the faces of Abraham Lincoln or George Washington.

Because we were so busy living, we didn't even have time to think of teaching my daughter the piano, nor did we have the finances to have her taught. Our children grew up without knowing what private lessons were.

One day, a certain pastor's wife gave us a small used piano that she had played before she got married. Perhaps it was because I hoped for such a thing that my daughter often played that piano. She played Beyer, the beginning piano book, and she would play hymns. And although she was quite late in learning the piano, she would also play the piano at church services. After my daughter was grown, she had the heart to learn the piano. So she went to the United States, met a famous professor and learned the piano. One time, I was listening to my daughter playing the piano, and I thought in my heart, "Wow, that professor is good," meaning that the sound of her playing the piano had changed.

A few years later, I traveled to Russia with my daughter. In the city of St. Petersburg, which long ago was called Leningrad; one of the world renowned cities for music, a world-class pianist named Isabella (Professor Isabella) received salvation. She was very happy to receive salvation, and my daughter began to learn the piano from her. After practicing the piano in Russia for many days, she returned to Korea. I wanted to see her so my wife and I went to meet her at Incheon Airport. I was very happy to see her because it had been a long time. She sat in the back of my car and I was driving. My daughter couldn't close her mouth because she was so busy talking about the things that had happened in Russia. Among them, she began to talk about the piano.

"Father, you know the piano. It doesn't work just because I am trying to control the piano. The piano and I have to become one. Father, before, I tried to play the piano well, but I can't do it when I have that heart. I have to empty my heart. The professor who taught me the piano always said to me, 'Playing the piano is like watering flowerpots. When you pour water into flowerpots, the water becomes absorbed. In the same way, you must be absorbed into the piano.' Father, this is exactly like spiritual life."

"Is that how it is when you play the piano?"

"Yes, Father. Even though you play the same piano striking the same keys, when you relax and play the piano, the sound becomes clean, pure, and light. You must be relaxed in order to have the touch that makes such sound."

"Hey, sounds are made when you strike the keys of the piano. How can you make the sound when you relax?"

"No, Father, it is not so. You must relax."

What do I know about the piano? Do, Re, Mi, Fa; that is all I know. People who play the piano for the first time play with all their might. They can play that way up to a certain point, but when they enter the next level, there is a secret to playing the piano. So what is the difference between people who have learned the piano in Korea and people who have learned the piano in a country of music? Inside Korea, they can't learn about this kind of a world.

One must not strike the piano with all his might to play it, but the person must relax and be absorbed into the piano. This is also true with all the principles of the world. This is true with swimming. At first, people swim using powerful strokes, but they do not move forward very well. They say you must relax to move forward smoothly. My daughter-in-law was a swimmer. That is why when she married my son, she had such wide shoulders that my wife only stared at them. When my son and daughter-in-law swim, they tell me, "Father, you must relax."

"Hey, if I relax, I am going to sink."

"That's not true. Relax."

This is a person who truly knows how to swim. Every principle of the world is this way. When a baseball player in the batter's box has too much strength, the commentator says, "He is forcing it. There is too much strength in him. That is why it is not working." In boxing, it seems that you must strike the person with all your might to knock him out. "There is too much strength in his shoulders. It's an open blow." That is what they say. It means that people must relax.

This is also true in the world of spiritual life. When people first enter the spiritual world, they only think about simply keeping the Ten Commandments, going to church on Sundays, reading the Bible, praying hard, and zealously being faithful. They busily do things. As they continue at that level of spiritual life, a change comes upon their lives. If they live their spiritual life without any thought, they just continue to labor with their own effort until they become old and die. But if people would think a little deeper, they'd conclude, "It is not going to work out because I do it with all my might. Ah, spiritual life doesn't work out because I am trying to do it with all of my effort. My spiritual life doesn't work out because I am pouring all of my heart into it." People are able to sense this. If people live their spiritual life thoughtlessly, they can't think like this throughout their entire lives. But in the middle of their spiritual lives, one day, people arrive at the point; "Ah, spiritual life will not work out just because I try hard, labor, or am loyal." From then on, their spiritual life begins to change.

I Will Never Deny You, Lord

Tonight, we read the words about Peter. One day, Peter was fishing at the Sea of Galilee and met Jesus. Just before Peter met Jesus, he had cast his net all night without catching a single fish, so he was washing his empty net. Right then, Jesus boarded Peter's ship. After Jesus told Peter to set his ship out from the land a little bit, He preached the words of God to the multitude from the ship. He told Peter to launch out into the deep and let down his net for a draught after He finished preaching. According to these words, Peter said, "Master, we have toiled all the night and have taken nothing. Nevertheless, at thy words, I will let down the net." And he let down the net and caught many fish.

Peter was shocked that day. Peter thought, "It seems that this man has never fished. How was I able to catch this many fish by listening to His words?" Peter was completely startled. So he said to Jesus, "Lord, depart from me for I am a sinner." Jesus said to Peter, "Peter, follow me. I will make you a fisher of men." At that instant, Peter threw his boat, net, and everything away, and followed the Lord. Peter had abandoned his ship, his net, and the fish he had caught, but he was not able to throw away believing in himself. That is why, even in following the Lord, he still followed his own thoughts.

When I read the Bible and see the lives of the powerful servants who have been preciously used by God, there was a certain point in their lives that allowed them to become used by God. Peter didn't reach such a point for a long time. He just lived on. In the words that we read this evening, he arrived at the capturing of Jesus. That evening, Jesus spoke to the disciples at the Last Supper, "One of you shall betray me."

Right then, the disciples became worried. Afterwards, Jesus said, "All ye shall be offended this night."

That was what He said, and right then Peter replied, "Lord, what do you mean? Though all men shall be offended because of you, yet I will never be offended."

And Jesus spoke again, "Peter, before a cock crows, you shall deny me thrice."

"Master, how can you say such a thing? If anyone would deny you, it would be Andrew, James, or John. Yet although I should die with you, yet I will not deny you."

Here it shows that Peter's thoughts were so different from

the thoughts of Jesus. When Jesus says, "You shall deny me thrice," to Peter, he should say, "Lord, will I deny you? Then, what am I supposed to do?" Saying, "Though I should die with you, yet I will not deny you," is a heart of believing in himself. If you believe in yourself as you believe in God, what kind of spiritual life would you have? People who believe in themselves, even if they believe in God, believe according to their own methods. That's why even though the Lord said, "You will deny me thrice," Peter said, "I will not deny you. I said that I will not deny you. Why do you keep saying that I will deny you?" and exerted his own thoughts.

When people begin their spiritual lives, they try hard and with the heart, "All I need to do is pray hard, keep the law and be loyal." They try to believe but when they actually try to do it, they arrive at their limits one day and they realize, "I can't keep the law." They realize they can't do things the way they make up their minds to do. People who have not experienced this say, "All I have to do is go to church on Sundays. All I have to do is be loyal. All I have to do is pray. I just need not to sin. All I have to do is be good." People who live this way, because they dwell within the spiritual life of trying to do everything themselves, can never reach the next level of spiritual life throughout their lives.

When people who play the piano reach a certain level as they sincerely play, they come to realize that the sound doesn't become better or clearer just because they strike harder. When they don't know this, they just play the piano mindlessly. As they listen to people who play the piano very well, they come to hear sounds coming from the piano that are completely different from the way they play even if it is the same piano. "How can that piano make such clear sounds? How are such sounds coming about? Why can't I do that?"

People who play the piano well, although they do not put any strength into it and simply play naturally, make beautiful sounds. They see this and come to realize, "Ah, things will not go well just because I put strength into it." With swimming, it is not necessary to stroke the water by putting great strength into it. People who swim well, even though they are simply relaxed, move forward really well. How can that swimmer move forward easily although he doesn't put much strength into it? Before seeing this, people think what they are doing is the best way. But once they see this, they enter into the next level.

Do you know what people who make money say? They say that you should not try to make money. If you try to make money, money will avoid you. They say, "Money has to come looking for you. You are not trying to make money, but the money comes looking for you. Then, you can make money. Don't follow after money to make money."

I read an interview in the IYF magazine about the famous hiker, Hong-gil Um, who conquered Mt. Everest. Upon reading his story, I thought in my heart, "If this man believes in Jesus, he will be very good at living a spiritual life." The words God and Jesus were missing, but he was speaking as someone that had attained high levels of spiritual life. One of his underclassmen who was very close to him was holding on to a rope on Mt. Everest and froze to death. To bring back the corpse, although it was extremely dangerous, he risked his life to climb Mt. Everest. He tried to bring the corpse of his underclassman all the way to Korea, but he was unable to do so and they had a burial on the mountain. What he said was, "I can't climb the mountain because I try to climb it. The mountain must permit me to do so." When he climbs the mountain, it already knows all about his heart. Unless he throws his ambitions away, the mountain will not give him permission. He tried to bring back the corpse of his loving underclassman to Korea. He thought in his heart, "This is as far as the mountain will permit me." He said, "Let us bury him here," and he buried him on the mountain and returned.

Everyone, in spiritual life there is a level we reach, and there is a level that God permits. No matter who it is, people who begin spiritual life for the first time think that if they pray hard, are loyal, and try hard, their spiritual life will work out. I listened to the sermons of many pastors on Christian television, and those pastors say, "Everyone, let us be loyal and let us serve God with all of our strength." But they are lying. Why? They have never done that. People who have tried know that they are unable to.

I once heard a person say that he read the Old and New Testaments of the Bible 175 times in one year. I knew right away, "That person has not once read the whole Bible." If I don't eat anything, and do nothing but just read the Bible all day long, it takes exactly one week to read the entire Old and New Testaments. So if you do not do anything but read the Bible, you can read the Bible fifty times in one year. But when I hear this man say that he read the Bible 175 times in one year, I know that he has not once read the Bible properly. People who have read the Bible know how long it takes to read the Bible through once. I don't read slowly. If I read the words with my eyes, it takes two minutes to read one page. The Bible is approximately 1,750 pages, so to read them all it takes a full 60 hours. But to have read it 175 times in one year, I recognized the fact that he has actually not read the Bible even once.

Everyone, people who say that they have gotten blessed because they were loyal to the Lord are people who have never done that. They are lying. Nowhere in the Bible does it say people were blessed for trying hard and sincerely being loyal. That is why people have a fake, hypocritical, and superficial spiritual life. They say that they fasted for several days and saw a vision while enchanted. Sure, you may see a vision, but that is not spiritual life. True spiritual life begins when you fail in directing your own spiritual life. People who do not fail in spiritual life try to do things themselves; then their spiritual life cannot work out. You have to fail in order to give up on yourself. When you give up on yourself, then faith to believe in the Lord comes. If you think you are great, try hard, and work hard, then faith becomes superficial and true faith absolutely cannot come about.

The Dream of the Prodigal Son

The story of the prodigal son in Luke chapter 15 reads, *A certain man had two sons: And the younger of them said to his father, Father, give me the portion of goods that falleth to me.* What is the meaning in these words? When a father gives his wealth to his son, if the son has no confidence, the son would say, "I am young so what am I supposed to do with this wealth? I don't know what to do." But in the prodigal son's heart, he had confidence. He felt strongly in his heart, "Father, do you think I am a little child? Come on, give me your wealth. I will do just fine." His father gave a portion of his wealth to his son. And not many days afterward, the son took that wealth and went to a faraway country and lived riotously. Then all of his wealth ran out and he began to be in need. A famine hit that land and there was nothing to eat.

And he went and joined himself to a citizen of that country; and he sent him into his fields to feed swine. And he would fain have filled his belly with the husks that the swine did eat: and no man gave unto him.

Even there, the prodigal son lasted as long as he could. Until when? Until his heart crumbled down.

Spiritual life is impossible because the tree called "myself" is wicked, dirty, and has fallen into sin. Spiritual life is cutting down the tree called, myself. You must deny the existence of yourself. I was thinking about what I should write on the front page of the sermon notes you have before you. I wrote the words, "Free from Sin." This is simply my testimony. Since I was young, without knowing anything, I zealously went to church. As I grew, I sinned. The church told me to repent whenever I sinned. "God, I committed such and such sins. Forgive me. I've committed such a sin. Forgive me," I would say, and I continued like that. I would sin and repent. And repent and sin. Repent and again sin. I continued living in this condition. This is not repentance. That is not turning from sin. That is not denying myself. After I received salvation, I saw that all the Christians of Korea, today, were living in this manner: repent and sin, and repent and sin.

When I was ministering at Hanbat Central Church, in Daejon, below our church was a small church named Calvary Church. Our church's early morning service is at 5:30 in the morning, but that church had their service at 5 o'clock.

Whenever 5 o'clock came, people from that church would cry. In the winter time, services are held with the windows closed, so it's okay. But in the summer time, it is hot, so the windows are open and we can hear all their crying. One early morning, a man took a flashlight and went into that church. Everybody was crying and he yelled out, "Let me sleep! Let me sleep!" Why were they crying? The Bible says, "Rejoice evermore. Pray without ceasing. In every thing give thanks." That's what the Bible says. Did it say, "Cry evermore. Sob without ceasing. In everything cry tearfully"? Is that what it says? Why do people do that?

Spiritual life is believing in Jesus. Because I can't do it myself, I believe the Lord will do everything in my place and I will leave my life to the Lord. People say spiritual life is tiring and wearisome, which means that you are doing it yourself.

I often travel on airplanes. I do not know how to fly an airplane at all, but it is not a problem in the least. It is because a skilled pilot is flying the plane. It is a problem when you are trying to live your spiritual life by yourself. If Jesus takes charge of your life and takes charge of your sin, and if He takes charge of your spiritual life and does everything for you, will there still be a problem? No!

The younger son took his father's wealth and went to a faraway country. He tried to do business himself. He thought he would do well running a business and the things his father did seemed insufficient. "Only if my father gives me the wealth, I can do well in business. I don't know why my father is like that. I don't understand him." But the father gave him wealth. And how excited he must have been! With that money, he would run a business and make a lot of money. If it were today, he would want to drive a nice Mercedes, honking the horn as he came home.

"Father, your younger son is here! How have you been? Why don't you come see my house?"

His father would ride in the beautiful car as his son drove into his estate. "From here, all the land within a 30 mile radius is my land."

"Father, from the entrance to the master bedroom is three miles. You have to ride a car to come in. On this side is my yacht harbor and on this side is my private jet. And on this side, there is my sedan. Father, all the trees in my house are tropical trees imported from South America. And all the gold fish I have cost 5,000 dollars per fish. And see all the antiques in my house? That piece over there was used by Qin Shi Huang a long time ago. And those were things that were used by emperors in Europe. Father, do you know how expensive they are? I have made a lot of money!"

This is what the son wanted to boast.

You, too, are that way. Like the younger son, you prayed well, you were loyal, you read the Bible zealously. And as you display all the things you've done you want to say, "God, look! I did all these things. God, I fasted for 40 days and prayed like this. And with my loyalty, we opened up a chapel. God, how do you like it? Great, isn't it? Let me into heaven." That is what people think. You all want this kind of spiritual life, but that is not grace. These are the wages for your effort. God knows that sin can't be washed away through the efforts of man and that man can't attain salvation through his labor. That is why no matter how loyal you are and no matter how much effort you make, He doesn't even glance at it.

The story of the prodigal son in the book of Luke was a

story Jesus made up. Let me ask you one thing. In actuality, aren't there many sons who did well taking their father's wealth and going to a faraway country? Even among your neighbors, there are many people who came to Seoul with nothing and became rich.

I once read the autobiography of Chu-yung Jung, the founder of Hyundai. It was long ago and I don't remember the story exactly, but Mr. Chu-yung Jung was born in North Korea and ran away, was captured, and put in jail. He ran away again and got a job delivering rice. Through that process, he succeeded and created the Hyundai Company. They call the city of Ulsan, the city of Hyundai.

Many cars are sold abroad and within our country, and that's why even though other cities may have fallen into a recession, Ulsan doesn't fall into a recession. This was how successful Mr. Chu-yung Jung was. But why does the Bible leave out the stories of people who have succeeded? Why does it include the story of the son taking his father's wealth, going out and staying with harlots, and herding pigs in a pigpen? Why doesn't the Bible speak of positive things?

The Bible was not written only for stories; it illustrates the world of our hearts. Among you here at the Olympic Gymnasium are some who make a lot of money, have good lives, and have succeeded in life. There may be some people who came to Seoul empty-handed, but through their hard work and labor, they made money, created a great business, became successful, and are helping many people. But to teach that spiritual life can't be achieved through one's efforts and labor, there is the story of the prodigal son becoming a beggar. If you, too, live a spiritual life of making an effort, laboring, and straining, you will become like the prodigal son.

Point of Change

The prodigal son one day thought, "There are so many hired servants in my father's house who have bread enough to spare. I perish here with hunger. I will go to my father and say to him, 'Father, I have sinned against heaven and before thee and are no more worthy to be called thy son. Make me one of your hired servants.'"

Everyone, this is a story of repentance. It shows what repentance is. Until that point, the younger son wanted to make money in business to show his father. But that didn't work out so he went down to the pigpen. Just because he went to the pigpen doesn't mean that he had given up on himself. "Even though I am like this, if I work a little harder, my master will acknowledge it. Then he will give me food and I will eat. And if I work a little harder, and if I gather the funds, and start doing business...." That is the heart the younger son always had.

One day a hunter went out to hunt and saw a fox sleeping. "I'd better catch it." And he thought, "What am I going to do if I catch it? I will sell my fox and buy a hen. If I buy the hen, it will lay many eggs. And with that, I will buy a female pig. When the female pig grows and has many babies, then I am going to sell them and buy a calf. The calf will grow and have many babies. Then I will sell them and buy land. I am going to buy a brick house and get married." He wanted to shoot the fox and aimed his gun. However, the fox had run away. The fox had been sleeping until then but had awakened and run away while the hunter raised many cows, built a brick house, and met a beautiful woman and married her. It was nowhere to be seen. So he had lost his chicks, hens, pigs, calves, a house and a wife; he lost everything. The fox had taken all of that with him.

Although the younger son lived in the pigpen, he had these kinds of dreams: "If I work a little harder, the owner will acknowledge it and give me some food, then I will work a little harder and make some money. Later on, I will start a business."

Everyone, people live their lives feeling the fun of these kinds of illusions. Gamblers gamble because they want to win. Everyone wants to win. There is no one who wants to lose. Who tries to lose when they gamble? They only think of winning and they never consider losing. That's why it seems that this time I will win, this time I will surely win. As men gamble away their money, they may even wager their wives and gamble. "What's so bad about wagering your wife and gambling? I am going to win." Isn't that so? Because they think they will win, they are able to wager anything. That's why people wager the ownership of their land, their houses, and their children's college tuition.

Foolish people, even they become like the prodigal son. "This time I feel like I am going to make a lot of money." Continuing along that way, how far did he go?

And he would fain have filled his belly with the husks that the swine did eat: and no man gave unto him. And when he came to himself, he said, How many hired servants of my father's have bread enough and to spare, and I perish with hunger!

It is that he should discover that the result of walking his path was death, and turning his heart from him. "This is the result of what I did and I will no longer do it myself, but leave control of my life up to my father. I will allow my father to do things." That's how his heart changed and that's why he was able to go back.

And he arose, and came to his father. But when he was yet a great way off, his father saw him, and had compassion, and ran, and fell on his neck, and kissed him.
And the son said unto him, Father, I have sinned against heaven, and in thy sight, and am no more worthy to be called thy son.
But the father said to his servants, Bring forth the best robe, and put it on him; and put a ring on his hand, and shoes on his feet: And bring hither the fatted calf, and kill it; and let us eat, and be merry: (Luke 15:20-23)

When did it become time for this son to wear good clothes, shoes, a ring on his hand, and eat the fatted calf? When he came to know that everything about him was a failure. It was when he gave up and denied himself, and it was when he left control of his life completely to his father.

Everyone, this is the point we must arrive at in spiritual life. As a pastor, when I meet many saints, it shows: "Ah, this person has not reached that point or this person has gone beyond that point."

Mr. Kim, a Shoe Salesman from Chicago

There was a man named Mr. Kim, from Chicago, in the United States. This person sold shoes at a shoe store in Chicago. He was a clerk in a large store. He was amazingly good at selling shoes. When customers would come and meet this man, he would send them away with at least a new pair of sandals. He would never simply let them go away. When I heard about this, I was amazed. What did he say that enabled him to do that? As a pastor, if I did not simply send people away, but send them all away changed, how nice that would be!

This person, too, had sins and he came to our Good News Mission Chicago Church and received salvation. After receiving salvation and having begun a spiritual life, he felt this in his heart: "What is the point of making money? What more can I do than feed myself? This gospel is so great and I want to become a preacher who preaches the gospel." So he applied to the missionary school in Korea. One day, he went to the shoe store owner and said, "Sir, I will work for one more month and then I will quit."

The owner was surprised. Mr. Kim was the driving force of the store.

"Mr. Kim, what's wrong? Is the treatment not good enough? Did we somehow disappoint you? Please tell me."

"It's nothing like that, but I want to go to missionary school in Korea."

"Why do you want to go to missionary school?"

"You don't understand, I must go there."

"Then go after one year. Mr. Kim, it is good that you are going to missionary school, but what's going to happen to our store? Who is going to sell if you are not here? Stay here a little bit longer, then go."

"I have made up my mind to go."

The owner was very disappointed. So before Mr. Kim left, the two of them got together over dinner.

He said to him, "Mr. Kim, when you go to Korea, study hard and become a great missionary. But if you run into hardships, come to our store anytime. We'll work together."

He got on the airplane to come to Korea. He threw his

job and everything away to become a gospel preacher, but he couldn't throw away the words, "Whenever you run into hardships, come to my store." He was studying in missionary school and was being trained in spiritual life. Other people were being trained with all of their hearts, but he thought, "The owner told me to come anytime. If this doesn't work out, I will just go and sell shoes. I am good at selling shoes." Because he was there with that heart, he couldn't be trained. It's just like a germ invisible to the eyes that enters the body and kills a person. This petty thought had entered him. The difference between him and the other missionary students after six months was like the difference between heaven and earth.

He had believed in himself. "I am good at selling shoes. I can cater to any customer's heart without upsetting him." After six months, even he noticed that there was such a great difference between the other students and him so he ran away. "If it doesn't work out, what am I going to do? It will be good to be a missionary, but if not, oh well. I will just go back to Chicago." He got off at the airport in Chicago and called the owner of the shoe store.

"Sir, I am back."

"Oh, Mr. Kim, you are back. Welcome."

From that day on, he went to the shoe store. But for some reason, whereas he was so good at selling shoes before, he couldn't sell them so well now. He would get into arguments with customers. But the owner thought, "That's because he hasn't done this for six months. I know he has great skills in selling shoes. He will be fine again." And the owner waited. For one week, shoes were selling in every corner of the store but not Mr. Kim's. Every customer who came got upset and angry and left. He wasn't like that before. Since he used to be so good, the owner trusted him. After two or three weeks passed by, it still wasn't working. One day after dinner, the owner asked him to have a cup of coffee. The two of them sat down and spoke over coffee.

"Mr. Kim, I have something to ask you."

"What is it?"

"Why did you come back from the missionary school?"

"Well…."

"Go back. No matter how much I think about it, I think God is blocking this. I really like you, Mr. Kim, but if you stay here, God is going to completely destroy our store. Please go back."

Oh, that confidence! "I am good at selling shoes. I always sell shoes to customers who come to me. The owner recognizes this. There is no one who is as good at sales in Chicago as I am. I am good at selling shoes." The heart of his believing in himself had not once been scratched, but that belief began to crack.

All men think, "Oh, my family is doing well because of me." That is why they always say to their wives, "If I listen to you, this family isn't going to do well. Because of me doing everything, we are living this well off at least."

A homeless father and son were walking along their way and saw a house on fire. All the people were just running around crying, not being able to go in. When they saw that, the homeless son asked the father, "Father, we don't need to worry about a fire, do we?"

"Hey, thank your father for that."

Everybody believes in themselves.

In the heart of Mr. Kim, the thought that he was a good

shoe salesman crumbled. "I didn't know I could be like this at times. I am good at selling. I am good. I didn't know I was this way. Even though I want to go back to the missionary school in Korea, because what I did when I ran away, I can't go back." One of our pastors in our mission went to America for a conference. One day, as Brother Kim gave that pastor his testimony, he said, "I have been arrogant." He repented tearfully.

That pastor called me and said, "Pastor Park, Brother Kim has broken his heart and repented."

"Tell him to come to Korea."

He came to Korea. The heart he had six months ago, "I am good at selling shoes, and if it doesn't work out in missionary school, all I have to do is go to the shoe store. I am different from the others," all came crumbling down. The thoughts that he could do it crumbled down. "If the Lord doesn't bestow grace upon me, everything I do is in vain. How foolish it was to believe in myself." He came to realize that fact.

Rather than during the training he received in the missionary school over the first six months, God had indeed showed him his true image while he was back at the shoe store for one month. He realized that he had sold shoes well until now by the grace of God. He came to know he was a human who was truly nothing. When the heart to believe in himself came crumbling down, he changed very much. He was trained in the missionary school and his faith grew so much that the others couldn't keep up with him. We sent him as a missionary to Anchorage, Alaska where many Eskimos lived. In the winter time in Anchorage, the sun rises at 11 am and sets at 2 pm. I heard that at night time, sometimes bears would come into the kitchen and go through things. When you drive your car around, sometimes you may run into different kinds of animals. He witnessed there and many people in Anchorage received salvation. So he stayed in rugged Anchorage for a few years, and a couple of years ago, he was sent to Hawaii. We can't say how beautiful the church in Hawaii has become.

Peter Who Finally Crumbled Down

You have to go through this process in spiritual life. People who do not go through this process trust themselves. "All I have to do is pray. All I have to do is keep the law. All I have to do is quit drinking, and all I have to do is give offerings." Because they are doing it themselves, why would God need to help them? When does spiritual life begin to work? Spiritual life begins to work when nothing else works even when you pray; when nothing works when you try to keep the law; and when nothing works when you quit drinking. When nothing works no matter what you do, that is when spiritual life begins to work. The prodigal son did not change through doing something well and pleasing his father. He changed when nothing worked out.

Confessing that you have stolen, committed adultery, and lied is not repentance.

"God, I can't do it. God I am a descendant of Adam. I am a seed of sin. If you plant a peanut, peanuts are borne. If barley is planted, barley is borne. If rice is planted, rice is borne. If cotton is planted, cotton is borne. In the same way, I am a seed of sin. There is no fruit I can produce other than sin. How could I, a tree of sin, produce any good? How can a peanut plant ever bear apples? How can beans be borne from barley? How can red beans be borne from rice? I am a seed of sin. The core of my heart is evil and dirty. Filthy and evil thoughts arise in me. I indulge in ambitions. Hatred arises in me. Time and time again, a lustful heart arises. I am an evil human who does wicked things! Oh God, have compassion on me! I am a dirty seed of sin, who has dirty sins springing up in me."

That is true repentance. If people don't know their core, people say, "All I have to do is pray hard and be a good person. All I have to do is not sin and keep the law. People who do not know themselves try to do everything on their own. All of this deceives our conscience. As you live your spiritual life, you will say the same thing Apostle Paul said: "Oh, wretched man that I am! Who shall deliver me from this body of death?"

"Why can't I ever do any good? Why does an evil heart arise in me? Why do I have a hateful heart inside of me? Why does such a dirty heart torture me inside?"

Just as David said, "I was shapen in iniquity and in sin did my mother conceive me," you must know that, by nature, you are nothing but sin. Everyone, the Bible says so. "Do men gather grapes of thorns, or figs of thistles?"

One time, I had spiritual fellowship with an elder from Washington D.C., in the United States. He told me that as an elder, he did many great things. I asked the elder, "Elder, in America do the thistles produce figs?"

"No, they don't."

"It is the same in Korea. By chance, are grapes borne from thorns in America?"

"No, they are not."

"That's right. It is the same in Korea. Then Elder, how did you produce good things on a tree of sin? You are very skilled."

His mouth dropped open and he was unable to shut it.

"Elder, the difference between you and I is that I am a seed of sin, so evil springs up in me and I am filthy and dirty and unable to do anything good. If I try to do something good, it seems as though it is going to work, but then it doesn't work. I can't do it because I am a seed of sin. But Elder, how did you bear such good fruit although you are a seed of sin?"

He was speechless. He had trusted himself. When you trust yourself, then you end up producing only fruit of sin. We must realize we are trees of sin. You must realize that no matter how hard you try, all you do is sin.

Peter did not know himself well. "All I have to do is not deny the Lord. All I have to do is throw my life away and follow the Lord." That night, as in the words we read tonight, Peter followed Jesus when Jesus was arrested. Everyone else ran away, but why didn't Peter run away? It was because he said, "Though all men shall be offended because of thee, yet will I never be offended," and that he would not throw the Lord away. He followed, saying that he wouldn't deny the Lord, and then he ended up denying the Lord. A damsel there said, "I saw this man with Jesus." But Peter denied it saying, "I don't know what you are talking about."

Before this, Peter didn't know himself. He thought that if he tried not to deny Jesus, he wouldn't. He thought if he tried not to lie, he wouldn't. And he thought that he would not do something if he made up his mind not to. He loudly boasted, "Though I should die with thee, yet will I not deny thee." But that day, he denied the Lord three times. Peter's heart of belief in himself crumbled down through seeing this.

"Foolishly, I had believed in myself and was like this. I had relied on myself. I had lived following these kinds of thoughts!"

Peter experienced how foolish he was, so he denied himself. Now Peter threw all of his thoughts away, and when he denied himself, his life became an amazing one in which Jesus Christ lead and guided his heart.

True repentance is not saying, "God, I lied. God, I stole. God, I had an abortion. God, I committed adultery. Forgive me." This is just speaking of one aspect. If you are a wild olive tree, it is not one branch that has to be cut off, but the entire tree trunk must be cut off and grafted onto a good olive tree. It is not that you must confess that you lied and stole.

But true repentance is saying, "God, I am a seed of sin, so that is why evil thoughts arise inside of me without end. So many dirty and lustful thoughts arise inside of me. Although I had not committed sin outwardly, in my heart, I endlessly committed adultery, murder, and lied. How can I, who am this way, ever be good? I cannot be. Therefore I deny myself. Loving Lord, now you take charge of my life. Lord, you rule over me now."

When you throw away everything that you are trying to do and leave your life and spirit to the Lord, from that point on, the Lord lives and works inside of you.

It is impossible for us to wash away our own sins. But when you leave it to the Lord, it is so easy for the Lord to wash away your sin. It is difficult for you to quit drinking, smoking, and taking drugs. But it is so easy when the Lord does it. It is difficult for you to do good, but it is so easy if the Lord does it. That is why true repentance is giving up on everything that you've done until now. It is leaving your life completely in the hands of Jesus because you can't do it yourself. True repentance is giving up on everything you are trying to do.

When such repentance is accomplished in you, the loving Lord begins to work inside of you. Repenting because you have committed adultery, thievery, murder, and having lied; repenting of such continual things is not true repentance. Because, by nature, I am a seed of sin, I can't be saved through me doing everything. I can't go to heaven by doing good. Giving up on what I do and leaving it up to Jesus Christ is true repentance and true spiritual life.

When this is accomplished inside of you, and if you truly repent, the faith to believe in Jesus naturally arises in you and God will work within you. And I believe that you will live a bright and blessed life.

2

Judas Iscariot's Repentance

2. Judas Iscariot's Repentance

Hello everyone, it's good to see you. Today's Scripture is Matthew chapter 27. I will read from chapter 27, verse 3.

Then Judas, which had betrayed him, when he saw that he was condemned, repented himself, and brought again the thirty pieces of silver to the chief priests and elders, Saying, I have sinned in that I have betrayed the innocent blood. And they said, What is that to us? see thou to that. And he cast down the pieces of silver in the temple, and departed, and went and hanged himself. And the chief priests took the silver pieces, and said, It is not lawful for to put them into the treasury, because it is the price of blood. And they took counsel, and bought with them the potter's field, to bury strangers in. Wherefore that field was called, The field of blood, unto this day. Then was fulfilled that which was spoken by Jeremy the prophet, saying, And they took the thirty pieces of silver, the price of him that was valued, whom they of the children of Israel did value; And gave them for the potter's field, as the Lord appointed me.

I read up to the words of verse 10.

Flower Blooms in the Land of Despair

In this busy generation, I am so thankful that God has given us this opportunity to put everything of us aside, to sit in this place to listen to the Word of God.

I will read from Genesis chapter one. *In the beginning God created the heaven and the earth. And the earth was without form, and void; and darkness was upon the face of the deep. And the spirit of God moved upon the face of the waters. (Genesis 1:1, 2)* In Genesis chapter one, verse two, the earth was without form and void and deep in darkness. Life was nowhere on earth, and there was no light anywhere. There were no flowers anywhere on earth. As the earth was cloaked in darkness without hope, some unknown period of time, perhaps thousands or millions of years, simply passed by.

One day, God said to the earth, "Let there be light." The earth changed and began to become renewed. As soon as the words of God came upon the earth that had been in darkness for thousands, millions, or billions of years, flowers bloomed, fruit was borne, butterflies danced, and birds sang in just a matter of days.

The earth changed into a beautiful world. I was very amazed once when I was reading Genesis. In my heart, I felt that the words in Genesis chapter one was so similar to the story of my heart. Before I met Jesus Christ, although I went to church, my heart was still in darkness and despair. No matter where you searched within my heart, there was no hope or light, and I lived a life of darkness, having no flowers or fruit anywhere in my heart. But just as God said to the earth, "Let there be light," one day, amazingly, the living words of God entered my heart. As those words began to work inside my heart, I saw flowers blooming in my heart one day. I saw fruit being borne in me one day. I looked within my heart one day, and I saw hope and joy. My heart was changing into a beautiful land.

Loving folks, the Bible is a mirror for our heart. It speaks to us concerning the things of our hearts. While you are attending this conference and listening to the words, when the words are trying to enter your hearts, at times you feel the desire to reject them, saying, "I don't think that's right." If you break that heart, however, and these words enter you, parts that were never purified no matter how you tried, will begin to become purified.

The Word is alive and powerful, and it is wonderful. The Word is truly amazing. The earth was without form and void and in deep darkness but changed into a beautiful world with flowers blooming, birds singing, and fruit being borne when the Word entered in. Likewise, there will be an amazing day of flowers blooming and fruit being borne in your heart as well when the true Word comes upon you, enters you, and finds room there.

This time, I want to talk to you about repentance and faith

and about spiritual life. Yesterday, I spoke to you about Peter's repentance.

Why doesn't spiritual life work out? There is a reason why it doesn't work out. A person who runs a dry cleaners must distinguish between the clothes that have been washed from the clothes that are dirty, and then hang the clean ones and give them to the customers. Even if clothes have been washed, if they are mixed with dirty clothes, then it is meaningless. With the world of your heart, if you distinguish precisely between the parts that are stained with sin and separate them, Jesus Christ, who is holy, will enter your heart and true repentance will be achieved. Then, even though you keep still, Jesus will come to you and He will cast out the filthy and dirty parts of the heart of old.

In John chapter 2, Jesus went up to the temple of Jerusalem. Before Jesus went there, the temple was filled with cows, sheep, and doves. It was just chaos with the sounds of cows and sheep bellowing and bleating, cows defecating and urinating, and the doves flapping their wings. When Jesus came in, all of those things were cast out. This was not only so with the temple of Jerusalem, but even in your heart, which is a temple itself. If Jesus enters, just as the cows, sheep, and doves were cast out, evil, filthy, lustful, and deceitful thoughts will be cast out. I believe the unimaginable, peaceful, and warm heart of faith and joy will arise.

There Is No Way He Would Like a Man with a Past like Mine

I held a Bible study every Monday in Daejon Prison. One

day, I was going there to once again preach the Word, and I took profiles of all the people who had come that day. I wrote down their names and their prison numbers, and I wrote down which department they worked in as well as their hometowns. As I was writing them down, there was a man named Se-won Oh. I wrote down his name, "Se-won Oh," and his prisoner number. I then asked him, "Where is your hometown?" And he said, "Seonsan in Gyeongbuk Province." I was very happy to see him because my hometown was Seonsan. I asked him, "Where in Seonsan?" And he said, "Jancheon Seonsan."

"My hometown is Seonsan-eup." From that point on, I became close with this person named, Se-won Oh.

He was a man with a lot of problems. He committed murder and ended up in prison. I asked him whether his family was still in town and he said they were, and whether he stayed in touch with them. He said that he couldn't keep in touch with them. After he had committed murder and came to prison, everyone in his family abandoned him. You may curse his family for doing that, but it is understandable because this man had caused them so much pain. That is why when he sends a letter home, it is never received, but they are all returned to him. For ten years he never saw his family, and not one person came to visit him; that is how he had lived.

However, his life has changed since he received salvation. When it was Bible study time there, I quietly told him, "Brother Oh, don't worry when your term is over. Come and stay at my church. Stay with me at my church." When I told him that, he was very happy. This man had many problems in prison, so he lived in solitary confinement for six years.

But after receiving salvation, he would read the Bible every day. He had changed so much.

One day, he was released after he completed his sentence. There was a room at my church and he stayed there with brothers from our church. He would go witnessing with the brothers and was doing well. But one day he came to me and said, "Pastor, I don't want to stay in the church. I want to go out."

"Why? Where are you going to go?"

He said that in every city there are facilities for people who are released from prison. Because they have nowhere to go, they continue committing crimes. This place is for those people to eat and sleep. It was called the Life Restoration Center.

"Hey, man. Why do you want to go to the Life Restoration Center? It's uncomfortable there. Stay here."

"I will go live there and witness there."

"Why don't you stay here and go there during witness time and come back after witnessing? Do you have to live there? Why don't you stay here and go witnessing? Why don't you just do that?"

"No."

He said that he wanted to go. Then I quietly thought about it. This brother was in prison, and after he came to our church and stayed together with us, I was not good to him in any particular way. It would make sense for me to be asking him to stay had I treated him well. I felt bad telling him to stay even though I was not good to him.

"Okay, Brother, you may go. Brother Oh, I haven't treated you well at all, but can we stay together? I wasn't able to treat you well or feed you heartfully, but why don't we just stay together like this?"

Right then, the brother's eyes began to well up, and he said that he would stay. I am inept, so I didn't know at the time, but later on, I found out that this brother had come to think of things this way:

"Pastor Park told me to come and stay at his church when I was released from prison. And now because he said that, he has no choice but to keep me here. There is no way he would like a man with a past like mine. Because he said for me to come, he has to take the responsibility. That's why he is letting me stay here. He probably doesn't like the fact that I am here; if so, I am going to get out of here."

That was the thought he had. Because I thought that church would be better than the Life Restoration Center for him, I told him to stay here with me. But that brother still wanted to go to the Life Restoration Center. In the end, I said, "Brother Oh, fine, you may go, since I can't treat you well in any way. But let's just eat and sleep together like family. Can't we live like this? Let's live like this." Upon hearing these words, that brother came to know my true heart. He thought, "Pastor Park told me to come here after I was released from prison even though he doesn't like me and I am a burden to him. He let me stay because he has no choice. Isn't that it?" But after knowing my heart, he completely changed his heart.

"Pastor, I apologize. I will stay here."

He was released from prison after ten years and his body began to hurt all of sudden. I told the brothers of our church, "Hey brothers, I drove my car around saw some places that sold good meat at good prices. A brother was released from prison and how can you treat him like that? Go and buy some meat for him. Let's cook it and feed him." And the brothers said, "You are right, Pastor. We never thought about that."

I called a sister who ran a pharmacy. "Hello Sister, one of our brothers was released from prison and his body is not in good shape. Do you have any good nutrients or anything at the pharmacy? What are brothers and sisters for? Come and bring some vitamins. Later on, bill me for the medicine." I still haven't paid for that medicine, but later on, I saw the brother receiving a few bags of IV fluid and I saw God blessing this brother.

Also in prison, because he didn't take good care of his teeth, it seemed that all of his teeth would rot and fall out. Our brothers took him to the dentist's office and one of them said, "This person served his term in prison for murder and now he has been released. Can you help us?"

The dentist said that he couldn't do it for free, but he charged only for the parts, and he treated him. It was extremely cheap because he only charged for the cost of the parts. When his new teeth were put in, his teeth changed his countenance. He was over the age of 40, so I felt he should get married. I said, "Brother Oh, it will be great if you get married."

One of the brothers at our church said, "Pastor, there is a sister at our church who is a widow. It would be great if he marries her." So I called that sister over.

"Did you call me, Pastor?"

"Sister, all the other people live with their husbands, but why do you live by yourself?"

"My husband died."

"Really? That's too bad. When?"

"Ten years ago."

"If it has been ten years, you should have remarried. Why did you always live by yourself? I get a headache whenever I see you. What's wrong with you?"

"Pastor, you're right. I have been wanting to get married, so Pastor, please send me someone to marry."

Inside I was thinking, "Alright, it is working out well."

"Then, will you marry the person that I tell you to marry?"

"Sure, I will."

"You will not say you are not going to get married, huh?"

"No pastor, if you tell me to, I will."

"Marry Brother Oh."

"What?" All of sudden, her eyes became big. "Pastor, everything is okay, but I am afraid to be married to a murderer and my heart is not drawn to him."

"You just said you would marry. Forget it then. Don't marry."

One week later, this sister came to me.

"Pastor, I will marry him."

And the two of them got married.

Everyone, a bachelor and a spinster getting married is great, but a widower and a widow getting married is quite a sight as well. But we overlooked that and kept on with our plan. The brother was rejoicing so much. However, even though he is so happy, he should act calm and gentlemanly, but he expressed everything. The sister acted as though she didn't feel that way but she was really happy as well. It makes me very happy to see such things. I am really happy that I have become a pastor. As the two of them live together, because he has a record, it is not easy for him to be employed. So he bought a car and the two of them would ride around in that car selling socks. When I saw what they did for a living, it seemed that they wouldn't make much money. Even so, they looked very happy.

There are many people in our church who were murderers who have received salvation and have married. Even now when I think of that brother, inside of my heart, I feel, "Had he left the church at that time and gone to the Life Restoration Center, would that brother have been able to get married the way he did? Would he be that happy?" I think about such things. Later, his family contacted him. The family heard that he was getting married and they came. They said that there was some wealth his father left behind for him when he passed away and with that money, he bought a townhouse. It was beautiful how everything was working out.

"Brother Oh, stay at our church." If I said that, all he needed to do was to accept what was in my heart.

But he had to rethink it: "Pastor Park is telling me to stay at his church, but why would he like someone like me? Although he hates me being here, he has no choice but to let me stay here. I'd be better off if I left here now before I become despised. I will leave while we are still on good terms."

A useless thought entered him, and had he really done so, what would have happened? Do you think this brother knew the end result of having these kinds of thoughts? No, he did not. Although it appears that we are good and truthful, all those things come from within us, and they continually ruin us and make us wicked.

Everyone, when Cain gave the fruit of the ground as an offering to God, within the heart of Cain there was an evil heart to kill his younger brother; yet Cain was giving his offering to God. Because the heart, "I should beat my brother to death," wasn't arising in him, but was hidden, he didn't know he was that kind of human being. When Cain worshipped God, and even when he was praying to God, his hatred and evil things were hidden. He was actually a dirty person.

I saw in prisons that many inmates used to attend church. As they attended services at church, do you think they planned, "Oh, I am going to commit murder"? As they went to church and had service, they never imagined even in their wildest dreams that, "I am going to commit crimes: commit adultery, steal and rob." When they are in the church service, they truly appear to be sincere and holy. I am sorry to be talking about this, but although you are here listening to the Word of God, at the bottom of your heart there is lust, evil, deceit, and hate. There are many other dirty things there as well.

But because we do not know about this very well, we repent outwardly of the sins we committed and we say, "God, I committed thievery, adultery, and I told lies. God, I cursed and hated other people." We only confess things that appear on the outside and beg for forgiveness. The things that are more serious than what has appeared on the outside are what are at the bottom of your heart. There are sins that are waiting for the opportunity to manifest themselves. You simply have those things covered. People try to turn only from those aspects, having stolen, told lies, and committed murder. That is why evil and sin continually proceed from you.

Did This Kind of Woman Really Kill Someone?

We gathered many Christian inmates at Suwon Prison and held a conference there on March 1st, 1988, which is the Korean Independence Movement Memorial Day. At that time, many inmates received salvation. Of them, there were people who have gone out as missionaries and there were many people who have changed. Because we had such good feedback, the Chairman of Religious Affairs in the prison asked me to hold a conference at a women's prison as well. So even at the women's prison cellblock, we gathered the female inmates and held a conference for a week. The inmates who attended had their hair cut short and they were wearing the same uniform with their numbers printed on the front. But the women were different from the men. They were more quickly absorbed into the Word than the men. Men think about all these things differently when we preach the gospel to them. "If I believe in Jesus like he tells me to, what would my in-laws say? What would my father say? What would my younger siblings say? What would my sister-in-law say? What would they say at work?" As they think about this, they are slow in obtaining faith. Woman was first to eat the fruit of the knowledge of good and evil. Likewise, they received salvation quickly. That is why people say that there are many women in church and there are many men in prison.

As I held the conference at the women's prison for one week, many prisoners were changed. Of them was a lady who appeared to be in her late thirties. She sincerely listened to the Word and I could see with my own eyes that she was changing. She was rejoicing and thankful and was very happy. But everyone, there is one thing I become curious about when I have Bible studies in prisons and become close with the inmates. What is it? What sin did they commit that they ended up here? I become very curious about that because that sister received salvation and appeared to be precious and lovely. Such a pure and simple-hearted sister, what sin did she commit that brought her here? I was extremely curious. On the other hand, it is an extremely rude thing to ask a person in prison what sin they committed to end up there.

One day, very naturally I came to know what crime that sister committed. That sister committed murder. She killed someone. She killed a person very brutally with a kitchen knife. I was absolutely shocked. She had a pretty face and a kind heart, and listened to the Word well. Her eyes were so clear. "What? This woman really killed a person?" I couldn't believe it as I listened to what happened.

This woman came to Seoul from the countryside. She met a man who loved her and the two of them began to live together. They lived together for a year when the man began to cheat on her. He came to know another woman besides her. This man's wife was very kind-hearted and was so simple-minded that she could be labeled a simpleton. She had no idea that her husband was cheating on her. She was always happy.

Then her husband began to dislike her. He wanted to live with this new woman so he brought her home. He also wanted to kick out his wife but he couldn't tell her to leave, so he overtly went around cheating. But his wife was so kind that she just let things be. The husband brought in his new girlfriend and they began to live together in the home.

Still, his wife let things be. When the husband would leave the house, only the two women would be at home and they would fight. The new woman wanted to kick the man's wife out so she could live happily with him. But the wife would not leave, so she fought her every day to kick her out. I don't know what it was that the wife heard one day, but the girlfriend had said something very degrading. When the wife heard this, she was very shocked. Later on, she saw that the woman was lying on the floor, bleeding. She didn't know what she had done but she was standing there with a bloody knife in her hand. Right then, she came to her senses. She had killed someone.

Even as I was hearing that story, I was wondering how such a kind, pretty, and simple-looking woman could kill a person. I couldn't believe it.

As I have visited prisons, the thing that amazes me as we have these Bible studies is how we think of murderers. We think of murderers as violent people with rugged faces, but there are not many like that. Whether it is a man or a woman, there are lots of people who appear to be kind and gentle. "How did that person end up committing murder?" I would think. There was a woman who received salvation at Jeonju Prison who killed two people. When you speak with her, she is so honest and clean. You may think a person who has killed other people may appear to be outwardly evil, dirty, and ruthless, but that is not so.

No matter how kind and sincere a person may appear, inside is a heart that can commit murder. No matter how smart or clean a person appears to be, there is a heart that is able to commit fraud. There are no sinister looking people among conmen or they wouldn't be able to con anyone. They appear to be gentle and pure. People think, "How can such a person commit fraud?" Those people are the ones who end up committing fraud.

The most difficult problem in our spiritual life is that at the bottom of our hearts we have the evil desires of sin although we do not address them because we are not aware that they are there. And when opportunity strikes, people commit murder, thievery, adultery, and they hate one another. The heart that drives us this way is dormant in all people, the descendants of Adam.

A long time ago, a famous artist wanted to draw a picture of Jesus at the Last Supper. He looked for the face of Jesus. Whose face looks like the face of Jesus? This person went all over the country looking for the person who could model the face of Jesus, looking for someone who looked kind, peaceful, and clean. There were people who appeared to be peaceful and good. When the artist would look closely, there was a kind of evil look in their eyes. That was why he was unable to find anyone he was satisfied with. One day, he was tiredly walking on his way when he saw children playing by a brook. Among the children there, one of them had a face that looked peaceful and good. "I should make his face the model of Jesus' face," he thought. So he approached that child, talked to him a little, and said, "I want to draw your face a little." He sat the child down and drew the child's peaceful face.

The artist finished drawing the faces of the disciples and Jesus, but he could not draw the face of Judas Iscariot, who betrayed Jesus. "What kind of face could be the face of Judas Iscariot?" So he began his journey once again. No matter how hard he searched, he was unable to find the face of a human being who was overflowing with evilness, dirtiness, filthiness, and violence. He looked for a face that had no peace, mercy, or kindness whatsoever. Finally, he went to a prison, and among the murderers he looked for such a face. Just because they were murderers, it does not mean they will have an evil face. But in a corner, he saw a man whose face was completely filled with evil. "That's right. That must have been the face of Judas Iscariot." The artist approached him and said he was an artist. He asked him if he could draw his face. That person laughed and allowed him to do so, saying, "Go ahead." When the artist finished drawing his violent, sinister, and ruthless face, that person began to talk to him.

"There is something I need to ask you."

"What is it?"

"Where did you find the face of Jesus for your Last Supper painting?"

"A long time ago, I was walking along when I saw children playing by a brook. Among them was a child who had a truly peaceful face and I drew his face as the face of Jesus."

"You did, didn't you? Didn't you just draw my face as the face of Judas Iscariot?"

"That's right."

"Don't you feel that the face of Jesus and the face of Judas Iscariot look somewhat alike?"

"Uh, yes! They do somewhat resemble each other."

"I was the child who played by that brook long ago. Back then, you drew my face as the face of Jesus, and now I have become the face of Judas Iscariot."

The artist was startled and looked at him closely. Indeed it was him. When the artist first drew the man's face in the man's youth, he was innocent and full of peace, but at the bottom of his heart, the characteristics that enabled him to kill someone and commit evil had been hiding.

When we realize our sin before God and repent, saying, "God, I stole, committed adultery, murdered, and told lies. I also had an abortion. Please God, forgive me," we are merely repenting of the sins from within that outwardly appeared. You only repent for the things that outwardly appear because you can't realize that your core is covered with sin and that you are a pile of dirty evilness. People pray and ask for forgiveness in that manner, but they commit sin once again because the evil comes out from within. They sin and repent again and again. They continually repeat this.

Because they live their spiritual life that way, they praise, "Oh happy day, oh happy day when Jesus washed my sins away," but live their daily life endlessly sinning and repenting. There is never a day when they can say, "The day Jesus washed my sins away." They always remain sinners. That is why Jesus Christ cannot live and work inside of them.

The Junk Cars in Africa Should not Be Repaired but Thrown Away

Once, I went to Ghana, Africa. An interesting thing was that all the used cars of Korea were in Ghana. One of the cars was a Stella from Hyundai Motors. It had Seocho Police Department written on it. There were some cars that read, "Kindergarten Bus," in Korean. Ghanaians wanted to show off that it was a Korean car, so they love it when such writing is on the car.

Those cars are such complete pieces of junk that when they go uphill, great amounts of smoke come out and you can't see the front of the car. When I told the Ghanaian people that in Korea you pay thousands of dollars in fines if smoke comes out from your car, they asked me if Korean cars don't have any smoke coming out of them. I said that there weren't and they said, "What car cannot have smoke coming out of it? It burns gas." I replied, "Black smoke doesn't come out, but there is a little bit of smoke that is so little that is unseen by the eyes. Once in a while, there are cars that have smoke coming out of them. If they are caught, they have to pay heavy fines." That is what I told them.

The first car I rode in while in Africa was a car owned by Sister Dasso. She brought it to the airport to pick me up. She was a sister who worked at a bank and she told me that while I was staying in Africa, I should use that car. I drove that car on a sightseeing safari. I put it to good use. On the day of my departure, as I was being taken to the airport, the car broke down and I almost fained as I opened up the hood. There was nothing there but the engine. The fact that I had driven that car almost made me faint.

You have to be careful when you ride in cars in Africa because sometimes your feet go through the bottom because there are holes in the floorboard. And you should never wear clean clothes when you are riding in a car because there is so much dust that the seats are all covered. Of course, there are some cars that are not like that. Nevertheless, there are lots of funny things that happen when you ride in cars in Africa. I heard that in Kenya not even one car has been junked since the country was formed. What that means is, no matter how junky a car may be, it will run as long as it has an engine. The owners continually drive the car; switching engines and changing parts.

Junk cars in Africa should not be repaired. People say that it is like fixing the teeth of the elderly such as grandmothers whose teeth are all rotted. When one is fixed, another is gone, and when that is fixed, another one falls out. We don't know what we should fix on those African cars. Because of that, windshield wipers do not work, yet nobody even tries to fix them. A broken window is also not a problem at all. Some cars have the problem of windows not rolling down. You can't roll the window down even though it is hot, so it is very difficult.

Everyone, such cars shouldn't be repaired; you simply need to get new cars. That's how it is in spiritual life. Let's open to Isaiah chapter 55. I will read Isaiah chapter 55, from verse 6. *Seek ye the LORD while he may be found, call ye upon him while he is near: Let the wicked forsake his way, and the unrighteous man his thoughts.* And then do what? Does it say, "Let the wicked repair his way and come to the Lord"? What does it say? What should the wicked do with his way and the unrighteous man with his thoughts? Let us answer together out loud. Do what? Forsake! Forsake!

> *Seek ye the LORD while he may be found, call ye upon him while he is near: Let the wicked forsake his way, and the unrighteous man his thoughts: and let him return unto the LORD. (Isaiah 55:6, 7)*

These scriptures are telling you to "forsake," and return to the Lord.

With junk cars, once you fix the windshield wipers, the windows won't roll up or down; and when you fix the window, the ignition won't turn on; and when the ignition is fixed, the blinkers won't work. When the blinkers are fixed, the brake won't work. When you fix the brake, you get flat tires. There will be no end to this even though you fix your car your entire life. To drive a car for one hour, you have to fix it for one hour. It takes about the same amount of time to drive the car as it takes to fix it. Having to repair your car every day and driving it for a little bit, and repairing it again and driving it, and repairing it again and driving it; that is a junk car. The car should not be repaired. You should get a new one. That car should be thrown away and a new car should be bought.

For most Korean churchgoers, their spiritual lives are exactly like driving around in a junk car. As they drive for a while, "Putt, putt, putt, stall. Putt, putt, putt, stall," the ignition turns off. "Why isn't the ignition turning on?" As they are fixing it with all their might, the engine vibrates then turns off. And if they repair that, they get flat tires. Junk cars continue to be this way. What kind of spiritual lives are like junk cars? Sinning and repenting, and after that, sinning and repenting; there is another sin. Asking to be forgiven and committing another sin, lying, and then, missing a Sunday service, and afterwards not tithing. When they have taken care of those sins, they fight other people and beg for forgiveness with their tears. Then they get angry because they don't get along with their spouses and they curse at their kids. These kinds of things will continue without end. This is exactly like driving a junk car.

That's why God says, "Throw away that spiritual life and gain something new." Your spiritual life will not work out by repairing the lying, stealing, drinking, and adultery you have committed. Your heart must be thrown away as a whole. Though you repair yourself, you sin endlessly; sin and repent; sin and repent. That is why, rather than getting new parts for a junk car, you would be better off getting a new car. In our spiritual life, we should not be trying to repair this and that, but our spiritual life should be made completely anew. That is true repentance. That is why when you are repenting, you should not be saying, "God, I stole, committed adultery, and I lied. Forgive me." Rather, you should say, "God, I committed adultery and I stole. Not only this, but by nature, I am a pile of sin. I am a cluster of sin. Because of that, everything that I do is evil. Therefore, I throw myself away," and receive the heart of Jesus. Then it can be a proper spiritual life. Amen? Amen!

Peter Who Threw Himself Away

Yesterday, we talked about Simon Peter. Simon Peter trusted himself, too. He didn't know how evil a human being he was. He thought that if he tried, he could do well. He thought that he could live his spiritual life well with his own heart. That is why, one day, when Jesus said, "You will all be offended because of me," Peter said, "Though all shall be offended because of you, but I will not be offended. Lord, I am not like Andrew. I am not like James. I am not like John. Though they may be offended, Lord, I will not. Why would I throw you away, Lord? I am not going to do that." He believed in himself.

Jesus said to Peter, "Peter, before a cock crows tonight, you will deny me three times." But still Peter believed in himself. "Lord, why do you say that? I am disappointed. I am not like that. I am not going to deny you, Lord." Peter thought he was good. He didn't know there was evil inside of him. He didn't know he was being dragged by Satan. Even though Jesus said, "Simon, Simon. Satan desires to have you, that he may sift you as wheat." Peter had the heart, "No, Jesus, I am not going to deny you. I am not going to throw you away, Lord. Believe me."

Only a few hours passed and Jesus was arrested. Peter followed Jesus from afar and followed him all the way to the high priest's house. Outside, the servants had a charcoal fire burning. Since Peter was cold, he, too, was warming himself by the fire. The people there said, "You are among the disciples, aren't you?" He calmly denied it. "I thought I wouldn't be like this. Why is this happening?" From inside of him, he wanted to shout, "That's right! I am a disciple of Jesus!" But that wasn't happening.

Among all the sins that I have committed, there is one sin that I will never forget in my life. The subject of my sin is a nail clipper. This is something that happened a long time ago --about 50 years ago. In our village, which was in Seonsan County, Gyeongbuk Province, there was only one nail clipper. That was the one at my house. I don't know how our house came to have acquired a nail clipper. Back then, they cut their fingernails with scissors, but only at my house, we could clip our nails with a nail clipper. It was great. Father also cherished it, so he tied a string to it, put a nail on the wall in the room where he would sleep, and that's where he hung it.

"Ock Soo and Jung Soo, don't ever take it outside. Okay? You must clip your nails here and hang it right back up here."

"Yes, sir."

But I wanted to take that nail clipper to school and show it off to my friends. One day, without anyone knowing, I put it in my pencil case and I brought it to school. After class, during a break time, I began to show off and cut kids' fingernails with the nail clipper. The kids in my class saw a nail clipper for the first time.

"Wow! That's great!"

"Who wants to have their fingernails cut? I will cut them!"

All the kids gathered together and it was amazing.

"Can that even cut wood?"

"Yes, it can."

We brought little pieces of wood that fit into the nail clipper and they were cut. That should have been the end of it, but another friend asked a question.

"Can it even cut a nail?"

I could have said, "Hey, how can a nail be cut?"

But I wanted to show off my nail clipper so I said, "It can cut through a nail!" One of the students brought a nail.

"Come and cut it!"

I knew what was going to happen, so I didn't want to cut it. But because of what I had said to my friends, I couldn't just stop there. I put the nail into the nail clipper and I pressed down. Was it cut? Because it wouldn't cut, I pressed down hard. The nail clipper snapped and broke.

Suddenly, I could see my father's face and I began to become dizzy. After school, if I said, "Father, today I took the nail clipper to school and while showing off, I did this and that, and I broke it," how nice that would be! But it seemed that I would surely be spanked by my father for this. I was so afraid. At that time, what I did while no one was looking, was put the nail clipper in my younger brother's pencil case in his bag and quickly closed it up. It was evening and when father came home, he looked for the nail clipper.

"Where is the nail clipper? Ock Soo, nail clipper."

"I don't know."

"Jung Soo, did you take it?"

"No."

"You guys are the ones who took it. Ock Soo, bring your book bag."

He looked through my book bag, but it wasn't there. Next, he searched through my younger brother's. Oh, the shocked expression on my younger brother's face, when the broken nail clipper was found as my father opened his pencil case! My father said, "You, rascal! Roll up your pant legs!" My father picked up a stick and spanked him. I had the heart to say, "Father, it was I who did it. Forgive me." But I didn't have the courage to do it and my younger brother was beaten badly. More than my younger brother who was beaten, I, who hadn't been beaten, was hurting so much. Therefore, this memory of what happened 50 years ago is vivid in my mind. After I became an adult, I once told my younger brother, "Hey, Jung Soo, such and such a thing happened back then. Did you know?"

"No, Older Brother. Really? I don't even remember." My younger brother doesn't even remember, but that sin remained with me as if it penetrated my heart. The Bible says that the sin of Judah was engraved with a pen with the point of a diamond. Truly, it was not erased from the tables of my heart.

This was so with Peter. He wanted to say, "I am a disciple of Jesus," but he was so afraid. Lastly, a certain servant said, "You are the disciple of Jesus. I can tell by your voice. I saw you together with Jesus on that mountain." Right then, Peter began to curse and deny it. Because the curse was not exactly recorded, we don't know what he said or what kind of swearing he used, but regardless, he denied Jesus. As Peter was slithering and slipping his way out, the cock crowed.

Peter said, "The Lord said that I would deny him. Although I disagreed, I ultimately denied the Lord," and realized how foolish it was for him to believe in himself. Peter didn't repent of the sin of denying Jesus, but he threw himself and the heart of believing in himself away: "I am a human who can't be believed. Denying Jesus is a sin, but this is the kind of human being I am. I am an evil and filthy human being. I can only deny the Lord."

In Peter, the faith to believe in himself came crumbling down. When the faith to believe in himself came crumbling down, Jesus' spirit came upon Peter. Not long after Peter denied Jesus, Jesus was crucified and killed on the cross. After Jesus resurrected and ascended, Peter was filled with the Holy Spirit on the day of Pentecost.

Peter was once going to the temple to pray, and there was a lame man sitting at the gate called Beautiful stretching out his hands asking for alms. The Holy Spirit was continually with Peter and told him to raise the man up. "What if I can't raise him up?" This is the heart Satan continually puts inside of us. Before, Peter believed in himself and he listened to his own voice, but now he has denied himself and he would not listen to his own voice. He spoke to the lame man according to the words of Jesus. "Look on us." As the lame man looked at him, he said, "Silver and gold have I none but that I have I give thee. In the name of Jesus Christ of Nazareth, rise up and walk." Peter took his hand, raised him up, and the work of God happened.

Silver and gold have I none,

But such as I have give I thee.
In the name of Jesus Christ of Nazareth,
You rise up, rise up and walk!

This is something that can only happen to people who have denied themselves. Even though God wants to work inside of you, within yourself, your voice says, "How embarassing it will be if we try to do that and can't raise him up?" People think, "What if I boasted that I prayed and it doesn't get answered?" This is what they listen to. You can't follow Jesus while you are listening to these voices of yours.

Peter had completely denied himself as a whole: "I am a dirty human being. I am a liar. I can only fall into sin being deceived by Satan." He knew that was how he was, and he denied himself. Afterwards, even if a thought arose inside of him, he would say, "This is my thought. I shouldn't believe it," and he followed the words of Jesus.

Judas Iscariot's Repentance

Peter repented of his filthy, dirty, and evil self. But what did Judas Iscariot do in the scriptures that we read today? Didn't Judas Iscariot repent? Didn't Judas Iscariot realize what he had done? Here in the Bible it says, *Then Judas, which had betrayed him, when he saw he was condemned, repented himself and brought again the thirty pieces of silver to the chief priest, and elders, Saying, I have sinned in that I have betrayed the innocent blood.* Did Judas Iscariot confess his sin or not? He did confess. Didn't he turn his heart around or not? He turned his heart around, returned the money that he had received, and thoroughly repented.

The problem is that Judas Iscariot repented of having sold Jesus, but he didn't discover how evil and filthy he was. He didn't throw himself away. He turned his heart around from having sold Jesus, but he didn't turn around from himself. Judas Iscariot would probably never sell Jesus again, but he was still believing and following himself. That is why he was so tormented that he killed himself. Why did Judas Iscariot kill himself? His committing suicide and following his own decision meant that he still trusted himself. Hanging and killing himself showed that he followed his own decisions and that he believed in himself.

We should not only turn our hearts around from stealing, committing murder, adultery, and lying, because even though we turn our hearts from them, a hundred and thousand times more of those evil and filthy things continually arise inside of us. That is why there is no end. That is why churchgoers today can't help but to sin and repent and sin and repent continually.

With repentance, there is the repentance of Judas Iscariot and the repentance of Peter. Judas Iscariot sold Jesus and Peter denied Jesus. Both of them committed sin. But through this, Peter was able to deny himself completely. He didn't believe in his own thoughts and he forsook himself. *Let the wicked forsake his way and the unrighteous man his thoughts.* From then on, Peter didn't believe in himself. No matter how correct the thoughts that arose from him were; no matter what good was inside of him, he only believed in and relied on the words of God.

Many people today turn their hearts around from having stolen, having committed adultery, and having lied, but they do not deny themselves. They do not deny their thoughts and then, they continue living and following after their own thoughts.

Everyone, suppose I unknowingly start to become close with a conman. And one day, the conman comes to me and says, "Pastor Park, let's do business together. You put in a hundred thousand dollars and I will put in a hundred thousand dollars."

So I put in a hundred thousand dollars, but that conman took it all and ran away. I have been conned. Afterwards, that person comes to me again.

"Hey you! Why did you rip me off last time?" I'd ask.

This person says, "What I did to you was wrong." He once again asks me to believe in him. I will distrust him for the fact that he committed fraud, but if I believe him again, then I will be tricked into being conned once again. If we become conned by a conman, being conned is only an incident. We should not believe in the person himself because he is a conman. Don't you think so? If I continue to believe the person even after I have been conned, I will continue to be conned.

Once at our church, one of our sisters had met a conman. The conman said, "Let's get married," and took all her money. After listening to this, I realized he was a conman, so I said this to the sister, "Sister, I don't think that man is a good man."

"Pastor, no, it is not like that. He is a good man."

"Then why did he do that?"

"Back then, it was because of the circumstances."

This sister could only continue to be conned by that man. Do you understand? Not only disbelieving the aspect of being conned once, she should not believe in that conman himself. In the same way, not the sin of how I committed theft, adultery, and lied, but I should not believe in myself as a whole.

Peter turned his heart around from himself and repented. Just like the words in Isaiah chapter 55, *Let the wicked forsake his way, and the unrighteous man his thoughts,* Peter threw all of his ways and thoughts away. But Judas Iscariot wanted to throw away the sin of having sold Jesus without throwing himself away. He had once again believed in himself. That is why when he heard the voice, "You sold Jesus. Commit suicide. Kill yourself. Kill yourself!" he listened to those words and he killed himself.

As I have lived a spiritual life, I, too, would always go to church and live a life of sinning and repenting. But one day, God bestowed grace and I was able to gain the eyes to see myself. Before then, I thought of myself as a good, sincere, and decent person. But I saw myself through the eyes of the Lord. I saw what a filthy, dirty, and wicked person I was. As I realized it, I distrusted myself. Because I was such a dirty, filthy, and evil person, I threw myself away. From that point on, the words of Jesus began to enter my heart as faith.

Because you believe in yourself, even if it is the Word of God, you accept the words that fit you and refuse the ones that do not. The life of following after your own heart cannot be true spiritual life. If you repent from and turn around from believing in yourself and following after your own heart, I believe that true faith towards Jesus will arise in you.

3

Apostle Paul's Repentance

3.
Apostle Paul's Repentance

Hello everyone, it's good to see you today. We'll look at the scriptures in Acts chapter 9. If you open to Acts chapter 9, I'll read from verse 1.

And Saul, yet breathing out threatenings and slaughter against the disciples of the Lord, went unto the high priest, And desired of him letters to Damascus to the synagogues, that if he found any of this way, whether they were men or women, he might bring them bound unto Jerusalem. And as he journeyed, he came near Damascus and suddenly there shined round about him a light from heaven: And he fell to the earth, and heard a voice saying unto him, Saul, Saul, why persecutest thou me? And he said, Who art thou, Lord? And the Lord said, I am Jesus whom thou persecutest: it is hard for thee to kick against the pricks.

And he trembling and astonished said, Lord, what wilt thou have me to do? And the Lord said unto him, Arise, and go into the city, and it shall be told thee what thou must do. And the men which journeyed with him stood speechless, hearing a voice, but seeing no man. And Saul arose from the earth; and when his eyes were opened, he saw no man: but they led him by the hand, and brought him into Damascus. And he was three days without sight, and neither did eat nor drink. And there was a certain disciple at Damascus, named Ananias; and to him said the Lord in a vision, Ananias. And he said, Behold, I am here, Lord. And the Lord said unto him, Arise and go into the street which is called Straight, and inquire in the house of Judas for one called Saul, of Tarsus: for, behold, he prayeth, And hath seen in a vision a man named Ananias coming in, and putting his hand on him, that he might receive his sight. Then Ananias answered, Lord, I have heard by many of this man, how much evil he hath done to thy saints at Jerusalem: And here he hath authority from the chief priests to bind all that call on thy name. But the Lord said unto him, Go thy way: for he is a chosen vessel unto me, to bear my name before the Gentiles, and kings, and the children of Israel: For I will shew him how great things he must suffer for my name's sake. And Ananias went his way, and entered into the house; and putting his hands on him said, Brother Saul, the Lord, even Jesus, that appeared unto thee in the way as thou camest, hath sent me, that thou mightest receive thy sight, and be filled with the Holy Ghost. And immediately there fell from his eyes as it had been scales: and he received sight forthwith, and arose, and was baptized. And when he had received meat he was strengthened. Then was Saul certain days with the disciples which were at Damascus. And straightway he preached Christ in the synagogues, that he is the Son of God. But all that heard him were amazed, and said; Is not this he that destroyed them which called on this name in Jerusalem, and came hither for that intent, that he might bring them bound unto the chief priests? But Saul increased the more in strength, and confounded the Jews which dwelt at Damascus, proving that this is very Christ.

We read to verse 22.

Before It Says, "Believe Ye the Gospel," It Clearly Says, "Repent"

Everyone, at this conference we're talking about repentance and faith and about spiritual life. When I meet and speak with people, those who have lived a spiritual life for a long time ask me about the problems of their faith that remain unresolved. Even this morning I had a conversation with a middle-aged woman after the sermon. It seemed that she was sincere and had believed with all of her heart. She knows that Jesus died on the cross for her sins and she also knows that her past, present, and future sins were washed away, but faith was unable to grow in her heart. Therefore she had conflict in her heart and came here. As I began to understand what her spiritual life was like, I didn't get to speak to her deeply, but this is what I said to her, "Lady, you know too many things without having gone through true repentance." I have met many other people who are like this lady.

There is a textbook you learn from in the first grade of most schools. There is another you learn from when you're in the second grade, another for the third grade, and grade by grade, step by step, you learn while you are in school. But church is not like school. When the pastor gives his sermon on Sunday, there are people who have been coming for 10 years who are listening to the sermon and there are people listening who have just begun to come to church. There are steps to be taken in order to grow in spiritual life. But churchgoers randomly jump back and forth among the steps, accepting whatever looks good. They just receive anything, and later on, they become completely confused. That is why, at times, they feel that they have good faith and they can go to heaven. They also think, "Will I be able to go to heaven like this, the way that I am?" Sometimes, it seems that Jesus has washed all of your sins away, and sometimes it seems that you have many sins remaining in your heart. The reason people live a poor spiritual life is because they have not climbed the levels of spiritual life, step by step.

In the Bible, it clearly says to repent before believing the words of the gospel. It says, "Repent ye and believe the gospel," to repent, turn around, and then believe in the gospel, but people do not know what true repentance is or what true faith is. That is why there are people who know many things about the Bible, who know that Jesus died for them, and who know that Jesus washed away all their past, present, and future sins. But those things do not enter or work in their hearts, lives, and spirits. Although they know this in their heart, they have no strength, and they are weak and lacking.

Saul Who Had not Known that It Was a Thought Put into Him by Satan

This morning, we spoke about Judas Iscariot's repentance. What did Judas Iscariot not know? What we actually must repent of is not that we have stolen, committed adultery, or lied.

When a person has leprosy, what is the true problem? Is the problem that his eyebrows are falling out, that his fingers are falling off, or that he has no feeling in his body? What makes the eyebrows fall out? Why is it that his fingers fall off, his toes fall off, and his arms fall off? Why does he lose all the senses in his body? Why does the person's face become disfigured and his nose collapse? It is the leprosy bacterium that is causing this to happen. Therefore, it is not that a leper must labor to keep his eyebrows from falling out. It is not that he should get a band-aid and tape his fingers to keep them from falling off. It is not that he should pull at and straighten his disfigured face. The disease of leprosy, itself, must be treated.

After Adam and Eve, all people were infected with the disease of sin. There are many mothers here. When you rear children, they are very pretty, beautiful, and cute. But when you see the evil hearts that arise inside of your children, you think, "Wow! They are so wicked." When I was in Daejon, our church had a kindergarten and the children were cute. Whenever I come home from conferences in America, I bring back chocolate bars and pass them out, one by one; they really love it. And when I see the image of the children eating the chocolate, it is beautiful, lovely, and cute. Once, I was looking at the children playing at the playground where there was a swing and a sandbox. I was watching them when one child picked up a handful of sand, threw it at another child, and pushed him down. "Wow! Who put that kind of heart inside that beautiful child? Where did it come from? How did that heart arise?" Outwardly, the children are beautiful, but their insides are not beautiful whatsoever. They all have evil inside of them.

Everyone, on Sunday, churchgoers put the Bible under their arms and say, "Pastor, how are you doing?" and they appear to be so gentle, don't they? But in reality, people are not good. I am at the Good News Gangnam Church, and before I came, Pastor Min-yong Moon was the pastor. Pastor Moon looks like a pure, clean person. Compared to Pastor Moon, I look like a fraud. One day, while reading Romans, I saw the words, *yea, let God be true, but every man a liar.* Then I thought, "Is Pastor Min-yong Moon a liar too? If the Bible says that he is a liar, then he is. How could a liar appear to be so pure?" After realizing this, he appeared to be more of a hypocrite than I am. Pastor Moon is here somewhere, but it is true.

Among humans, there is no one who is good. There are many people who appear to be good and sincere, but there is no one who is good and sincere when seen through the reflection of their conscience. But people hide the fact that they are evil, filthy, and dirty by nature. They only confess sins such as stealing, committing adultery, and lying that appear on the outside.

I spoke about this yesterday evening. Simon Peter's repentance, after he denied Jesus three times, was not that he repented of the deed of denying Jesus, but he repented from himself: "I cannot help but to be this way. I am filthy.

I am dirty." But Judas Iscariot, on the other hand, when he realized something deeply and was tormented in his heart for having sold Jesus, he threw the money he received into the temple. He only repented of the deed. He did not know that he, himself, was dirty and filthy. Because of that, he did not know that he was not worth believing in and continued to follow his own thoughts.

When I give such a sermon, there may be people who say, "Pastor, if I'm not supposed to live following my own thoughts, then am I supposed to live following somebody else's thoughts? Pastor, I don't understand. If I'm not supposed to live following my thoughts, then how am I supposed to live?"

Okay, let's talk about this. This evening, we read about Saul. What it says in the book of Acts is…. Let us read Acts 26:9-10:

I verily thought with myself, that I ought to do many things contrary to the name of Jesus of Nazareth. Which thing I also did in Jerusalem: and many of the saints did I shut up in prison, having received authority from the chief priests; and when they were put to death, I gave my voice against them.

Here is what Saul says: *I verily thought with myself, that I ought to do many things contrary to the name of Jesus of Nazareth.* So, in Saul's heart, the thoughts, "I'd better go against Jesus. I'd better persecute Jesus. I'd better capture and kill those who believe in Jesus," arose in his heart. And he, alone, considered that heart to be correct.

"Jesus freaks. They are all a bunch of liars because I know Jesus died. How can they all lie saying that He came back to life? Such people should be put to death."

He thought to himself, "Surely those Jesus freaks are all a bunch of frauds and heretics." Who placed those thoughts he had in him? Satan had put this sin in him, but Saul had no idea and did not realize that the thoughts he had were wrong.

The Thief Who Became a Missionary

Once, I went to Daegu, a brother came to me and said, "My older brother is here and he refuses to come inside. He will only stay in the car. Pastor, would you please come with me for a little while?" "Sure," I replied, "it doesn't cost me anything." I went out and I saw that this brother's older brother and his wife were sitting in a van. So I greeted them, "Hello." The two of them were sitting there looking very serious. I spoke to them for a little while and I asked them to go inside and talk. I brought them inside. I was sitting there speaking, but the older brother all of a sudden said to me, "Pastor, I committed robbery." And I wondered, "What did this person do that he would say he committed robbery?"

Detail by detail, he began to tell me. He said that when he was laid off from work, he came out boasting loudly, "So what? I can still eat and live without this job!" but it was so difficult for him to live in this world. Therefore, he had no choice. He got a job as the security officer of an apartment complex. Because he worked as a security officer, the ladies who lived at the apartments despised him very much. Because his old job was pretty good, it hurt his pride so much that he felt he could not continue like this. Naturally, he had a heart of wrath and a heart of rage against the supervisor who laid him off. One day, in order to take revenge, he went to his former supervisor's apartment.

On his way there, all of a sudden he rang the bell of the house next door. From inside someone asked who it was and when he said that he was from the security office, she opened the door for him. He went in and saw that the woman was there by herself. He put a knife to her throat and ordered her to give him money. It was his first time committing a robbery and he became afraid. "What am I going to do if this woman attacks me?" He first made sure he had his knife. Then he told her to put her arms behind her back and tied her up. He was also afraid that she would scream, so he took a rag and stuffed it in her mouth to keep her quiet. But the woman who had been obedient to that point, all of a sudden bit his hand. His hand began to bleed and he panicked. He didn't know what to do, so he just ran out.

He closed the door and ran. The car he had parked was nowhere to be found. Later on, he discovered that it had been parked illegally and the police had towed it away. He came home and told his wife everything that had happened. His wife said, "Honey, why did you do such a thing? Now we are completely ruined," and the two of them held each other's hands and cried all night long. He became very worried and it seemed as if the police were going to come and capture him. At that time, he thought, "Pastor Ock Soo Park often goes abroad to have conferences. If I tell him about this, then he will find a place abroad to which I can flee. Let me go abroad and live there and never come back." He had come looking for me in that state of mind.

Earlier that day, I had read about the prodigal son in Luke chapter 15:

And he said, A certain man had two sons: And the younger of them said to his father, Father, give me the portion of goods that falleth to me. And he divided unto them his living. And not many days after the younger son gathered all together, and took his journey into a far country, and there wasted his substance with riotous living. And when he had spent all, there arose a mighty famine in that land; and he began to be in want. And he went and joined himself to a citizen of that country; and he sent him into his fields to feed swine. And he would fain have filled his belly with the husks that the swine did eat: and no man gave unto him. And when he came to himself, he said, How many hired servants of my father's have bread enough and to spare, and I perish with hunger! I will arise and go to my father, and will say unto him, Father, I have sinned against heaven, and before thee, And am no more worthy to be called thy son: make me as one of thy hired servants. And he arose, and came to his father. But when he was yet a great way off, his father saw him, and had compassion, and ran, and fell on his neck, and kissed him. And the son said unto him, Father, I have sinned against heaven, and in thy sight, and am no more worthy to be called thy son. But the father said to his servants, Bring forth the best robe, and put it on him; and put a ring on his hand, and shoes on his feet: And bring hither the fatted calf, and kill it; and let us eat, and be merry: For this my son was dead, and is alive again; he was lost, and is found. And they began to be merry.

Before I was born again, when I read the Bible, I used to simply think, "Oh I guess that's what the Bible says." But after I received the forgiveness of sin and Jesus Christ entered my heart, the Lord would often have me realize the truths of the Bible. That day, while reading about the prodigal son in Luke chapter 15, one of the images that came to my mind was that this story seemed like a well drawn work of art.

Everyone, when creating a painting, for a beautiful red flower to stand out, there must be green leaves in the background. Just because the color of the flower is pretty, the entire canvas should not be painted in the color red. In art class, a teacher told the children to draw and one student turned in a completely blank, white sheet of drawing paper. "Hey, you little rascal, what is this? Why didn't you draw anything?"

"I did draw."

"What is it?"

"This is a scene of snow falling."

"Don't draw that. Draw something else."

Afterwards, he completely colored the entire sheet of paper black and turned it in. The teacher asked, "What is this?"

He said, "I drew the black board."

Everyone, it is the basics of drawing to use contrasting colors so that the opposing colors are shown.

In Luke chapter 15, there are truly contrasting colors that are being used. There is a scene where the prodigal son is wearing filthy clothes in a pigpen and he is eating husks along with the pigs because he is so hungry. This is a scene of extreme darkness and self-pity. After this, however, there is a scene of him wearing the best robe, with a ring on his hand, shoes on his feet, eating the fatted calf. This is a scene of true and bright glory and beauty. Luke chapter 15 creates a truly beautiful picture by putting together these two scenes.

While reading the Bible I thought, "Is it the same son? On

one hand, he has to live pitifully in a filthy and dirty pigpen. But on the other hand, why is it that he gets to share joy and happiness in the midst of glory at the party with music and have killed the fatted calf?" The Bible speaks of this very clearly. This story distinguishes between the times when the son is at work and when the father is at work. When the younger son was trying hard to do something, the results of his work were wearing dirty clothes, shivering in the cold at the pigpen, and eating the husks that the pigs ate. In his hunger, he could only say, "I will die. This is how I will die." It was such a pitiful scene. However, the father worked when the prodigal son returned and when the father spoke, the dirty rags were taken off and he was able to wear new clothes. When the father commanded the servants to put the best robes on the prodigal son, do you think they put just any robe on him? Do you think all that they did was put a robe on him? They quickly took him to a bathtub, turned on the hot water, and washed his hair. They gave him a hair cut, a shave, and scrubbed his back. They wiped him clean, put underwear on him, put good clothes on him, and made him look very spiffy. The father continued to further say, "Put a ring on his hand. He is my son." Then he said, "Put shoes on his feet. Kill the fatted calf, and let us have a party."

I thought, "Ah, that's right. This is spiritual life."

When we are at work, the result is us dying pitifully. When the father is at work, it results in everything truly becoming glorious. That day, while reading the Scriptures, I searched through other parts of the Bible. In all the 66 books of the Bible, the results of man trying to do something himself ended pitifully. But when God did the work, everything ended so beautifully. We don't even need to ask the reasons of people who cannot live a spiritual life; of people who live difficult spiritual lives; of people whose spiritual life is tiring; of people whose prayers are not answered. It is because such people are trying to do everything themselves. There is no reason for us to ask why people do not change, or why people are unable to quit drinking, smoking, or doing drugs. They are people who are trying to live spiritual life by themselves.

But no matter what kind of a person you are, it is so easy if God works. A long time ago, Elder Hyung-mo Lee's grandfather was a pastor, so he had gone to church from a very young age. When he became an adult, he would often drink. Then, one day, he came to our church and received salvation and even after he received salvation, he drank. One time, he went to go drinking with his friends. After they had one drink, two drinks, they became drunk. He said that one of his friends said, "Hey, hold up. I have something to say," and he began to boast about himself. Then another person said, "Shut up. Listen to what I have to say," and then he went on to speak all about the things he was proud of. Before alcohol entered them, they were reserved and reputable people. But once they began drinking, they were each boasting about their own greatness, and it was so childish. And that's how he too was until now. At that place, after receiving salvation, he saw that he had always been as childish as these people. With that thought, he became sober and from then on, he didn't drink anymore. Thus it was not Elder Lee who had quit drinking on his own; God made him quit.

I have ministered for a long time as a pastor. It is not I who has been ministering. I cannot even pray well; I cannot understand the Bible well; and I cannot give good sermons.

There's nothing that I'm good at, but God is doing the work, and that was what is so amazing.

Upon listening to the words of that man who had committed robbery, the words of Luke that I had read that morning came to mind. "Mr. Jong-ryul Kim, listen to what I have to say. You have lived by your own zeal until now and the end result has been nothing more than you becoming a robber. Now leave your life in the hands of God. Then God will lead you."

He said that he would do that. At that moment, they brought in the dinner table. We had a portable gas burner and I roasted meat for him, asking him to eat. I told him, "Tomorrow, go to the Busan police station and turn yourself in," and I also said, "If they sentence you to 10 years, serve it. If they sentence you to 20 years, then serve it. And if they sentence you to death, be executed. From now on, leave everything to God and let go of everything." I told him to see whether God will work or not, and he said that he would do that.

But his wife, who was right next to him, shouted, "No way! No, not that!" I asked her why she shouted, and she said, "I cannot tell my son that his father is a robber." And she said, "My son will be a robber's son, and I cannot allow that!"

I said, "Shut your mouth! How can you say that in this situation?"

I am very loud when I speak through a microphone like this, but without a microphone, I often scream. I asked him, "Are you going to do it?"

He said that he was going to do it. He spent the night, and the next day he went to the Busan police station and turned himself in. I recommended that he hire a lawyer and go together when he turned himself in. He did that. He learned that the police had already searched the home and had collected three of his fingerprints. In a few days, his identity would have been known and he would have been arrested. After he turned himself in, from that point on, God began to work.

I don't have time to tell you all about it this evening. He was sentenced to two years in prison and three years of probation. But miraculously, he was released after one month. He called me immediately.

"Pastor, I just got out of prison today. I will come see you."

I told him not to come. "Since you were released today I am sure you have much to do. Take a bath and put on new clothes. Go home and have dinner with your family. Get your affairs in order, and after about 10 days, when things are settled down and you have some time, come and see me."

He said that he would, and later on, he came to see me. He spoke to me about his past. While in prison, God helped him moment by moment. He thought that it was a premeditated robbery and that probation was impossible, but that's how he was sentenced and released. He was very thankful and said, "Pastor, I wanted to leave Korea and go to a foreign country and live there. Now, I want to go abroad and live as a missionary." He entered our missionary school, and right now, he is a missionary in Japan. He is working as such a precious missionary.

"Ock Soo Park, You Dirty… You Conniving… You Wicked…"

There is such a difference when God is at work and when

I am at work. When my wife is cooking Doenjang stew, because I trust her, I am not concerned about it whatsoever. Once, my wife wasn't at home, so my daughter, who was in the seventh grade at the time, cooked Doenjang stew. I told her, "Hey, is that how you're suppose to cook that? Do this and do that." I said this because my daughter didn't know how to make it, but when my wife is cooking Doenjang stew, I do not say, "Honey, are you going to let the Doenjang stew broth boil that much? Put in some more pepper. Oh, don't make it like that."

If you have faith that Jesus will take charge of your life and that He will lead it well, there is nothing for you to do. Many people today pray zealously and try hard, not because they have faith, but it is the opposite; because they do not have faith. If you leave your life to the loving Lord, how beautifully He will take care of everything! Everyone, the prodigal son came back. What does it matter whether he has a lot of pig dung on his clothes or a little pig dung on his clothes? In his own eyes, it matters whether he has more or less dung on him. But in the eyes of the father, they are clothes that are to be thrown away anyway. Isn't that so? If Jesus cleanses you and washes your sins away, what does it matter whether you have many sins or a few sins? We do not become too concerned when we catch a cold, but we become extremely distressed when we get cancer. To God, healing a cold or healing cancer is the same; wouldn't it be? Can you say amen to that? Yes, that's right. Everyone, if you have faith to believe in God, there is no need for you to wrestle against sin. There is no need for you to wander and labor because of sin.

I am the pastor of Good News Gangnam Church. Only

extremely good people are our church members. Other pastors know the houses and addresses of their church members, their birthdays, and even their family's birthdays. I lag behind in that. I don't even know the houses of ten of my church members. Birthdays? I'm sorry. I am afraid that my wife might be here listening. We finished the conference in Gwangju and were on our way home. The next day was my wife's birthday. I didn't know. I heard my son was going to come over to eat breakfast. I asked myself, "Why is he going to come?" and my wife seemed to be very disappointed in something. It was later on that I found out it was her birthday. The next day, I was eating breakfast and something felt strange. So I thought quietly, "What is the date today?" It was my wife's birthday. Because people's ages change every year, it is difficult to remember. Although birthdays don't change, it is difficult for me to remember.

Whether I was in Daegu, Daejon, or in Seoul, I did not do any of the work in my ministry. Our church members believe that God is with everything that Pastor Ock Soo Park does because they actually see and experience it. Mine was a wretched life; and then I met Jesus. I didn't believe in Jesus because I wanted to, nor did I go to a mountain, fasting and saying, "Lord, I believe you," while holding onto a pine tree and laboring to believe that way. I knew I was the most pathetic person in the entire world. I knew that I was the most evil and dirty person in the world. I was so filthy. In addition, I saw no light whatsoever on the roads laid ahead of me in my life. The painful thing was not that I was poor, hungry, or had many difficulties. I was sick of the situation and I would be able to live on if there was any hope that tomorrow would be better. However, there was no hope that tomorrow would be better.

The final choice that I made was to volunteer to go into the army. I took my physical at Daegu First Army Hospital. Because my front tooth was broken, I failed the physical. "Even the army hates me." I fell into despair. But one day, I saw myself and I was truly a wicked, dirty, and filthy person. Before that, I thought I was clean and good. I looked at my face in the mirror and shouted, "Ock Soo Park! You are so dirty! You are so conniving! You are so wicked!" Before this, I hadn't taken a good look at myself. I thought that if I tried to be good, I would become good. And I thought that if I tried to be honest, I would become honest. I thought that if I prayed hard and read the Bible, I would become a better person. Because I was so filthy and dirty, I strained to live as a good person, but the more I tried, the more I saw it was not working. One day I saw myself as God sees me. I saw that I was an evil, filthy, and dirty person. The heart of believing in myself crumbled down.

Before, I tried to do everything myself: "I am going to pray hard. I am going to zealously read the Bible and labor to become a good person. I am going to become a great person." I would say this, but I was unable to do it. "Why am I a person who isn't able to do this to begin with?" Afterwards, I didn't even try to pray or read the Bible. I didn't try to live as a good person. I've come to know I was truly a wicked person. One day, when I was nineteen, I distrusted myself. When I looked at the life that I was living until then, I, who didn't know anything, had made every decision concerning how I lived my life. I saw that it was so foolish. How would I know anything? I didn't even know a single thing, but I acted according to my own decisions and I had been deceived into thinking that all of my decisions were right. I had been so foolish. I had been so stupid. After realizing this fact, there was nothing for me to do whatsoever.

Then, the world appeared different to me because the entire world was made up of lies.

"Genius is 99% perspiration and 1% inspiration."

Before, I would say, "Those are great words. If I, too, try hard, I could become a genius." Later on, I realized that those words were a bunch of baloney. Is a genius made from 99% perspiration? You know, perspiration works for those it works for, but for those for whom it doesn't work, no matter how hard they try, it doesn't work. A bird brain will not become a genius just because he studies. If he studies all night, nothing is going to happen, except his hair will fall out. Everyone, a person who knows how to sing should try to learn, but the more a tone-deaf person sings, the more he makes an unbearable sound.

I opened my eyes and saw that the entire world was this way.

"Even though the earth should see the end tomorrow, I will plant an apple tree."

When this person died, he didn't plant an apple tree. He has to plant an apple tree the day before he dies. He had said this with his mouth, but his actual life was not this way. People consider these words to be great and write them down and post them on their desks, but they all live their lives being deceived. If the end of the world comes tomorrow, I will never plant an apple tree. If the end of the world is coming tomorrow, will I be crazy enough to be planting an apple tree?

Here's something I read from a text book at school.

George Washington's axe was so good when he was young that he excitedly chopped down a cherry tree. Later on, his father came to him and asked, "Who chopped down this tree?" I heard that Washington answered, "Father, it was I." The father then patted George Washington's head and said, "The honesty you have shown is more precious than the cherry tree that has been axed," and he commended him. Such stories come about because Washington became the first president. If he had grown to become a bad person, then they would have cursed him saying, "That scoundrel was a person who chopped down the cherry tree to begin with. No matter how good the axe was and no matter how much he wanted to use the axe, what kind of person would chop down a fine cherry tree? Such thoughtless people should be spanked. They should be spanked until their calves are completely swollen." They speak well of him now because he later went on to become the President of the United States. But what he actually did was not something good at all.

In the world, they call such tales good stories. My perspective of the world has changed. But the amazing thing is that my perspective of the Bible has also completely changed. People are hypocritically reading the Bible. They deal with the Bible only on its surface. I've come to realize that people don't believe the Word of God that is contained in the Bible. From then on, the words of the Bible began to enter my heart anew. Before, I thought I was great and smart, and I thought highly of myself. I was standing so upright that even though I was brought up with the Bible, only the aspects that fit my heart entered. I couldn't accept the things that didn't fit my heart. When I came to deny myself, the words of the Bible began to enter my heart exactly as they were, without being filtered.

One day, Elijah appeared before the widow at Zarephath. This woman was starving to death so she wanted to eat her final piece of bread and die. Then, Elijah said, "Bring that to me first, and then, from your jar, meal will continue to spring forth."

"The meal that was in the jar was already eaten, how could more meal be in the jar? Please cut the nonsense. This old man is trying to outwit me to take my bread." In our thoughts, that was what the widow at Zarephath should have thought.

When I first learned from the Bible at church, I thought that if you did good things and listened intently to the words, you would become a better person, more and more. But when I saw the true meaning of the Bible, I was far from becoming a good person. Even when I tried, in reality, I couldn't do it. And even though I attended church, what can a bunch of friends do in the countryside? In the evening, I would go play poker or attack an orchard. Especially about this time of year, they hang out dried persimmons. On dark nights, we would steal and eat those sweet, delicious dried persimmons. From then on, we would be afraid because of the guilt of having stolen. We would then go to early morning service the next day and repent. In the countryside, I always did bad things. When I didn't know what kind of person I was, I thought that if I prayed, read the Bible, and tried to live like a good person, then I would become good. That was what Satan taught me; and I was deceived. Today, there are so many Christians in Korea who are deceived by Satan. They think that if they labor, they can become good because they are trying hard to live as good people. They are people who do not actually believe in God. They have a false idea about belief in God.

One day, when I distrusted myself and read the Bible, I saw the Bible was completely different from what I had thought. Before, I picked out only the parts that fit my heart, so the Bible fit my heart then. Now I saw that the Bible was so different from my heart. What the Bible says is that there is no righteousness in men. What the Bible says is that there is no good inside of men. What the Bible says is that there is nothing good or righteous whatsoever inside of men. There is no good and there is no righteousness inside of us, so how can we produce any righteousness? Many people labor to do good and they labor to produce righteousness.

One day, I realized this fact: "That's right. I only have evil and there is no good in me. All I have is dirtiness. I have no righteousness. Then, I can't do good even if I try." I thought about the past. I came to know the reason why I couldn't become good no matter how hard I tried. It didn't work even though I would cry and repent early every morning and try to become good. By nature, there is no good in me, so how can I do good? There is no way for it to work out. From then on, trying to do good on my part ended.

"Jesus, I am a dirty human. I am an evil human who can only go to hell. I am a human who can only be destroyed because of sin. Lord, you have to cleanse me. Lord, whether you cleanse me or whether you allow me to go to hell, there is nothing I can do. If you do cleanse me, I would be thankful."

Right then, I was able to give my life completely to Jesus. Amazingly, from that moment on, Jesus Christ entered my life and began to work. Hallelujah! I praise the Lord.

That Pastor Is a Liar!

I once saw a child playing the piano, and I said to my daughter, "Eun-sook, why didn't you help that child playing the piano?"

"Dad, I cannot teach that child."

"Why not?"

"In my eyes, she's not very good at playing the piano, but she thinks she is better than me at playing, so I cannot teach her."

"Is that so?"

I did not say anything more.

After service yesterday, a member of our church brought his son to me. He is a child with a lot of problems. I spoke to him for a long time and saw that this child despised me very much, so I asked him, "Why do you despise me? You can't even go to high school right now, who do you think you are to despise me? Do you know my son? My son studied in America. He's a lot smarter than you, and he speaks English fluently, but my son doesn't even despise me. Why do you despise me? How then am I supposed to help you?"

That student thought that he was much smarter than me, so no matter what I said, it did not enter him, and he only spoke of his own opinions.

"Think deeply about this once if you are really smart. If you're so smart, then why aren't you in high school? What's wrong with you?"

You may not despise Jesus, but every one thinks that they are great people. People feel insecure leaving their lives up to Jesus and they hold onto everything themselves. That is why Jesus cannot do any work inside of their lives.

There is one thing you must know precisely. It is that you cannot do anything good, no matter how hard you try. Even now, the people who do not know this are trying to do good. Many pastors in Korea, today, stand at the pulpit and shout out, "People, let us be good! Let us live as good people!"

When I was in Daejon, an army major had received salvation. His wife had gone to church for 20 years. She was attending the church on the base where her husband was stationed and her husband attended our church. After services, the husband would go home and ask his wife a question.

"Honey, what did the pastor of your church preach about today?"

"Oh, he preached about the Bible."

"Which story in the Bible?"

"Oh, he preached the Word of God."

"Oh, which Word of God?"

There was not one thing remaining inside of the wife. Then he would tell her, "Pastor Ock Soo Park of my church talked about this, this, and that."

On Sundays this brother would first drop his wife off at the base church and then he would come by himself to my church. One day, his car was low on gas, so he took a right turn to go to the gas station. When he did that, his wife thought that he was forcefully bringing her to our church, and when she thought that, she opened the door to jump out of the moving car. The husband was stunned.

One day, he and his wife were watching TV together. It was May, which is the month for family in Korea, and there was a certain pastor giving a sermon. He said, "Everyone, love your wives. Don't be angry at your children. Even to this day, I have never once said anything to break my wife's heart. And to this very day, I have never once said a word that upset my children." That was what this pastor said. Then the wife looked at her husband and said, "You heard him, right?"

The husband replied, "That pastor is a liar! In the Bible, it says, 'If any man offend not in word, the same is a perfect man.' Do you think that this person really is perfect? If he's so perfect, why does he believe in Jesus? He should believe in himself. That person is lying. How can you never make any mistakes? There's no one who never makes any mistakes when he talks, but his saying that he has done it perfectly must be a lie."

The wife was completely surprised. It was the same person, but the way the husband saw him and the way the wife saw him were completely different.

We are not good. We are not holy. This evening, if there's anyone among you who still thinks that you can do good and become holy by doing good, you have to suffer a little bit more. Go ahead and try it. However, the time when faith arises inside of you, is when you say, "Ah, I cannot do this." You come to believe in Jesus because you cannot do it through your own effort.

Deceived People Who Think It Will Work This Time

I once went to Germany. It was in September, and there were many students who boarded the plane with me who were going to study abroad in France and Italy. A while after the airplane took off, one student pulled out a watch, and asked, "What time is it in Germany right now?" He wanted to change his watch to German time. However, he said, "I can't change the time," and he was not able to change the time on his electronic watch. The students around him were also unable to do it as well. And inwardly, I thought, "Gee, these college students can't even set the time on a watch? I'm good at that." Then that watch began to circulate around the airplane. One student tried and could not do it, and passed it on to the next student. And that student could not do it and passed it onto the next student. I was thinking inside to myself, "I hope that they don't do it. Let it come to me. I'll set the time, and show them." Then the watch came all the way to the student sitting next to me.

"Why can't I do this?"

"Student, give it to me. Let me try."

I don't know what kind of watch it was, but even I couldn't set it. It had four buttons and I pushed them all, but I couldn't do it. I ended up not being able to set the watch. Think about it. Could an old gentleman be as good as these young students?

Yesterday, my wife sent me a text message on my cellular phone while I was riding in the car with her because she wanted to play a joke on me. I have never once sent a text message. Since someone bought a phone for me, I carry around a very nice cellular phone, but other than making phone calls and receiving them, I have not once used the other functions. Because I asked, "How do you send a message?" my wife and my daughter told me how. So for the first time, yesterday, I sent a text message to my wife. My wife sent me a text message saying, "A stupid old man is sitting in the back of the car," so I sent her a message saying,

"The stupid old man's wife is sitting in the front of the car."

College students can do this much better than I, but I had the heart that if I tried, I could do it. After trying for a while, I told them, "I cannot do it," and returned the watch to them. The watch then began to circulate again and again. Another thought that came to me was, "Ah, what kind of heart did the watchmaker make the watch with? If I set the time thinking about that, then I could do it." The watch went all the way around once more, and again, back to me. "Let me try one more time." And again, I could not do it.

Everyone, spiritual life is exactly like this. If you cannot do well this time, it seems that if you try harder you will be able to do it. It seems that if you become more determined and work harder you can do it, or if you quit drinking and pray you can do it. People are deceived by this and they continue to try. Jesus cannot work while people are this way. While the prodigal son was working, the father did not do anything. When the prodigal son rested, the father worked. That's how it is in the Bible.

I am a person who does not know anything. I don't know the Bible and I truly lived wickedly. I said, "I am truly a dirty person. What a wicked man I am! I cannot do good even though I try to," and I deeply realized that I was a sinner and a helpless man. Because I knew that no matter how hard I tried, I could not do it, I was able to let go of things from my hands. Right then, Jesus Christ worked with power and my sins were washed away. I was sanctified; my life became bright; and I was able to see God working inside of me.

Everyone, if there is a reason that Jesus cannot work inside of you, it is because you think that you can do it yourself if you try. All I have to do is go to church on Sundays, keep the law, read the Bible, and live as a good person. How can such a person rely on Jesus? He cannot. After I discovered my own image, Jesus Christ lived inside of me and began to work.

In our mission, we want to send 700 college students all over the world as missionaries next year. This is something tremendous. A female student came to me while we were training those students, and asked me, "Pastor, will we be truly changed upon receiving the training? Will we be changed?" Many students with problems came and this is what I say to those students:

"God never works together with us. God works when we let go of things from our hands."

When we truly know ourselves and let go, from then on, God works. If that happens, everything works out so amazingly and beautifully. However, because you are deceived inside an illusion, thinking that you can do something if you try hard, you do not try to let go of what you are trying to do.

Abraham's wife Sarah brought another woman to her husband's bedroom. What kind of a woman would allow another woman into her husband's bedroom? Do you know why Sarah allowed another woman to enter into Abraham's bedroom? It is because she had clearly known that she could not have a son. If there was any chance that she could have a son, would she be crazy enough to send another woman into her husband's bedroom? That would be nonsense.

Jesus works from the point that you know it cannot be done with your effort. Amen? However, in many churches, today, they teach spiritual life backwards. They continually deceive people, saying, "Let us be faithful. Let us love. Let us live by faith. Let us zealously serve the Lord. Let us give an offering." People continue to do this because they are deceived.

After people who gamble lose money, they think that they will win the next time. After losing more money, they think that they will win the next time. They never think about losing, but only about winning. That is why they continue to gamble even if they lose their wives. "So what if I lose my wife? I'll just win her back." It's only a problem when he loses, so even though he is risking his wife for however much it may be, it's not a problem if he doesn't lose. The reason that he does this is because he only thinks of winning. That's how it is. People who live that kind of spiritual life think that it may not have worked last time, but they feel that this time they can do it. They feel that if they start the New Year off by fasting, it will work out. They also think that they can do it if they pray for 40 days. And they think that they can do it if they do the 100 day early morning prayer. It doesn't work out because they try to do it and hold onto it with themselves as the lord.

On an airplane, there are two pilot seats. One seat is for the main pilot and the other seat is for the co-pilot. When the main pilot says, "I got it," and takes the controls, the co-pilot must let go of the stick. When the main pilot says, "You got it from here," he hands the stick to the co-pilot. Then the main pilot must let go of the stick. The airplane cannot be flown with both pilots holding onto the stick. It must either be you who solves the problems of your life, or Jesus who solves the problems of your life. It must be one or the other, but not both. When you leave it entirely up to Jesus Christ, then the loving Jesus works upon you, and amazing works occur.

I Thought It Would Be Right to Put Him in Prison and Kill Him

Before Apostle Paul received salvation, when he was Saul, he captured people who believed in Jesus, put them in prison, and killed them. What did Saul say in Acts chapter 26 that we read today? *I verily thought with myself, that I ought to do many things contrary to the name of Jesus of Nazareth.* He was thinking by his own means and he believed in his own thoughts. People who believe in themselves believe in their own thoughts. If someone continually rips me off and I no longer believe him, then no matter what he says, I will not follow his words. Because Saul trusted in himself, he followed after his own thoughts, captured the people who believed in Jesus, and killed them. He put them in prison. And he persecuted them.

"These Jesus freaks! This Jesus died and they go around ripping people off saying that He is alive. These liars! These people are a menace to society. They should be killed. They should be destroyed."

In Jerusalem, he captured people who believed in Jesus and locked them up in prison. Now, he was going to Damascus to capture people who believed in Jesus. But on his way to Damascus, there was a great light and Saul fell down. At that moment, he heard a voice.

"Saul, Saul, why persecutest thou me?"

Saul was absolutely stunned.

"Lord, who art thou? Who are you that you say I am persecuting you?"

"I am Jesus of Nazareth whom thou persecutest."

"What? Jesus? Then is it really true that you are alive? I

thought it was a lie when Christians said that you were alive. I thought that was nonsense. But is it true that you are alive?"

Saul came to know that his thoughts and his judgment were wrong. Before then, he thought to himself, "Jesus freaks! They're a bunch of liars. How can Jesus, who is dead, come back to life? These people are a menace to society. They should be killed and gotten rid of." Following those thoughts, he captured Christians, locked them in prison, persecuted them, and beat them. However, he came to know how ignorant and evil those thoughts were. Right then he heard the voice of Jesus.

Arise, and go into the city, and it shall be told thee what thou must do. (Acts 9:6)

Saul had lived with his own decisions, his own opinions, and his own thoughts. But upon hearing the voice of Jesus, he realized that his own judgment was wrong. "Ah, how dangerously wrong it was that I acted and simply followed after my own thoughts, without precisely looking into things!"

Not just anyone can become a general in the army. A person with much combat experience and knowledge can become a general. A person who just entered the army yesterday cannot be a general and lead the army. Not just anyone can become a minister, Prime Minister, or a mayor. And not just anyone can become the president of a company. But sadly, we establish ourselves, who know nothing of our future, as kings in the kingdom of our heart, and we have done everything according to the decisions we have made ourselves. Saul was saddened that he had lived his life this way.

"Simply following my own thoughts, I thought that it was a

lie that Jesus resurrected, without looking into it. I had been so useless. I had been so arrogant. Why did I do something so wrong? The people I put into prison; the many people I persecuted; I had truly done wrong to those people! Why did I believe in myself? I should not have simply followed my thoughts, but I should have looked further into it, confirmed it precisely, and then gone about things!"

Saul had now become afraid of following his own thoughts. He had no choice but to let go of his own thoughts. Right then Jesus said, "Arise, and go into the city." Now Saul did not arise through his own thoughts. He arose and was entering the city through Jesus, and through the words of Jesus.

Loving folks, do you live through the Word, or do you live through your own thoughts? Because many people still believe and rely on themselves, they do not live spiritual life through the Word, but through their own thoughts, experiences, and methods. When they choose a church, they choose one that fits their own heart. And they also choose a pastor that fits their own heart. In the same way, because I was the king of the kingdom of my heart until now, Jesus Christ could not work inside of me. Therefore, spiritual life cannot work with your effort.

For Jesus to work inside of you, you must truly realize that you are evil. You must realize that you are filthy and dirty. You must deny yourself. You must know it can't be done with your zealous effort. That is why, though you may fail, or though it may not work, you must be able to leave it in the Lord's hands. If a certain person is healthy and the doctor wants to cut his stomach open, would he allow that? On the other hand, if a person can only die of cancer, he has no choice but to leave his body up to the doctor. You can believe in Jesus when you have no methods of your own. Everyone, the reason faith does not arise in you is because you are following your own ways.

Satan deceives you to make you believe in your ways in order to keep you from entering into faith. "Okay, all you have to do is work hard. Just pray. Live nicely. Keep the law. You'll be fine." And because you try to do it that way with that kind of heart, you cannot believe in Jesus. People who receive the grace of God discover exactly who they are.

"I am a seed of sin. There is evil inside of me. Even though I am trying to do good, it will not work. I can only be destroyed when I hold onto it. I can only go to hell."

Therefore, they leave themselves up to Jesus. When you leave your lives in the hands of the Lord, from that point on, Jesus will work powerfully.

4
Cain's Repentance

4.
Cain's Repentance

Hello, everyone. This morning, we will read the words in Genesis chapter 4. Please open to Genesis chapter 4. I will read from Genesis chapter 4, verse 1.

And Adam knew Eve his wife; and she conceived, and bare Cain, and said, I have gotten a man from the LORD. And she again bare his brother Abel. And Abel was a keeper of sheep, but Cain was a tiller of the ground. And in process of time it came to pass, that Cain brought of the fruit of the ground an offering unto the LORD. And Abel, he also brought of the firstlings of his flock and of the fat thereof. And the LORD had respect unto Abel and to his offering: But unto Cain and to his offering he had not respect. And Cain was very wroth, and his countenance fell. And the

LORD said unto Cain, Why art thou wroth? and why is thy countenance fallen? If thou doest well, shalt thou not be accepted? and if thou doest not well, sin lieth at the door. And unto thee shall be his desire, and thou shalt rule over him. And Cain talked with Abel his brother: and it came to pass, when they were in the field, that Cain rose up against Abel his brother, and slew him. And the LORD said unto Cain, Where is Abel thy brother? And he said, I know not: Am I my brother's keeper? And he said, What hast thou done? the voice of thy brother's blood crieth unto me from the ground. And now art thou cursed from the earth, which hath opened her mouth to receive thy brother's blood from thy hand; When thou tillest the ground, it shall not henceforth yield unto thee her strength; a fugitive and a vagabond shalt thou be in the earth. And Cain said unto the LORD, My punishment is greater than I can bear. Behold, thou hast driven me out this day from the face of the earth; and from thy face shall I be hid; and I shall be a fugitive and a vagabond in the earth; and it shall come to pass, that every one that findeth me shall slay me. And the LORD said unto him, Therefore whosoever slayeth Cain, vengeance shall be taken on him sevenfold. And the LORD set a mark upon Cain, lest any finding him should kill him.

I read up to the words of verse 15.

God, Give Me a Pair of Gloves!

I have ministered until now and have seen how loving Jesus changed the lives of many people. I saw Him blessing them. When a new person comes to my church, I carefully search his heart. Then, with the eyes of my heart, I mark him. How will he be changed in one year after receiving the forgiveness of sin? How much will he be changed in two years? I am happy just imagining that. Before I became born again, I had earnestly attended church, but no matter what I did, nothing went well. With my lips, I said, “It is a blessing to believe in Jesus. It is a joy to believe in Jesus. I can go to heaven.” But in reality, there was absolutely nothing that was going well. One day I received the grace of the Lord, and my life was changed. From that point on, there was nothing that did not work out in my life.

I entered the military in the winter of 1965 and was in the middle of training. I slept one night and woke up in the morning. I was going to put on my gloves for training, but my gloves were missing. I had folded my gloves and left them next to my helmet. But while I was sleeping that night, somebody had stolen them. I was extremely worried because of this problem. “Now, what am I going to do?” In the military, everybody receives the same gloves and it was not long before that I had received those gloves. It would not be difficult for me to say that I am going to the bathroom and quietly steal someome else’s pair. But the Lord inside of my heart would not permit me to steal.

However, in my carnal heart I thought, “Still, you have no choice. This is the army. You have to steal here.” That was the heart I had. In the morning, I went out for training carrying my M-1 rifle. We were going along singing the cadence, “I Was Born a Man.” Out of the forty people in my platoon, thirty-nine of us had gloves on and were raising camouflaged hands. I was the only one lifting up bare, red hands. It was no problem that my hands were cold, but I was worried that my platoon leader would say, "Where did you sell your gloves?" At that time, beatings were very severe. From time to time, in my platoon, I had often seen some of my colleagues being beaten with a stick by the platoon leader. I became very afraid when I thought about that.

"God, give me a pair of gloves!"

When you lose your things in the army, you can never say that you've lost them. You should not say a word and go steal it back. Then it becomes yours. If you say that you've lost something and then go and steal, then the person who loses the same thing will come looking for you. I, too, went three days without saying that I lost my gloves. I worried for three days. I made up my mind saying, "I can't go on like this. I'd better go steal some gloves." But from my heart, "I am going to be in the military for three years to preach the gospel. If I get caught stealing gloves, how will I be able to witness? Even if I do not get caught, if I carry on this way, will I be able to preach the gospel while I am in the army?" That was the heart that stirred up, so I completely lost the heart to steal gloves. I lay down to sleep that night and I prayed. Even when we sleep at the training camp, we don't just sleep. We must go to sleep lining our heads up perfectly at the head of our beds. We weren't allowed to lie on our stomachs nor were we allowed to kneel down. So I lay straight on my back and prayed.

"God, give me a pair of gloves. If I get caught by the platoon leader for not having gloves, even though I may get badly beaten and go through hardships, I will not steal. Please, give me a pair of gloves."

While praying that night, I decided not to steal any gloves. The next day, we had grenade throwing training. It was training where we would remove the pin from a grenade and count, "One. Two," throw it, and then lie on our stomachs. After 50 minutes of training, we took a ten minute break. While all the other colleagues were smoking, one colleague approached me.

"Ock Soo Park, why don't you have your gloves on?"

"Hey, I have a problem."

"What?"

"While I slept one night, somebody stole my gloves."

"Man, you should have told me."

"Why? Do you have two pairs of gloves?"

"Yeah, I have two pairs."

"Hey, where did you steal them?" I am sorry, but that is how they talk in the army.

"Steal?"

"Then how can you have two pairs of gloves if you didn't steal?"

"My brother is a company commander. He gave me another pair because I have frostbite on my hands. Hey, this is what's good about being army buddies. Let's share these gloves."

That friend took off his gloves and gave them to me. When I received those gloves, I thought, "Are these really gloves?"

Everyone, I have lived a spiritual life since I was young, but in my spiritual life, a clear line was drawn. Before that line was drawn, no matter what I did to live a spiritual life, although other people were able to do it, I could not. From that day on, though, that line was drawn. Whether I was in the army or wherever I was, the hand of God never left me. For me to talk about such things, I won't be able to mention them all to you even though I may talk all night long.

Send Yeong Kook Park to the Stockade!

When I talk individually to the people who attend our church, I can see exactly what problems they have in their spiritual lives.

"Ah, this person's problem has not been solved yet. That person is still under the law trying to do things by himself. This person is still caught in his own works."

When I speak to them for just a little while, I can clearly see this. I, too, used many humanistic methods before I received salvation. God made me realize in my heart that it was useless to use them. After I let go of those humanistic methods, it was easy for me to see that God was working inside of me. But some people are still trying to use humanistic methods as they live their spiritual life. "Ah, if he does that, he will fail, but he still doesn't know it." When I speak to the individuals I meet, I talk to them about that step. When they go beyond that step, I can see that the Lord who worked inside of me works inside of them with the same power. This is something that is very fun. I can see these things clearly through stories of how God helped businessmen and the stores they run.

I served three years in the army as a regular soldier and was discharged. I was very happy being together with Jesus over those three years. I was so thankful for the times I preached the gospel on my base that even if I were to be told to be in the army for the rest of my life, I would want to.

My son went into the army at a late age; the age of 26. Someone came to me and said, "Pastor, Yeong Kook is going into the army. Should I call someone I know in the army to help him out a little?" I told him, "What are you talking about? God is leading him. You must absolutely leave him alone. I want to see how God works." My son must have been burdened because all his friends had already been discharged while he was now entering the army at a late age. However, he said, "I have to go anyway." Therefore he departed with these words, "I hope I won't get into the Special Forces." The day he finished his training at the training center in Nonsan, I was holding a conference in America. I then heard the news that he was sent to the Special Forces.

After being assigned to the Special Forces, he would call home once in a while. "Father, there are two public phones in our training base. I skipped dinner tonight and waited 30 minutes in line. That's what I had to do to call you today."

"Mom, I twisted my ankle, can you send some bandages?" It seemed that he was having a very difficult time. Upon finishing his basic training for the Special Forces, he was assigned to the base where he would serve. They called out all the names of his training colleagues and assigned them to their bases, but they didn't call his name. At the very end, they called out his name: "Yeong Kook Park; Secretary of the commander."

All of his colleagues said, "Wow!" He became the secretary of a three-star general. Later on, my son gave a testimony:

"Father, I didn't become the commander's secretary through any connections, nor did I try to become the secretary."

You see, in the Special Forces, everyone at the base must receive special training. When the commander's secretary was being discharged, they had to calculate the dates of soldiers at Nonsan basic training center and calculate the dates of the start of the Special Forces training. They also gave an English test to all the soldiers in training who fit those dates. Of them, my son placed first, and it was decided that he would become the commander's secretary. My son gave a testimony of how he was living in the army. Anyone hearing the testimony could clearly see God was helping my son.

Shortly after he had become the. commander's secretary, my son was alone in the office after the commander left work one day when a senior serviceman from his base came into the office. The serviceman fearlessly used the commander's phone to call his girlfriend in Japan and spoke to her in English. His girlfriend was North Korean-Japanese and the phone call was caught by communications security. The commander became angry and yelled at those in the secretary's office.

"Who used my phone to call his girlfriend in Japan, speaking in English?"

All the workers in the secretary's office said it was my son, Yeong Kook. The only one at the secretary's office who could make a phone call in English was Yeong Kook. "Bring Park, Yeong Kook over here!" My son was summoned. "Why did you make a phone call in English to Japan with my phone?"

"Sir, I did not do that, sir."

"You punk, you think you can lie here? Send him to the stockade!" My son was to be sent to the stockade. When my son was in the army, he didn't pray much. But because he was to be sent to the stockade the next morning, he couldn't sleep, so all night long, he knelt down and prayed before God.

"God, help me. Why are you allowing this to happen to me?"

Through this, my son's faith grew immensely. The next morning, everything was prepared for him to go to the stockade, but the chief of staff, who was a one-star general called him over. "Yeong Kook Park, come over here."

"Sir, yes, sir."

"Did you make the phone call?"

"Sir, I did not, sir."

"You believe in God, don't you?"

"Sir, yes, sir. I do, sir."

"Your father is a pastor?"

"Sir, yes, sir. He is a pastor, sir."

"Can you swear in the name of God that you didn't make the phone call?"

"Sir, yes, sir. I can, sir."

"Can you swear on your father's name?"

"Sir, yes, sir. I can, sir."

"Bring over all the workers at the secretary's office." He then asked all the workers, "You. Did you see Yeong Kook making the phone call?"

"Sir, no, sir. I didn't see him making the phone call, sir."

"Did you see it?"

"Sir, no, sir. I didn't see him making the phone call, sir."

"Did you see it?"

"Sir, I did not see it, sir."

"You rascals, why did you lie and say that he made the phone call?"

The chief of staff met the three-starred commander.

"Commander, I don't think Yeong Kook made the phone call."

"Chief of staff, you don't know about this. He did do it."

"None of the workers in the secretary's office said they saw him do it."

"What? They didn't see him do it and they said that Yeong Kook did it? Tell them all to get over here. Hey, you! You didn't see him do it? And you, you didn't see him do it?"

That was how my son avoided being sent to the stockade that day. My son had clearly experienced the power of prayer.

God places faith into people who have no faith from the moment they are connected with God. If God puts faith in, then can faith not be put in? When you put rice into a rice sack, can it not go in if it doesn't want to?

I Have Set Before Thee an Open Door, and No Man Can Shut It

Everyone, there are people within whom God works and there are people within whom God doesn't work. It is not difficult at all to figure this out. People who do not have God working in them put much effort into living a spiritual life on their own. But people who have God working in them do not try to do things themselves. God does everything. People who don't know this say, "Then should I just open my mouth beneath a persimmon tree and wait for good luck to roll in?" However, if God works, it is possible. You don't even have to leave your mouth open.

As a pastor, when I look at the members of my church for people upon whom God works, even the things that should not work out, work out so easily. That is so amazing. On the other hand, for people upon whom God doesn't work, even things that should go well do not. I saw an ad for a book in a certain newspaper. The ad headline read, "In a house where everything goes well, watermelons are borne even on eggplant bushes." But in a house where things do not go well, watermelons are not borne even on watermelon vines. Therefore, people whom God helps do impossible things through God, but people whom God doesn't help are even unable to do the things that everyone else can do. It is this way so often.

In my spiritual life, I have almost never started something that was possible; I mostly did things that couldn't be done. In 1985 and 1986, I broadcasted sermons. At that time, there were two Christian broadcasting stations: Far East Broadcasting and Asia Broadcasting. At Asia Broadcasting, I preached on a program called "A Message to Our People in North Korea" at 4:15 in the morning. One time, the broadcasting station called me and asked me to change my time slot. At the Asia Broadcasting station, where their slogan was "Asia Broadcasting: Spreading the Good News," their prime time was a two hour time slot called, "The Good News." At that time, Pastor David Cho had a 15 minute slot, and I had a 30 minute slot. Because there were so many people making requests to the broadcasting station, "Please send me the sermon tapes of Pastor Ock Soo Park," they had to make a department for sermon tapes. I had received many letters from pastors all over the country saying, "I prepare for my sermons by listening to your sermons."

At that time, it had not been long since I, as young a man as I was, had moved to Seoul. I had recently moved from the countryside. I was then leading the most important program on the broadcasting station and people were becoming jealous. From then on, they began to accuse me of being a heretic.

The employees of the Far East Broadcasting and Asia Broadcasting stations said, "We have thoroughly investigated the past of Pastor Ock Soo Park. There is nothing wrong with him and there is nothing wrong, whatsoever, about his perspectives on faith. There is nothing biblically wrong with his sermons. They are very good. If you would like, the station can arrange for you to meet Pastor Ock Soo Park."

But there was not a single person who stepped up to do so. Instead, they continued to pressure the broadcasting stations. "If you continue this, then we will no longer listen to your broadcasts. We will cut off all our support." The employees of the broadcasting stations cried and said, "Pastor, wait a while and we will broadcast your sermons again."

Ultimately, we stopped broadcasting. Therefore, we decided to publish a book. We wanted to publish a collection of sermons titled, *The Secret of Forgiveness of Sin and Being Born Again*, but we didn't have a publisher. At the time, publishing was the realm of the Korean President, President Doo-hwan Chun. There were basic laws regarding the press, so it was very difficult to get a registration permit for publishing. Because it was a religious book, it had to be published at a religious publishing house. There was no one from the Christian Publishing House who wanted to publish my book. All the Christian publishing houses in Seoul considered me a heretic. The funny thing is, that people who had never met me or never once come to me to determine whether I was a heretic, began to call me a heretic. That led to other rumors, which ultimately made me out to be the chief of heretics.

We had to publish a book, but there was no publisher who was willing to publish our book. One Saturday, I prayed and prayed all day long.

I fasted, and prayed, "God our Father, allow this book of the gospel to be published. God, if you are pleased, I believe there is nothing you cannot do."

After praying this way, I was told, by chance, to meet a Dr. Young-ho Park at the Christian Literature Mission located at Bangbae-dong Intersection. I was told to meet him, so I did. While talking with him, we had a very interesting conversation because all the people he knew, while he was studying in England, were people I knew as well. Nowadays, we can put everything on a disk, but back then, we had to organize everything into a transcript. We brought him the huge transcript and told him that we would like to publish it. At that moment, he said, "I'm sorry. We published some books last year and ended up incurring 40,000 dollars in losses. Therefore, the editor-in-chief decides what books should be published." He picked up his phone and called the editor-in-chief. The editor-in-chief came in and though it was my first time meeting him, he greeted me happily. "Pastor, what brings you here?"

"I'm sorry. I don't remember who you are."

"Of course you don't. I have been to your conferences, Pastor Park, many times. I have received the forgiveness of sin, and I am born again."

He then went on to say that throughout his life he had published an uncountable number of books, but he said that he would publish Pastor Ock Soo Park's book with all his heart. He then asked me, "How many would you like to publish?"

I said, "Ten thousand."

He replied, "Pastor, we have never published ten thousand books before. So let's just print three thousand."

But I said, "Let's print eight thousand." As soon as the book was published, all 8,000 copies were sold out within a week. For the second printing, we printed another 8,000. They were all sold out on the spot. Then, there was a great commotion: "Why did the Christian Literature Mission publish the books of a heretic?"

Pastor Young-ho Park who was the head of the Christian Literature Mission clearly said, "I am a theology professor. You don't think I can recognize heretics? Have you read this book? This book contains no biblical discrepancies. You, too, should read this book and repent."

The common churches strongly pressured him.

When I met a person from the mainstream mass media, he said to me, "There is something that I would like to tell you, Pastor. Korean churches, starting from the large churches to the small ones in the countryside, have all become rotten, every single one of them. When my son gets married, I told him that I will allow him to marry anyone he wants to, but I will not allow him to marry a person who goes to church."

The thankful thing, however, is that although many people try to block me, He who opens the door no man can shut, opens a way for me. Who can stop me? Even as I am holding this grand conference here at the Olympic Gymnasium, I am deeply touched. The citizens of Seoul are changing. When we were first holding a conference in Jamsil, people called us heretics and they tore down our posters and placards. Now, this has decreased considerably. While preparing for this conference, there were many people who said, "I heard the sermons of Pastor Park." The number of people who have called us bad is getting smaller and smaller. Now the citizens of Seoul are changing.

When I was first called a heretic, all the churches in Korea would preach that all are sinners. Pastors would say they were sinners. Deacons, elders, and every one of them would say they were sinners. A man who was a so-called "pastor" wrote, "I declare, that am a sinner until the day of my death," as he slandered the book I wrote, *The Secret of Forgiveness of Sin and Being Born Again.* Since then, Korean churches have changed. They used to call us heretics because we said that we received the forgiveness of sin and have become righteous. Many pastors, today, read our books and teach that they are righteous. So, there are pastors who teach that they are sinners and there are pastors who teach that they are righteous. There are many pastors now who teach, "If the Good News Mission asks you, say that you are righteous. Say that you are born again and say that you don't have sin." But even as they do this, they call us heretics.

The important thing is the fact that they are using humanistic methods proves God is not with them. The works of God can't be compared to the works of men. Therefore, there is no need for me to use such methods when I see the works of God.

Cain Who Was Cursed by God and Cain Who Was Protected by God

Today, we read about Cain in Genesis chapter 4. In the story of Cain, a clear line can be drawn. Until Cain had reached a certain point, God was constantly criticizing Cain, chastising him, and speaking words that condemned him. But when Cain had come to reach that point, God clearly changed His heart. God had changed into one who was comforting, helping, and protecting Cain. Even you are divided into these two kinds of people. There are those who are still in the position of Cain, in which God is chastising and condemning them and there are those who are in the position to receive the blessings of God. Let's talk about this as we read the Bible.

Let's look at Genesis chapter 4. First, let us look at the relationship between God and Cain in verse 3.

And in process of time it came to pass, that Cain brought of the fruit of the ground an offering unto the LORD. And Abel, he also brought of the firstlings of his flock and of the fat thereof. And the LORD had respect unto Abel and to his offering. (Genesis 4:3, 4)

Although it was the same Cain, there was a time when God did not respect him, help him, nor was God with him. Yet there was a time when God helped, respected and blessed Cain. It is the same in regard to you. When you are in the position of Cain at the beginning, no matter what you do, God won't help you. Even when you hold services, you may rejoice on your own because you held a service, but God takes no joy or satisfaction in what He received from your service. Even when you do business, the business doesn't go well.

What did Cain do afterwards? Cain huffed and puffed and his countenance fell.

Let's look at the verse 6:

And the LORD said unto Cain, Why art thou wroth? and why is thy countenance fallen?

Here, God was not receiving Cain's offering. We know that God is speaking here in a position of chastising Cain, trying to turn his heart around from being on the wrong foot.

Let us read on a little more. Verse 8:

And Cain talked with Abel his brother: and it came to pass, when they were in the field, that Cain rose up against Abel his brother, and slew him.

Verse 9:

And the LORD said unto Cain, Where is Abel thy brother? And he said, I know not: Am I my brother's keeper?

We can see God is continually not respecting Cain by pointing out Cain's sin and pinpointing Cain's wrongdoings and chastising him.

Verses 10-12:

And he said, What hast thou done? the voice of thy brother's blood crieth unto me from the ground. And now art thou cursed from the earth, which hath opened her mouth to receive thy brother's blood from thy hand; When thou tillest the ground, it shall not henceforth yield unto thee her strength; a fugitive and a vagabond shalt thou be in the earth.

Not once did God speak soft words or bestow His grace, mercy, or compassion on Cain. God refused Cain's offering and chastised him such that his countenance fell. Then God interrogated Cain, asking, "Where is Abel, thy brother? You killed your brother, didn't you?" God continually scolded Cain, chastising him and cursing him.

But as soon as Cain reached a certain point, we see that God completely changed His own heart. It is so amazing. What did Cain say?

Verse 13:

And Cain said unto the LORD, My punishment is greater than I can bear. Behold, thou hast driven me out this day from the face of the earth; and from thy face shall I be hid; and I shall be a fugitive and a vagabond in the earth; and it shall come to pass, that every one that findeth me shall slay me. (Genesis 4:13,14)

As soon as Cain said this, God, who had scolded, chastised, cursed, and had no respect for Cain until that moment, all of a sudden, changed His heart. He told Cain, "That is not so. You will not be cursed. You will not be killed. Cain, whoever kills you will receive punishment sevenfold." God then gave Cain a mark in order for him to avoid death from whoever he met.

And the LORD said unto him, Therefore whosoever slayeth Cain, vengeance shall be taken on him sevenfold. And the LORD set a mark upon Cain, lest any finding him should kill him.
(Genesis 4:15)

We can see that God had taken Cain's side, protecting and guarding him. Although Cain was the same person, before, in verse 14, God was continually chastising Cain and giving him a difficult time. In verse 15, however, God's heart is completely changed, and He says, "No, Cain. You will not be cursed. You will not be killed. No one will be able to kill you." He placed a mark upon Cain, and gave him words of comfort.

There was a time when Cain was in the position of receiving the chastisement of God, and there was a time when he was in the position of God forgiving his dirty self for killing his younger brother. God didn't punish him for that sin and kept him from dying by protecting him. As a pastor, when I come to church and see the brothers and sisters in the church, I can see what positions they are all in.

Once, I was hospitalized at Hanyang University Hospital because I had a skin infection and was sent to the dermatologist. An intern with a scalpel scraped my skin and said that he would examine it under a microscope. He looked at it and asked me, "Is this a heat rash?" However, the chief dermatologist recognized my condition and said, "Oh, this patient is suffering from the side effect of an antibiotic." He then told the intern, "You have to give him a different antibiotic. Let's find out what kind of antibiotic he has been taking until now." He looked at the chart and prescribed some medicine for me. When I took the medicine, I was healed immediately. Don't you think that to be the chief dermatologist at a university hospital he has to be that good? When you are the chief dermatologist, after just one glance you can recognize things like, "This is a fungus. This is leprosy. These are side effects from an antibiotic. This is a heat rash." From a single glance, they recognize this.

The condition of my heart was bad once, so I was examined in the United States. An elderly doctor walked in and examined me. He had already retired and would only come in to look at patients with special cases. He could barely walk and his back was hunched over. Two young doctors were supporting him in order to bring him to my room. He told me to get on the treadmill and walk. Then he told me to run. As he saw the EKG graph of my heart beat on the monitor, at once, he said that electricity was leaking. Even at the Hanyang University Hospital, they placed recording mechanisms on me and observed me for 24 hours, but they couldn't figure anything out. However, this doctor figured out the problem immediately. He was an expert.

Pastors see the spiritual lives of people. "This person is living a Nicodemus type of spiritual life as found in the book of John. This person's style of spiritual life is exactly like that of the Samaritan woman. This person's spiritual life is exactly the same as the man with an infirmity for 38 years. This person has a spiritual life like the woman taken in adultery." We can see this right away. Then where does the treatment come from? It is all in the Bible. How was the woman treated who was taken in the act of adultery? What treatment was given to the man who had an infirmity for 38 years? What was the treatment for Nicodemus? It is all there.

Cain is one man, but there was the figure of Cain who was unable to receive the mercy of God, and there was the figure of Cain who did receive the mercy of God. This is how it is with the people who live spiritual life. You cannot simply pray; you must receive the grace of God. If you pray within the grace of God all night, then those hours of prayer would be the most precious time. But if you don't receive grace, those hours become a time of sleep. At that time you become the sleepiest and the most bored. Whenever I give sermons, while reading the Bible, I come to feel, "I didn't know this. I'd better preach these words." And with that, I speak of how the Lord lives in my heart. That is why I am most excited when I give sermons from behind the podium.

People Respected by God Are Happy in Spiritual Life

When it was my tenth wedding anniversary, Elder Jong-cheol Kim, from Jeonju, invited my wife and me to come down. "Pastor, I know you are busy, but please come to my house for three days." That was 20 years ago. I went to his house for the first time. He and his wife are public officials. Though they were busy, they received some time off. Back then, sedans were very hard to come by, but they had prepared a sedan for me to drive. They told the brothers and sisters that the pastor should have some rest and told them not to come. He said to me, "Pastor, rest comfortably." He then took me to Mt. Nejang. Consequently, since it was monsoon season, we were heavily rained on and came back. They were serving us with all sincerity, but I felt uncomfortable in my heart, and later on, I couldn't bear it any longer. "Tell the brothers and sisters to come." That evening, when I preached the words in front of the brothers and sisters, I was filled with strength, and I was so excited.

If you try to give a sermon without the grace of God, you would say, "What am I going to preach now?" In order to find things to preach about, people watch movies and read newspapers. Yet they still can't solve the problem, and they end up copying sermon booklets. That is how it is with all things. Even with giving offerings, when you know your life belongs to the Lord as a whole, then you pray and God gives you money. When you know this, you don't feel it is a waste to give all of what you have. People who do not receive grace feel that it is such a waste to give offerings. "Should I skip giving my tithe this time? But what if I get cursed for doing that?" It is a burden to them. This is also true with witnessing and their spiritual lives are this way.

When I think about it, people in Seoul, nowadays, work themselves to death all week long, and when the weekend comes, they go to see the foliage of Mt. Seorak. I am very thankful that even though I don't go to Mt. Seorak, at the Olympic Park, the foliage of the ginkgo trees are so beautifully displayed. In the countryside there is not a drop of gasoline, but you consume gasoline all day long to get to Mt. Seorak, suffering through lots of traffic. People drive five to six hours to get to Mt. Seorak and they just take a quick look at the foliage, take a few pictures, barbeque, and come back home. What fun is that? When one person receives eternal salvation through your preaching the gospel to him, seeing that person change and rejoice, how wonderful it is!

There is a program where we train college students that is called the Good News Corps. One day my wife was there actively going back and forth. She is an old grandmother.
"Honey, what are you doing here?"

"I am a teacher here. Why?"

"Who made you a teacher?"

"What do you mean who? The Lord made me a teacher."

"I didn't see you on the teachers' list."

"I am a teacher, too, honey."

I was very thankful that the wife of a pastor was teaching the students about the Bible. So I left her to do so. After the training, we came home and were about to go to sleep, but my wife wouldn't go to sleep. I have to go to sleep at a certain time to wake up at a certain time.

She said, "Honey, today I met a student and spoke with her. The condition of her heart was like this, but it changed like that, and like that." I saw how happy my wife was.

Throughout our marriage, I gave a gift to my wife only once. It was a blouse I had bought for her early in our marriage. After finishing a conference, the people there gave me some transportation money to thank me for the work I had done. Since I had never bought my wife anything, with that money, I bought a gift for her. I didn't know what to buy, so I thought hard. And for the first time in my life, I bought a blouse. I thought my wife would be very happy and thankful. But when I pulled it out, my wife looked at it and asked, "How much did you pay for this?" I thought, "Should I say I got it at a lower price? What should I do?" Then I honestly told her the price. She said, "You paid that much for this? With that money, we could have done this and that." That day, she really gave me a hard time. Then, I made up my mind, "I am never going to buy you a gift again."

After that incident, I never bought another gift for my wife. After I do conferences, they sometimes buy me scarves, blouses, or makeup for my wife. When I tell my wife, "Honey, I went to the mall and I bought this gift for you," and then bring them out, my wife knows everything already. She'd say, "There is no way you would buy all these." I've never once seen my wife happy with the gifts that I bought her. But as my wife cried together with many college students who had lots of problems and as she spoke with them, those students changed and were set right. As she saw that, she was so happy. We were staying up all night long and I told my wife, "Honey, always be a teacher. Do this until you are 100 years old. Do this until you die of old age. Stay a teacher."

It is a happy thing to serve God. It is joyful. The same way that a heart to love your grandson, your children, and your wife arises inside of you, it is a joyful and thankful thing to be working for God. But God doesn't give happiness to the people He doesn't respect. To such people, giving sermons is wearisome and tiring, and ministering is also a wearisome and tiring thing.

Last spring, I went to Germany and led a conference there. My impression of Germans was that they were very stiff, rigid, and arrogant. The Gracias Choir sang and all the Germans were so touched. They were once again touched when they listened to the sermon. They said it was their first time hearing such sermons. Because Germany is a Christian nation, everyone pays religious taxes. They pay pastors' salaries with those taxes. Because pastors are employees receiving salaries, they get paid even when they are not doing church work. Therefore, they like to do things such as getting away on vacation, so they aren't always working. Because they are obliged to give 15 minute sermons, what could they possibly say in 15 minutes? They would say such things as, "Be good. Do well. Be great." The people who have been listening to such heartless sermons came to our conference. They listened to sermons that came from the heart and their hearts were all opened. That day, many Germans raised their hands and came forward and received salvation. When I saw how the German people's hearts were softened and opened to the Word of God, I was very thankful before the Lord.

Is It Millet or Is It Rice?

There are levels in spiritual life. To a certain point, even though you do things with all of your might, God doesn't even look at it.

"I don't want it. I don't want that offering. I am not going to receive this offering."

"God, receive this offering that I am giving you."

"I don't care for it."

There is no response regardless of whether you gave offerings or prayed, and regardless of whether you witness. I was able to see such things as I was reading the Bible. Surely God had no interest, no matter what Cain was doing. When he arrived at a certain point, though, God poured all of His heart unto Cain.

"Cain, it is okay. Don't worry about it. Nothing will happen to you. Surely you will not die. I will protect you. I will give you a mark. I will not allow anyone to kill you."

God had changed. The heart of God towards you must change. If that is the case, everyone, then how does the heart of God change? Will God's heart change when you try hard and you are loyal? When you put forth lots of effort, will God be so moved by this that His heart will change? Not so. That is why the spiritual life of a person who has lived a spiritual life for 30 or 40 years turns into formality and is corrupted. Although they have believed for more than 50 years, they say they don't know whether they will go to heaven or not. An elder who supposedly had good faith curses Jesus as he dies. Such things happen because God had no interest in them. They want to receive grace and go to prayer houses and pray all night long. There are many people who come back demon-possessed the following day. This is not something to laugh about. Do you know how many people there are who became demon-possessed through praying in the mountains? Or how many people go to revivals and end up becoming demon-possessed? There are a number of those like that among the people I have met. It is that God has no interest in those people. On their own, they believe in God. But they have a faith that has nothing to do with God.

There was a certain turning point in Cain's life. Until he got beyond that turning point, God was not with Cain, even though Cain dug the ground, farmed, and brought forth his best crops and said, "God, receive this." God didn't care for it. He doesn't even look at them. "God, receive this prayer." God doesn't receive it. Everyone, when you have service, do you know whether God receives your worship or not? You just simply think that God receives it as you offer it to Him. You are oftentimes like Cain.

Because I am a pastor, I searched into which instance God had no interest in Cain, and which instance God helped and bestowed His grace upon Cain. I was able to discover God did both according to a precise rule.

When I was young, my father would plant rice on the farm. Before planting the rice, he would tell us to remove the millet from the field. You people from the city can't distinguish rice form millet, can you? Other than people who have farmed, you would not know about this. When my father told me to remove the millet, he plucked out a bunch of millet and a bunch of rice. He said to me, "This is millet and this is rice. Find the difference between the two." At a glance, millet and rice appear to be similar, but when you look closely, there are differences. Rice leaves are slightly wider, while millet leaves are a bit narrower. Rice is black, while millet is yellowish and it has a reddish tip. Rice also has fuzz on its stem, while millet does not.

"Father, I found the differences."

"Tell me."

"The millet has a reddish tip, and it is slightly narrower than rice. And, it has a yellowish tint."

"Good."

"Another thing is that rice has some fuzz on its stem, while millet doesn't have any."

Father smiled and said, "You have learned well. You are ready to remove millet from the field." From then on, I began to remove millet. From afar, I would check and see whether the tips were red and I would check to see if there was fuzz on the stems. If there weren't, I would pluck them.

A long time ago, veterans of the Korean War went through close quarters combat against North Korean soldiers at night. They would become exhausted, pass out, and fall asleep. When they woke up from their sleep, they could see North Korean soldiers sleeping next to them. Since it was dark, they couldn't see anything. They were unable to distinguish the North Korean soldiers from themselves. Back then, there was an exact method used to distinguish North Korean soldiers from South Korean soldiers. The North Korean soldiers shaved their heads completely, while South Korean soldiers only shaved their heads halfway. While a soldier was sleeping, you would take off his helmet and feel his head. If his head was completely shaven, you'd think, "Aha! This is a North Korean soldier." If his hair was a little longer, you would think, "Aha! This is a South Korean soldier." That was how you would distinguish between the two.

When I first entered the military, a person from personnel who had participated in the Korean War came and told us stories. It was so much fun listening to him for an hour, and we listened to him with open mouths. In one of his stories, a trainee came in for the first time, and after putting a bullet in an M-1 rifle, he fired the weapon. "Bang!" The shell was released and the gun's breach was opened. The trainee then said, "Platoon Commander, the gun opened its mouth and won't close it. What am I supposed to do?" I had so much fun listening to these kinds of stories.

Just as North Korean soldiers and South Korean soldiers could be distinguished by their hair lengths during the Korean War, there is a method for pastors to distinguish between the people who are born again and those who are not. There is a method used to distinguish between the people whom God is with and those whom God is not with. Without knowing this, people simply think that if they do good things, are diligent and work hard, they are saved. And they think if they do bad things, they are not saved. From time to time, diligent people commit fraud and run away from God. Then what is that? That is nonsense. Okay, everyone, inside the Bible, which kind of people did God not care for and just left alone? To which people did God bestow His grace? This aspect talks about true repentance. Cain tried to give an offering to God; tried to serve God; and tried to be loyal to God all by himself. How do you feel seeing Cain's heart? If we dissect Cain's heart, inside of him, there is a heart to serve God and a heart to be thankful to God. But also within him, there was a heart of wrath, a heart to kill his younger brother, and a heart to lie. But is there a heart to kill his younger brother inside of God? Is there a heart to lie inside of God? Is there a heart to rebel? No, there is not.

Even though one may outwardly worship and serve God, and even though all men may do this, at the bottom of man's heart is evilness. One day, evil will spring forth. That is why no matter how sincerely you worship God, He will not even look at it. Though you may sacrifice your body, God will not even look at it. What kind of work did God continually do upon Cain? God led Cain so that he would crumble apart and break down and deny himself. That is why Cain went through many, many hardships.

Everyone, when you try to exalt yourself and do well, God doesn't help you and has you fall into sin. He continually works to keep everything from working out for you. The reason for this is that the heart of man is so dirty. God doesn't accept the heart of man.

One day, when I went to the Red Cross blood center I talked a little with a person working there. He said that the cleanest blood is from female juniors in high school. The Red Cross tests all the blood that is donated. If they receive 100 donations from the general public, there is quite a large amount of blood that is contaminated with germs. So the Red Cross goes to an all-girls high school. They do not take blood from seniors because they are too busy preparing for college. Instead, they receive blood donations from juniors. Their blood is mostly clean, but on rare occasions, they have hepatitis or some sexually transmitted disease such as syphilis. If this occurs, they don't keep that contaminated blood in the bank, but store it separately. The reason is that if they transfuse that blood, then the hepatitis would spread, or the sexually transmitted diseases would spread. No matter how clean the blood may seem that blood must never be transfused. It must be kept separate. The blood may be used for plasma or for medicinal purposes, but it can't be used for transfusions. If one hepatitis virus or a single syphilis bacterium is found in the blood, no matter how sorry you may feel throwing it away, it can't be used and it must be discarded.

No matter how much God wants to receive you, He can't accept you if He sees the smallest bit of sin in your heart. It is exactly the same with receiving blood contaminated with germs. However, you generally overlook this without much thought. Because God can never accept such things, He continually works to have you crumble down.

Cain Who Finally Realized How Ruined He Was

Cain, himself, didn't crumble down. He tried to please God with his own efforts, but God hated all the offerings that came from Cain; the prayers that came from Cain; and the praises that came from Cain. I knew that. Although I am a pastor, if I try to go before God through my success, being diligent, doing good deeds, and being loyal, God hates it. Therefore, I threw myself away. I realized that I was a person who could only have been destroyed, and received Jesus into my heart. When I worked with the heart of Jesus, I could experience God helping me out with a thousand out of a thousand things and ten thousand out of ten thousand things that I did.

Cain, however, wanted to exalt himself. Through God receiving his offerings, he wanted to be recognized. He wanted to be acknowledged as having a good spiritual life. That is why, with his diligence, he prepared an offering and offered it. It had infuriated him when God ignored his offering. Because he didn't receive any recognition, he killed his younger brother, Abel. That is the heart of Cain, not the heart of God, isn't it? Is there murder in the heart of God? Is there hatred in the heart of God? Is there jealousy in the heart of God? There is not. Such evil appeared because it was in the heart of Cain.

Everyone, if you live with your heart, at times you are

good, but evil will reveal itself. But there is no evil in the heart of God. There is no curse in the heart of God. There is no hatred in the heart of God. Because of this, when you go out with the heart of God, you can give an offering that God is pleased with. For God to appear in you, you must be denied.

One day, Cain beat his younger brother to death. This came from man. God knew this. God broke Cain down through this. If Peter had not denied Jesus three times, he would not have been broken down. He would still have believed in himself. That is why God doesn't want you to be diligent and do good, but for you to crumble down and deny yourself. God left you to fall into sin. Didn't you all commit sin? Didn't you all fall into wickedness? You have never done good deeds, but have committed sins and evil deeds that are worthy of being cursed. So you must discover yourself, saying, "Ah, that is the kind of human that I am." But without realizing this, if people still try to be recognized through fasting and staying up all night praying, then God will continue to throw those kinds of people away. He hates such people and does not accept them.

God asked Cain, "Cain, where is your younger brother Abel?"

"I do not know. Am I my brother's keeper?"

Even though he had committed sin, he was still back talking. That is how men truly are.

Once again, God precisely pointed things out saying, "What have you done? The blood of your younger brother cries out to me from the ground. The earth has opened its mouth and received your brother's blood from your hand and you shall receive the curse of the ground. Although you may plough, the earth will not give you its strength, and you will be a fugitive and a vagabond on this earth."

Cain was a ruined person to begin with, but only then did he realize that he was a person who was ruined. He was a person who could only be cursed.

Although an evil heart is inside of men and we can only be cursed, we are deceived into thinking that if we do well, we will not be cursed but blessed. It is not that humans have to work hard to receive the blessings of God; Jesus Christ must work. God does not accept anything other than the work that Jesus Christ has done. No matter how well you may have done, God does not accept any good that is coming forth from men.

"Where is your younger brother Abel?"

"I don't know. Am I my brother's keeper?"

"What hast thou done?"

Only when Cain heard such words from God did he say, "I am a person who can only be cursed." He realized the fact that he was ruined.

For people who own businesses, when their companies run into difficulties, it is a problem for them to pay back loans they have taken from the bank. If someone makes a decision, saying, "It is not going to work," and declare bankruptcy, then he will be comfortable. People feel that if they can only last a little longer, they could do well, so they bring in money they got from their in-laws. They pull in money from their younger brothers and uncles to prevent bankruptcy. The following day, another bill arrives and they try to cover those bills. Now, they have borrowed all the money they can from their relatives and they still can't make ends meet, so they start borrowing money from loan sharks. They feel that if they just pay off one debt, everything will be okay. It becomes a great burden to them. They pay huge amounts of interest and use the money from loan sharks to pay off those bills. But then another bill arrives. And when they fail after doing this, from then on, it is so agonizing. If they fail to begin with and file for bankruptcy, they will be okay.

We must also become bankrupt. Then our spiritual lives will move to Jesus. You think, "Oh, I must fast. From this year on, I must do well. From now on, I should read ten pages of the Bible a day. I should wake up at 5 o'clock in the morning." You say this because you are not yet bankrupt. That was how Cain was. But after Cain killed Abel, and after listening to the Word of God, he became bankrupt. So the heart of wanting to do well, the heart of wanting to exalt himself all came crashing down.

This is an important step. When the prodigal son returned to his father, this was how he had returned. Before then, he thought, "I am the son of a rich family. How can I go back wearing these filthy rags? How can I go back holding a beggar's can? I should make some money and wear fine clothes. I should return with a gift for my father." And he thought, "I should go back with good shoes on." One day, the prodigal son realized that he was ruined. In his current situation, he returned to his father's house. When he entered the village, the people said, "Isn't that so-and-so's son? But why is he wearing those filthy clothes? Are they filming a movie? Is he an actor? What's wrong with him?" They would say unkind things and make fun of him. "Go ahead. Make fun of me. I am a ruined man." It was not a problem. When the prodigal son was returning to his father's house, his being mocked was not a problem because he had returned to eat. When you arrive at that level, and when you have been crumbled down, that is when grace comes.

Everybody, people do not crumble down just by listening to this kind of sermon. In people's hearts they still exalt themselves. That is how Satan supports you. This morning, you must acknowledge you have failed in your spiritual life from the core of your heart. Everything you do must fall apart. Your praying zealously, reading the Bible zealously, witnessing zealously, and being faithful; all these things must crumble down.

"I can't do it. I can only be destroyed. I am a dirty sinner who can only go to hell."

That is true repentance. When repentance is accomplished, from that point on, you will let go of everything and God will begin to work inside your heart. When God begins to work inside your heart, you will change and you will become a person with power.

For Faith, One Must Go Through the Process that Cain Went Through

People generally bypass true repentance. They just pass it by and say, "Oh, Jesus washed away all of my past, present, and future sin. I have no sin. I can sin as much as I want." That is what they say. People are so sly in not crumbling themselves down. Do you know what God said about that? He said, "Though thou shouldest bray a fool in a mortar among wheat with a pestle, yet will not his foolishness depart from him." If you put wheat or other grain into a mortar and grind them with a pestle, shells and peels come off. This means that foolishness is this difficult to peel off. It is saying that it has to be ground that much more with a pestle. Getting into a car accident; getting divorced; or becoming bankrupt; all these things are getting ground, one by one, with a pestle. But if those things still do not become loosened, then they won't loosen. How bad must this have been that God said this in His Word?

Had Cain earlier said, "That's right, God. You will not receive my offering. That is because everything from me is evil," and had given up, he would have received the grace of God. Even after having beaten his younger brother to death, he continued to resist. When he could no longer resist, and when he had collapsed, that's when God helped Cain.

Spiritual life doesn't just happen. People who don't know anything say, "Let's pray hard. Then, it will be accomplished. If I just read the Bible, it will be okay." It can never be done by doing this. Even so, outwardly, pastors say, "Do good deeds. Work hard. Be loyal and pray." No matter what part of the Bible they open to, that is the only thing they say. Upon hearing these words, no matter how hard they try to do it, churchgoers are unable to do it. That is why they corrupt. I want to bring about an age in Korea where such pastors will not stand at pulpits. Because such pastors stand up and say only those kinds of nice things, people say, "Wow! The pastor of our church is spiritual and full of grace." But that does not bring about faith in people's hearts in the slightest.

Faith is the process that Cain went through. Can you understand? I don't have much time, but from time to time, I turn to the Christian broadcasting station and listen to the pastors' sermons. They are all the same. Whether they read from Genesis and speak; whether they read from Exodus and speak; or whether they read from Revelation and speak;

all they ever say is to do good. There is no need to listen to that. Is it because you don't want to do good that you don't do good? You don't have to do well in spiritual life, but you must totally give up. Believing in God is not "I" doing everything, but believing that God will do it. Believing that I can do it all is believing in myself: it is not believing in God. Amen?

Loving folks, will you deny yourself because you have no other choice, after having killed your younger brother and standing before the curse like Cain? Acknowledge now that you are ruined.

"God, I am a sinner. I have not kept the Ten Commandments. A deceitful heart arises, a heart of hatred arises, and from time to time, a lustful heart arises as well as other evil. My heart is full of things that you hate, God."

Confess that. Do not bring the things that you have done well before God. God will not be deceived. God was not deceived by Cain and He will not be deceived by you either. No matter how much you bring out the things that you are good at, God doesn't care for them. The same way you hand over your failed and bankrupt company, you must hand over your life to Jesus Christ. When you are crumbled down and everything of yours is handed over, the problem of your sin, diseases, gambling, drinking, and spiritual life will all be handed over to the Lord's hands. When they are held in the Lord's hands, the Lord puts them in a clean, beautiful order, and your life will begin to change. And I believe the works of God will arise inside of you. Do you believe this?

Cain repented when he arrived at the final step, "My punishment is greater than I can bear." His trying to exalt himself, and his trying to be recognized by doing well crumbled down. And as he gave up on himself, from that point on, he left his life in the hands of God. That is why God kept Cain from being destroyed and cursed. And He led Cain to be blessed.

In Korea, Christians today say that they believe in God, but it is difficult for them because they think of themselves. It is because you try to do everything yourself that your sins are not washed away. If God does it, then they will be washed away. It is a problem because you are holding onto them. However, if God is the one who does it, then everything will be taken care of beautifully.

Early on I realized I was full of myself and realized that I was full of wickedness and that I was dirty, so I let my hands go of everything. From then on, Jesus became the master of my life. And from the day that Jesus became the Lord of my heart, I could experience my life becoming truly beautiful, holy, and blessed.

Today, crumble down and make Jesus Christ your Lord. Throw away your trying to do well; your trying to keep the law, and say, "Lord, now I leave it in your hands. Whether I fail or succeed, I will let go of everything. Jesus, now you do it." Say this and leave it all to Jesus. I believe that Jesus will then work inside of you with power.

5
David's Repentance

5.
David's Repentance

It's good to see you, everyone. Today we'll read from 2 Samuel chapter 11. If you have found it, I will read to you from verse 1.

And it came to pass, after the year was expired, at the time when the kings go forth to battle, that David sent Joab, and his servants with him, and all Israel; and they destroyed the children of Ammon, and besieged Rabbah. But David tarried still at Jerusalem. And it came to pass in an eveningtide that David arose from off his bed, and walked upon the roof of the king's house: and from the roof he saw a woman washing herself; and the woman was very beautiful to look upon. And David sent and inquired after the woman. And one said, Is not this Bathsheba, the daughter of Eliam, the wife of Uriah the Hittite? And David sent messengers, and took her; and she came in unto him, and he lay with her; for she was purified from her uncleanness: and she returned unto her house. And the woman conceived, and sent and told David, and said, I am with child. And David sent to Joab, saying, Send me Uriah the Hittite. And Joab sent Uriah to David. And when Uriah was come unto him, David demanded of him how Joab did, and how the people did, and how the war prospered. And David said to Uriah, Go down to thy house, and wash thy feet. And Uriah departed out of the king's house, and there followed him a mess of meat from the king. But Uriah slept at the door of the king's house with all the servants of his lord, and went not down to his house. And when they had told David, saying, Uriah went not down unto his house, David said unto Uriah, Camest thou not from thy journey? why then didst thou not go down unto thine house? And Uriah said unto David, The ark, and Israel, and Judah, abide in tents; and my lord Joab, and the servants of my lord, are encamped in the open fields; shall I then go into mine house, to eat and to drink, and to lie with my wife? as thou livest, and as thy soul liveth, I will not do this thing. And David said to Uriah, Tarry here today also, and tomorrow I will let thee depart. So Uriah abode in Jerusalem that day, and the morrow. And when David had called him, he did eat and drink before him; and he made him drunk: and at even he went out to lie on his bed with the servants of his lord, but went not down to his house. And it came to pass in the morning, that David wrote a letter to Joab, and sent it by the hand of Uriah. And he wrote in the letter, saying, Set ye

Uriah in the forefront of the hottest battle, and retire ye from him, that he may be smitten, and die. And it came to pass, when Joab observed the city, that he assigned Uriah unto a place where he knew that valiant men were. And the men of the city went out, and fought with Joab: and there fell some of the people of the servants of David; and Uriah the Hittite died also.

We read up to verse 17.

If Only I Could Erase My Past

Everyone, I am continually speaking about repentance and faith. We repent because, if true repentance is accomplished in our lives, it creates a relationship where we become one with Christ through receiving the forgiveness of sin by faith. Many people go to church and repent, but there are many people who have not been freed and cleansed from sin. But everyone, if true repentance is accomplished inside of you, not a single sin will remain. Every last sin will be washed away and you will become as white as snow.

In 1981, I received an invitation from a pastor from Yeosu Aeyangwon Church. We gathered with the church deacons, elders, and other church staff and had a retreat at Mt. Jiri. I really liked that retreat at Mt. Jiri. All morning long, I preached to them through the book of Genesis how our sins were forgiven. After lunch, the deacons would come to me, one by one, and receive spiritual counseling. When I saw them returning after receiving the forgiveness of sin and rejoicing, it brought so much joy to my heart.

One day, after fellowship, I had been sitting down for a

long time and I felt a little stuffy. So, I was going outside the tent to get some fresh air, when a lady who seemed to be in her late twenties came to see me. "Pastor," she called out to me. She was standing there ashamed of something. I sat this lady down and explained the Bible in detail to her and the process whereby our sins are washed away.

After finishing what I had to say, I read some verses in Hebrews to her.

And their sins and iniquities will I remember no more. Now where remission of these is, there is no more offering for sin. (Hebrews 10:17, 18)

Upon hearing these words, this lady began to weep and sob. "Why is she crying?" I thought. I hadn't told her anything special. Even though I told her to calm down, for a while, she was bent over, sobbing. Because she was crying like this, I didn't know what to do, so I went and got some fresh air. When I returned, she was still hunched over, crying. I calmed her down, telling her to stop crying. She stopped her crying and told me more about herself.

She said that in middle school, her mother passed away and her father remarried. However, she did not get along with her stepmother, so she took her tuition and ran away to Masan. But heaven help her, this girl, who was just a student, was sold to a brothel. There, she lived as a prostitute for many years. And while she was there, she met a man one day. That man told her to simply follow him. She without giving it any thought followed him, and he turned out to be a son of lepers from the Aeyangwon Leper Colony. The two of them got a place there and got married. Although he was a son of lepers, he was a healthy man. And because he had loved such a filthy woman as her, she was so thankful and she lived happily. Her parents-in-law loved her. She experienced two years of happiness that she had never known before in her entire life.

Those two years passed with her parents-in-law waiting for a grandchild, but she was unable to conceive. We don't know from whose mouth it came, but word went around that because their daughter-in-law was a prostitute, she was not able to have children. Afterwards, not her father-in-law, mother-in-law, nor anyone would look her in the eye. Whenever she would set dinner on the table, they would turn their faces away from her. When she left, then they would eat. The parents-in-law would not look her in the eye. This lady became extremely saddened. Now, nobody in her household would speak to her, and nobody would look her in the eye. This woman began to blame her past, saying, "If only I could erase my past. If only I could erase my memory…." She lived her life saying these things. She would attend church, but was too ashamed to look people in the face there. She would enter long after the service had started and sit in the back and listen to the Word. To keep anyone from knowing that she came to the church, she would quickly run out before the other people started to leave.

Even the day she listened to the Word from me, she came and listened to the Word alone because she was so ashamed. But the great thing about the Word of God is that it brought freedom from sin even to this woman.

And their sins and iniquities will I remember no more. (Hebrews 10:17)

Upon hearing these words, this lady became freed from those sins that she had so badly wanted to erase.

"Although my past cannot be erased from my father-in-law's memory, my mother-in-law's memory, my husband's memory, or from my own memory, it has been erased from God's memory." She was very thankful.

After the Mt. Jiri retreat, the people from Aeyangwon Church returned to their homes. All the people who attended the Mt. Jiri retreat were changed and renewed. So at the Aeyangwon Church, a Mt. Jiri sect was formed. At that church they said, "Let us not be like this. Let's invite Pastor Ock Soo Park to our church so we all can listen to the Word together." So, in the fall of that year, I went to Aeyangwon Church and held a conference. At the Aeyangwon Church, there is a really good persimmon tree in the garden of the church's parsonage. I guess that it must have been late fall because I have memories of plucking and eating the persimmons in the afternoon while reading the Bible.

Once, I was leaving after finishing the sermon, and while people were crowding out in the dark night, one person tugged at my sleeve. I looked to see who it was, and it was that lady. "Pastor, my husband came to church today for the first time ever." All of the worries and pain on her face were gone and she truly had a bright face.

During that conference, I preached the Word early in the morning, later in the morning, and in the evening. And in the afternoons, as I rested, I had counseling sessions with the elders and deacons. When I asked the people who would like to receive the forgiveness of sin to raise their hands and come forward after every sermon, a hundred to a hundred-fifty people came forward. I preached about the forgiveness of sin. These people received the forgiveness of sin, rejoiced, and gave testimonies. Most of them were lepers. One elder was so joyful; he did not know what to do. He gave his testimony, saying that he had committed a sin that he could never wash away throughout his entire life.

He had been in much pain. A long time ago, when he lived in the countryside, he lived right next to a chapel. He wanted to build a fence around his house and work, but he did not have a hoe, so he took the church hoe and worked with that. After finishing the work, he wanted to return the hoe, but because of this and that, he couldn't put it back and thought of putting it back the next time he had the chance. A rumor began to go around the church saying that someone stole the church hoe. Whenever he would meet the church people, they would ask, "Who stole the hoe? Who stole property from the temple of God?" All he needed to say was, "Oh, that hoe? I took it because I needed to use it. I'll put it right back." But he couldn't do that because he was afraid of being accused of being a thief. So he hid it because he was afraid that the church members would one day discover the hoe at his house. So he dug a hole in the ground and buried the hoe. Although forty years have passed since this incident, the sin of stealing property from the temple of God had pierced his heart. Even though he would cry and cry, it seemed that that sin would never be washed away.

There was another person who said that he had contracted leprosy and stayed in the village where he used to live. Eventually he could not live there anymore so he ran away. He went to the harbor; stole a boat; and rowed away. He said, "At that time, a boat would cost a person his entire wealth." But he boarded the boat, rowed away, and just simply discarded the boat elswhere. He said that he had been suffering from the guilt of that sin.

People go to church and they pray repentance prayers,

asking for forgiveness of sin because they do not know exactly how to go about it. But biblically, our sins are washed away. Because they didn't receive the faith that their sins are washed away, it seems that their sins still remain. Besides that, they have conflicts and they are wandering. There are many people who live spiritual life that way.

When I read the Bible, after receiving forgiveness of sin and becoming born again, the amazing thing was that my ability to understand the Scriptures had completely changed as I read Genesis, Exodus, Leviticus, and so on. In the Bible, God is telling us so clearly how He has forgiven us of our sins. After realizing this, I had the heart, "Wow! How amazing this is! The forgiveness of sin is so clear in the Bible. But why do people not know about this? Why do they live being tied down to sin?" Afterwards, I began to speak about the forgiveness of sin and people have received the forgiveness of sin.

This evening, a person came to me and said, "Pastor, do you have nothing to talk about other than the forgiveness of sin? Please talk about something else." That's all I know. But there are still so many people on this earth who have not received forgiveness of sin and they are living tied down to sin. That is why God opened the way for me to preach this gospel.

Do You Know How David Had His Sins Forgiven?

The words we read tonight are of how David committed adultery with Uriah's wife. I have spoken a lot about these words as I've had spiritual counseling sessions with many people.

"Deacon, do you know the story of David committing adultery with Uriah's wife?"

"Ah, yes I do know."

"Elder, do you know the story of how David committed adultery with Uriah's wife?"

"Yes I do, I think it's in 2 Samuel."

When I ask deacons, elders, or pastors if they know the story of David committing adultery with Uriah's wife, most of them say that they do. There is almost no one who does not know. Then I asked them another question: "Pastor, do you know how David received forgiveness from the sin of committing adultery with Uriah's wife?"

"Well, he probably repented and was forgiven."

Some people say, "He was forgiven by crying all the night and making his bed swim in tears."

In Psalms, there is a psalm that mentions how David made his bed swim with tears and that he had watered his couch with his tears. But these are not words about how he was suffering from the sin of committing adultery with Uriah's wife. They were words about how he was making his bed swim and watering his couch with tears because of his enemies. But there are people who stick these words in places where they don't belong and say that because he cried, his sins were forgiven. Many people know this to be the case. I guess they don't know the hymn that says, "Weeping will not save me!" Sins are not washed away just because you cry.

The story of David committing adultery with Uriah's wife is found in the Bible in 2 Samuel. God did not record these words without a reason, but He recorded these words to have us realize what we must do to have our sins washed away. The reason is that if He simply talks about how sins are washed away, we may not understand. Starting from 2 Samuel chapter 11, step by step, the process of committing sin has been told. God has recorded this process all the way through, and afterwards, shows us the process of how sins are washed away. Sadly, however, this is hidden from people's eyes. They know the story about David committing the sin of adultery with Uriah's wife very well, but they do not know how that sin was washed away.

Once, two monks came out from their temple and entered the village to collect alms. As the two of them were walking, they came upon a large creek. Most creeks nowadays have bridges across them, but a long time ago, it wasn't that way. They had to roll up their pant legs to cross. When they approached the creek, they discovered that it had a pretty strong current. A pretty young woman was standing on the creek bank not knowing what to do. Both the monks rolled up their pant legs, and one started to cross the creek, but the other monk turned around and said to the woman, "Miss, you're trying to cross the creek, aren't you?"

"I am so embarrassed, but yes, that's right."

"Miss, get on my back. I will carry you on my back across the creek."

It was very different back then. The interaction between men and women was very restrictive. It was said that men and women should be separated from the age of seven. So, even though he was a monk, how can she just get on the back of someone she does not know? That would not be tolerated, but what was she going to do if she didn't get on his back? She couldn't just stand there all day. So this woman was saying, "What should I do?" And she wound up saying, "I'm sorry, but there is nothing else I can do," and she got on his back. The monk carried the woman on his back and crossed the creek. He crossed the strong flowing creek and let the woman down on the other side. "Well, Miss, farewell."

"Thank you," she said and the woman went on her way.

The two monks then continued on their way to go collect donations. The monk who had carried the woman was in front and the other monk followed, and from behind, the monk began to speak.

"You know, you are learning the ways of Buddha, but have you slyly kept women in your heart? You waited for that woman to ask you to do that, didn't you?"

He was yelling at him. The other monk didn't say a word and continued walking. A while later, the monk who was following from behind said something else, "Imagine if the people of the village saw this. What do you think they would say? Don't you think they're going to say, 'Oh, the only thing those monks do is carry women on their backs'?" But that monk still remained silent. And after a little while, the monk who was following from behind began to speak again. "Hey, what if our master finds out about this? Do you think he is going to just let this go by? You really are a sly one. You don't care about the ways of Buddha. All you care about is women!"

Right then, the monk that was walking in front, stopped and turned around. The monk who was following from behind was a bit stunned. "After I carried that woman across the creek, I let her down on the other side. But even now, why can't you let that woman down from your heart?"

"Humph!"

He took a direct hit and he was unable to say anything;

and they went their way. I heard that there was a story like this.

Everyone, carrying the woman on his back was not a problem, but if the woman remained in his heart, then she would continue to remain in his heart. If your sin is not resolved in your heart, then it still remains in your heart. That is why people cry and pray, saying, "Please, forgive me of this sin," early every morning. If faith enters, and those sins become clean like new fallen snow, then it is not a problem in the heart. But people still have sin remaining in their hearts even though they pray and go to church service. How can Jesus dwell inside of that heart? How can the holy heart of God dwell within such a heart? How can God live and work inside that kind of heart?

Tonight, God is making the heart of each and every person sitting here into the temple of God. As He dwells there, He wants to take care of all of your problems and create peace, joy, faith, and love inside of your heart. However, God is not dwelling in our heart, but sin dwells in our heart; filthy thoughts dwell in our heart. And because of those sins, God cannot enter our heart. Because God is not inside of our heart, deceitful, lustful, filthy, dirty, and ambitious things crawl up from within. No matter how much you suppress them, you cannot, and they spring out. People become ashamed of that sin, and they become afraid that others will find out. Because of this, people begin to lose confidence.

That is why God wants to become the true God inside each and every person here. He wants to cast distrust and pain out from your heart, and He wants to create faith, joy, and hope inside of you, so that you may praise God in the midst of faith, joy, and love. This is what He sincerely wants. Therefore, He has precisely recorded the path to accomplishing this in the Bible step by step. But Satan has closed our eyes, so we think about other things when we read about them.

I hope you will listen to the sermons of this conference one more time on tape. We charge 1,000 won per tape, and since there are people who do not have spare change, they don't buy any, so we decided to just give them to you. During this conference you must receive forgiveness of sin and begin a new life. If you listen to the sermon once, it seems that you're listening to everything, but that is not so. During my sermon, when I talk about leper colonies, then inside of you, Satan makes you fall into the thought, "That's right. One of my cousins had leprosy, and he had a very tough time." And when you have these thoughts for about twenty minutes, the sermon just passes you by. When I talk about how David committed adultery with Uriah's wife, and while you think, "Oh yeah, my friend's brother-in-law cheated on his wife, and he lost his wealth and got a divorce," you cannot understand the meaning of the words I am speaking. Satan works very hard to keep you from listening and comprehending my words. When my church members listen to the Sunday sermon on tape one more time, they become amazed. They ask, "Did he talk about that?"

During this conference, I am trying to preach the Word so that anyone may have their sins washed away, as white as snow, and become born again. But while you're listening, you miss a lot of things. If some awkward thought comes in, or if sleep comes to you, then you miss things and the words are not well connected. Do middle and high school students get a hundred percent if they take the test on what they have studied? Sometimes they make a seventy. Sometimes they make a fifty. Sometimes they even make a forty. Even young students who are very smart are this way. But you who are older; who are way past the age of being a student, when you listen to the sermon, though you are trying to accept everything, there are parts that are disconnected. So, when those parts that should connect become disconnected, you don't understand the parts that we speak about afterwards.

Psalm 51: the Path of Forgiveness of Sin David Speaks of

This evening, we're speaking about how David committed adultery with Uriah's wife. David was very diligent, but one day, his heart became arrogant. I looked in the Bible and the Bible says that he didn't go out to battle, but woke up from his bed in the evening. He should have woken up in the morning. Why did he wake up in the evening? Many of our church pastors wake up at 4 o'clock in the morning. As they minister, after breakfast they have to meet with church members, or they receive many phone calls, so they cannot pray. So early in the morning is the only time for them to pray. Early in the morning they wake up, fight their sleep, read the Bible, pray, and meet God. We think, since David woke up in the evening, surely that night he must have had drinks and danced and enjoyed himself all night long. That was why he woke up in the evening, don't you think?

In the middle of a war, David is becoming corrupt. He has become relaxed. When he wakes up in the evening, since he's the king, there were so many things he had to do. He needed to decide on things; he needed to organize things; and he needed to take care of things. There were things he needed to delegate. If he woke up in the evening, he should have zealously gotten to work, saying, "Is there anything I need to decide on? Hurry up and bring them to me." Nevertheless, he was just walking back and forth on the roof of the palace. Then the devil said, "This is my chance!" And when David was relaxed in his heart, and when he was distant from God, Satan felt, "If I tempt him, then David may fall." He allowed a woman to appear in David's eyes. David saw that below the palace, behind the wall of a house, a woman was bathing and pouring water down her body. A long time ago, in the country of Judah, when the days of a woman's separation ended, they had to bathe at sunset. Did they have public bathhouses or showers back then? They would just lock their doors and bathe behind their walls. But since he was looking down from the roof of the palace, he could see so well. David drooled and said, "Wow, she's pretty." If there was a proper servant nearby, he would have said, "Your Majesty, think of your reputation. Turn your eyes away. How could you watch another man's wife bathing? This is unfit for the king of a nation. Turn your head, Your Highness." But near the king, there are always servants who love to kiss up. "Isn't she pretty? Should we bring her to you?"

David became distant from God. He had gotten drunk, he slept late, and he had become corrupted. So he brought her over and slept with her. But the woman became pregnant. He was stunned when he heard that she was pregnant. Later on, he discovered that she was the wife of one of his soldiers. The fact that a king had violated the wife of one of his soldiers was something horrendous, so he told her husband to return from battle. He told him, "Go home for a day. Take a nice break and rest well." He wanted to deceive Uriah. If Uriah sleeps with his wife for one night and goes to battle, when he returns after years of fighting and sees a child, he would think that the child was conceived that night. However, her husband would not go home. He thought, "Right now our country is in the middle of a war and all of our generals are out in the battlefield. How can I go home to my wife? I cannot do that." The next day, David wanted to give him liquor and send him home, but it still didn't work. So David arranged for him to be killed on the battlefield. He killed a woman's husband. He committed a terrible sin. So up to this point, it is the story of how David sinned.

Afterwards comes the story of how David had his sins washed away. The prophet Nathan was sent by God and went to David and scolded him about his sin. After being scolded, David said, "I have sinned against the Lord." Then Nathan said,

And David said unto Nathan, I have sinned against the LORD. And Nathan said unto David, The LORD also hath put away thy sin; thou shalt not die. (2 Samuel 12:13)

As soon as David said that he had sinned against the Lord, the prophet Nathan said, "The Lord has put away your sins."

"I have sinned."

"Your sins are put away."

I have sinned, your sins are put away, this is so easy. If we look, not only at these scriptures, but the other scriptures related to this, this process has been recorded precisely. For you to clearly understand this story, there is one scripture that you have to see. Where is it? It's in Psalm 51.

I hope that you will open to Psalm 51. I will read from verse 1.

[To the chief Musician, A Psalm of David, when Nathan the prophet came unto him, after he had gone into Bathsheba.]

Have mercy upon me, O God, according to thy lovingkindness: according unto the multitude of thy tender mercies blot out my transgressions. Wash me thoroughly from mine iniquity, and cleanse me from my sin. For I acknowledge my transgressions: and my sin is ever before me. Against thee, thee only, have I sinned, and done this evil in thy sight: that thou mightest be justified when thou speakest, and be clear when thou judgest. Behold, I was shapen in iniquity, and in sin did my mother conceive me. Behold, thou desirest truth in the inward parts: and in the hidden part thou shalt make me to know wisdom. Purge me with hyssop, and I shall be clean: wash me, and I shall be whiter than snow. Make me to hear joy and gladness; that the bones which thou hast broken may rejoice. Hide thy face from my sins, and blot out all mine iniquities. Create in me a clean heart, O God; and renew a right spirit within me. Cast me not away from thy presence; and take not thy Holy Spirit from me. Restore unto me the joy of thy salvation; and uphold me with thy free spirit. Then will I teach transgressors thy ways; and sinners shall be converted unto thee.

I read up to verse 13.

Everyone, this psalm contains all the central parts needed for David to receive forgiveness for committing sin with Uriah's wife, killing her husband on the battlefield, and trying to hide that sin.

David surely committed adultery with someone else's wife, and he committed the terrible, terrible sin of killing her husband. However, in the Bible, David surely had that sin washed away. This evening, every single one of you must have sinned. There are those of you who must have lied; there are those of you who must have stolen something; and there are those of you who must have committed adultery, like David. There must also be people who have hated others. It does not matter what sin you may have committed or what evil you may have done. If your heart flows in the same direction as David's committing adultery with Uriah's wife and having that sin washed away, you too will receive the forgiveness of sin. Is that so? Is that true?

Everyone, your popularity or your reputation, throw all of that away this evening and stand before God, not in front of Pastor Ock Soo Park. But for your own souls, stand in front of God. Do you understand? Please answer me. You must stand in front of God. Can you say amen to that? Everyone, we must not simply listen in theory, but we must participate in this with our hearts. There is a great difference between the two. I am so joyful that I have received forgiveness of sin, that I am telling you about the path to receive forgiveness of sin. I am hoping that you will not just listen to this in theory, but I hope that you will actually become this way.

Now, if you've committed adultery like David; if you've committed murder like David; then you can receive forgiveness of sin like David. God has recorded these words here because, no matter what sins you may have committed, God wants to wash those sins away. In the exact same way David received forgiveness of sin, your sins, too, can be washed away. If you know the Word precisely and believe, then just as David had his sins washed away, your sins, too, can be washed away.

Romans chapter 4 records what David said:

Even as David also describeth the blessedness of the man, unto whom God imputeth righteousness without works, Saying, Blessed are they whose iniquities are forgiven, and whose sins are covered. Blessed is the man to whom the Lord will not impute sin. (Romans 4:6-8)

Even though you have sinned, God sincerely wants for the words, "God does not recognize my sin. God does not impute my sin upon me. My sins are covered. My sins have all been washed away. I am not a sinner. Thank you, all of my sins have been washed away," to echo from your heart, even tonight. Hallelujah! Amen? God wants this. Do you want this, too? Yes? Then all is well.

Now let us read Psalm 51, verse 1:

Have mercy upon me, O God, according to thy lovingkindness: according unto the multitude of thy tender mercies blot out my transgressions.

Here, David says that God is forgiving his sins. It is not because he prayed or fasted, nor was it because he was faithful. Only according to God's lovingkindness and His tender mercies are your sins forgiven. Your sins are not washed away by laboring to do something well, but your sins are washed away through the tender mercies and lovingkindness of the Lord.

Verses 2 and 3:

Wash me thoroughly from mine iniquity, and cleanse me from my sin. For I acknowledge my transgressions: and my sin is ever before me.

Verse 4:

Against thee, thee only, have I sinned, and done this evil in thy sight: that thou mightest be justified when thou speakest, and be clear when thou judgest.

These words tell us how David's sins were washed. They were washed clean. He was made clean enough that he could be called righteous. Do you understand?

And in verse 5:

Behold, I was shapen in iniquity, and in sin did my mother conceive me.

Yes, this is what it's all about. Everyone, this time I am speaking to you about repentance. People say that they repent, but in the Bible, repentance should be connected with the forgiveness of sin. However, there are so many people who repent, but their sins are not forgiven. Why is that? It is because they don't do true repentance. True repentance is not confessing, "I have lied. I have stolen. I have committed adultery. I have murdered." That's not it. Confessing that you are a seed of sin, however, that is true repentance. The fact that you've stolen, committed adultery, and murdered is important. However, you have the trait and characteristics of sin inside of you, since you are human, and you can only commit sins. That is what I have continually talked to you about this week. When Peter realized this, he realized that he was a dirty sinner. But because Judas Iscariot only realized the act of selling Jesus, he did not deny himself. He therefore followed his own thoughts and committed suicide.

David didn't merely say, "I have committed adultery and committed murder," but said, "I was shapen in iniquity and in sin did my mother conceive me." He acknowledged that he is bundled inside of sin. It's not that he has done this or that, but that, as a whole, he is a pile of sin; a cluster of sin. That is what David acknowledged and prayed that God would be responsible for and have compassion on him as a whole.

Purge Me with Hyssop

Now let's talk about the next thing. Let us read the words of verse 7 together:

Purge me with hyssop, and I shall be clean: wash me, and I shall be whiter than snow.

What do these words mean? Everyone, these are very important words. What is hyssop? It is a kind of plant that grows up the walls of Israel. It is the smallest and ugliest plant. But why does it say here, purge me with hyssop? When the Israelites were coming out of Egypt, they killed a lamb, dipped hyssop in its blood, and put the blood upon the side posts and upper post of the doors of their houses. What, "Purge me with hyssop," implies is that on the tip of the hyssop is the blood of the Lamb of God. The hyssop, in David's time represented the blood of the lamb that died for sins. But in the New Testament, it is talking about the blood of Jesus Christ, who was crucified and killed for our sins.

David should not confess to sleeping with his soldier's wife and killing the soldier to have his sins washed away. There must be blood shed in order for that sin to be washed away. There has to be blood on the hyssop for that sin to be washed away. Then why does blood wash sins away? It is because the wages of sin is death. Whosoever sins, the punishment for his sins, which is death, must be accepted in order for that sin to be washed away. The blood implies that the punishment for that sin, death, has been paid. Amen? That is why David's sin of committing adultery with Uriah's wife and killing Uriah wasn't just washed away, but it was washed away by the blood of Jesus Christ.

Jesus had not yet come to earth during the time of David,

but through the revelation of the Holy Spirit, David knew that Jesus Christ would come to this earth. He knew that hundreds of years later Jesus Christ would come and would die for his sins.

My sins have not just simply been washed away, but through dying on the cross, Jesus received the punishment for my sins. For that reason are sins washed away. And when that happened, David said, "I shall be whiter than snow."

Purge me with hyssop, and I shall be clean: wash me, and I shall be whiter than snow.

Let us read it out loud together:

Purge me with hyssop, and I shall be clean: wash me, and I shall be whiter than snow.

Everyone, David committed the terrible sins of committing adultery with Uriah's wife and killing Uriah. If somebody is killed as punishment for the wages of a sin, then that sin is washed away. Isn't that so? Then as a mark that somebody was punished and died for that sin, the blood of the dead animal must be put on the door posts.

This is how our sins are washed away as well. They are not washed away because I confess them or ask for forgiveness for them. Sins are not washed away because I am tormented and suffer for the sins of my past. Sins are washed away when someone dies for them. Who can die for our sins? No one can. For this reason, Jesus Christ died for our sins. For this, He shed his blood.

The blood Jesus Christ shed and the death that He died on the cross washed away the sins that David committed. Jesus was crucified on the cross for the sins of the woman taken in the act of adultery. For you who are sitting here, Jesus did not die only for your sins of stealing or committing adultery, but He died in our place for all the evil that arises from us. Amen? Then if the blood that Jesus shed is put on the hyssop then that means Jesus died for my sins. The price for all my sins has been paid. It testifies that all of my sins are gone. Therefore, when we accept this into our hearts, we are able to say that our sins are gone. All my sins have been punished on the cross. David said, "Because of Jesus, who will come and be crucified on the cross, these sins of adultery and murder have been washed away." For us, Jesus, who already died 2,000 years ago, received the punishment for all our sins, so we are able to know and believe that all of our sins are gone. It is proof that the blood of Jesus washed all our sins away! Amen? Amen!

Let me ask you once more. *Purge me with hyssop, and I shall be clean: wash me, and I shall be whiter than snow.* In this verse, who does the blood on the hyssop belong to? It was the blood of the lamb that was shed to wash away the sins of David. It represents the blood of Jesus Christ: Jesus, who was being crucified on the cross. He's not talking about paying the price for the sins of adultery and murder. But just as David confessed, "Behold, I was shapen in iniquity; and in sin did my mother conceive me," He had paid for the sins of us, who are piles of sin by nature. Through Jesus being crucified on the cross, Jesus received the punishment that you, who are piles of sin, should have received. He shed His blood. It is proof that His blood has washed your sins away. The prophet Nathan knew this fact and said, "The Lord has put your sins away." And David said, "Amen," and believed it.

David received the forgiveness of sin. This evening, not the prophet Nathan, but Pastor Ock Soo Park, as the servant of God, is speaking to you. Your sins, no matter which sin you may have committed, were all washed away through the blood of Jesus Christ, the son of God, who was crucified. So just as David said, *Purge me with hyssop, and I shall be clean: wash me, and I shall be whiter than snow,* you can know that God has already made you clean with the hyssop. God has already purged you with hyssop. This becomes proof that the blood of Jesus on the hyssop has already covered your sins. Why was Jesus crucified? And why did He shed His blood? It was not only for your sins of stealing, lying, murder, or adultery, but it was even for the sins that have not yet come out from within you, and the piles of sin that will eventually come out. For those sins, our Lord was punished on the cross! That is why God tells us, "You have no sin! You're clean! You're righteous!"

Whether you know it or not, through the fact that Jesus was crucified on the cross, your sins have already been made whiter than snow. But Satan makes us say, "No. My sin of having an abortion must remain. My sin of adultery probably remains. My sin of lying to others probably remains." And Satan continually deceives us. I hope that you will not listen to these voices, but believe in the Word of God. The Word of God has recorded that the blood on the hyssop has made our sins as white as snow. Amen?

Oh! I know I'm alive in the Lord, and I strive
Unto blood with the sin that would damn;
As I walk in the light there is strength for the fight,
I'm redeemed by the blood of the Lamb
I'm redeemed, I'm redeemed,
Jesus saves me and keeps me just now, Hallelujah,

And I join with the throng round the throne in the song,
I'm redeemed by the blood of the Lamb.

Do you believe it? Hallelujah! Everyone, we believe that the blood of Jesus forgave our sins. Amen? Many people say that Jesus forgave their sins, but they say, "Lord I'm a sinner." If your sins have been forgiven, but they still remain, what kind of forgiveness is that? David was excellent at sinning, but he was also excellent at receiving forgiveness. Some people suffer forty years for stealing a hoe, or suffer their entire lives for stealing someone else's boat. Although David slept with another man's wife and killed her husband, he had his sins immediately washed away by faith and said, "God, I am clean. Amen." This may seem presumptuous, but it is true that his sins were washed away.

Like David

Psalm 51, verse 9 says,

Hide thy face from my sins, and blot out all mine iniquities.

Now we'll look at verse 10:

Create in me a clean heart, O God; and renew a right spirit within me.

He says this because all of his sins were washed away. Before, a lustful heart arose inside of him, but in verse 12, he was saying:

Restore unto me the joy of thy salvation; and uphold me with thy free spirit.

David was a dirty sinner, but through the hyssop, he was already purged, and he was rejoicing in the joy of salvation.

He had entered the process of dwelling in the free spirit; of being upheld in the free spirit. This is exactly the same with us. We are like David! Do you understand this, everyone?

Behold, I was shapen in iniquity, and in sin did my mother conceive me. Because of this, does sin continually come out of us, or not? It does. For the pile of sin that will come out from us, Jesus shed His blood and died on the cross. Jesus, who died for David, died for us as well. David saw that the blood on the cross forgave his sins before it happened. He saw it beforehand and believed it. But after it happened, we see that the blood shed on the cross has forgiven us all of our sins. By believing this, we are able to obtain eternal life. Amen? Do you believe it?

Raise you hand if you're still a sinner. There's no one here who is a sinner? "Now my sins are all forgiven. I am clean. I have become whiter than snow." That is what the Bible says. The blood of Jesus has purged me. Raise your hand if you believe it. Amen, hallelujah! Hallelujah! I praise the Lord. This is believing in Jesus. If you do not believe that the blood Jesus shed on the cross forgave your sins, you are not truly believing in Jesus, but are only believing Him outwardly.

For a long time I had suffered inside of sin. I wanted to be freed from sin, but I sinned and repented everyday. I continually repeated the cycle of sinning and repenting. But I'm not like that anymore. Why? It is because Jesus eternally forgave my sins 2,000 years ago on the cross. I think of the sins I committed in my heart. I told you the day before yesterday how I broke the nail clippers and put them in my younger brother's pencil case, right? I did that when I was about ten years old. It's still vivid in my memory even though 52 years have passed. I once told my younger brother, "Brother, a long time ago it was I who broke the nail clippers."

He said, "Brother, did that happen?" He said that he doesn't remember anything about it. But when I saw my younger brother being spanked by my father, I felt so guilty and I was tormented by my conscience. I thought that that sin would never be washed away my entire life. But even that sin was washed away on the cross. That is why I have become whiter than snow.

Sins of years are wash'd away,
Blackest stains become as snow,
Darkest night is chang'd to day,
When I to the fountain go.

Although this is how people sing these hymns, they say, "God, I'm a sinner."

Happy day, happy day,
When Jesus washed my sins away

After singing hymns like this, when we tell them to pray, they say, "God, forgive me of my sins." They only sing and pray through lip service, they pray prayers and sing hymns that are not from their hearts.

Everyone, let us believe in Jesus now. Let us believe that the cross of Jesus is not powerless and that He has forgiven all our sins. Now, you are not sinners in the eyes of God. It is true that you committed many sins. But because the blood that Jesus shed on the cross washed all of your sins away, in the eyes of God, you are holy, righteous, and pure. God says that He does not remember your sins anymore. God has recorded the story in detail of how David committed sin to teach us this fact. David may say, "How embarrassing. Is he talking about that again?" Because David sinned, his story taught us the path to receiving the forgiveness of sin. When we go to heaven and meet David, we should say, "King David, thank you!"

Just as the blood of Jesus forgave my sins and the sins of David, and just as Apostle Paul's sins were forgiven, your sins, too, are forgiven. I believe that. That is why you are not a sinner. You are holy. You are righteous. Amen. I'll read one more verse and I will end. The words of 1 Corinthians chapter 6, verse 10:

Nor thieves, nor covetous, nor drunkards, nor revilers, nor extortioners, shall inherit the kingdom of God.

Next, verse 11:

And such were some of you: but ye are washed, but ye are sanctified, but ye are justified in the name of the Lord Jesus, and by the Spirit of our God.

It says, *And such were some of you.* It means that you have committed such sins, but you are washed. You are sanctified. *Ye are justified in the name of the Lord Jesus, and by the Spirit of our God.* This is what God is saying to you. You have committed these sins, but He is saying that through our Lord Jesus Christ, in the name of our Lord Jesus Christ, and inside the Spirit of our God, you have been washed; you have been sanctified; and you have been justified. Simply believe this. Don't add or take anything away from it.

He is telling you that you are washed. He's telling you that you are sanctified. He's telling you that you have been justified.

That is why I say that you are holy. But people began to speak against me, saying, "Who says things like this? Look at that heretic. He says that he is holy."

"Yes, I am holy."

"What? You don't sin? Are you holy?"

"Aren't you holy?"

"I'm not holy, I'm a sinner."

"I'm holy. God says that I'm holy."

God says that I am holy, so what else can I say? If God says that I am holy, then I am. But they all believe in their own thoughts. I don't know what kind of thoughts you have tonight or what kind of sin you have, but throw all of your thoughts away now. Repent of all of your thoughts. Throw them all out and believe the Word of God. If He says that you are holy, then believe that you are holy. If He says that you are righteous, then believe that you are righteous. If He says that you are washed whiter than snow, then believe that you are washed whiter than snow. Bless those who believe. Those who do not believe this fact should be cursed. Do you believe? Hallelujah! Raise your hand high if you believe that Jesus Christ has purged you of your sin. Thank you.

My sins are washed away! I was a dirty human, but now I am righteous! I am holy! I am a child of God! I can go to heaven! Amen. Hallelujah! I praise the Lord.

Everyone, salvation is not gained through our efforts. It is accepting into our heart what God has done. I had accepted this fact into my heart 43 years ago. From then on, Jesus was always with me. Inside of you, who accept this fact, Jesus will dwell in you as well. I believe that He will lead your lives to become blessed and beautiful.

6

The Chief Butler's Faith

6.
The Chief Butler's Faith

Hello everyone. Today, we will look at the words in the book of Genesis. I will read to you from Genesis chapter 40, verse 1.

And it came to pass after these things, that the butler of the king of Egypt and his baker had offended their lord the king of Egypt. And Pharaoh was wroth against two of his officers, against the chief of the butlers, and against the chief of the bakers. And he put them in ward in the house of the captain of the guard, into the prison, the place where Joseph was bound. And the captain of the guard charged Joseph with them, and he served them: and they continued a season in ward. And they dreamed a dream both of them, each man his dream in one night, each man according to the interpretation of his dream, the butler and the baker of the king of Egypt, which were bound in the prison. And Joseph came in unto them in the morning, and looked upon them, and, behold, they were sad. And he asked Pharaoh's officers that were with him in the ward of his lord's house, saying, Wherefore look ye so sadly to day? And they said unto him, We have dreamed a dream, and there is no interpreter of it. And Joseph said unto them, Do not interpretations belong to God? tell me them, I pray you. And the chief butler told his dream to Joseph, and said unto him, In my dream, behold, a vine was before me; And in the vine were three branches: and it was as though it budded, and her blossoms shot forth; and the clusters thereof brought forth ripe grapes: And Pharaoh's cup was in my hand: and I took the grapes, and pressed them into Pharaoh's cup, and I gave the cup into Pharaoh's hand. And Joseph said unto him, This is the interpretation of it: The three branches are three days: Yet within three days shall Pharaoh lift up thine head, and restore thee unto thy place: and thou shalt deliver Pharaoh's cup into his hand, after the former manner when thou wast his butler. But think on me when it shall be well with thee, and shew kindness, I pray thee, unto me, and make mention of me unto Pharaoh, and bring me out of this house: For indeed I was stolen away out of the land of the Hebrews: and here also have I done nothing that they should put me into the dungeon. When the chief baker saw that the interpretation was good, he said unto Joseph, I also was in my dream, and, behold, I had three white baskets on my head: And in the uppermost basket there was of all manner of bakemeats for Pharaoh; and the birds did eat them out of the basket upon my head.

And Joseph answered and said, This is the interpretation thereof: The three baskets are three days: Yet within three days shall Pharaoh lift up thy head from off thee, and shall hang thee on a tree; and the birds shall eat thy flesh from off thee. And it came to pass the third day, which was Pharaoh's birthday, that he made a feast unto all his servants: and he lifted up the head of the chief butler and of the chief baker among his servants. And he restored the chief butler unto his butlership again; and he gave the cup into Pharaoh's hand: But he hanged the chief baker: as Joseph had interpreted to them. Yet did not the chief butler remember Joseph, but forgat him.

We read the words up to verse 23.

The Day I Can Never Forget for All Eternity, October 7th, 1962

When we read the Bible, it seems that it is a collection of some stories and incidents. Amazingly, however, our images and the way of spiritual life are illustrated precisely in those words. When people are asked, "Can you go to heaven?" Oftentimes they answer, "We have to get there to know. How can we know? You have to die to know. How can you not go there and be sure if you can go to heaven?" There are many people who say, "What if you think that you are going to heaven and end up not going? What are you going to do?"

When you look in the Bible, there are people who go to heaven and people who don't go. There are people who are saved and people who are not. It is not an unclear distinction between the two, but rather, the distinction is very precise. It unmistakably illustrates the kind of who people walk the path to heaven and the kind of people who cannot walk the path to heaven. Early yesterday morning, I led the service at a funeral. A very old woman had passed away. I was told that the people were leaving for the cemetery at 5:30 in the morning, so I woke up in the morning, got in my car, went to the funeral home, and preached the Word. I spoke about how I had an intestinal obstruction a long time ago.

My grandmother had passed away in my hometown and because I was the chief mourner of the funeral, I had to return to my hometown to attend the funeral. In Korea, the body is kept at the funeral home for three days immediately after the death and funeral services are held there. After the three days, the burial is held. Many guests arrived over the three days, so I barely got any sleep at night and lasted the three days drinking only coffee. There was a conference starting on the evening of the day of the burial. After depositing my grandmother's coffin to her grave, it was about 1 o'clock in the afternoon. I told the people there that I was extremely busy and had to leave early. I asked them to understand and I quickly got in my car and drove to the conference site. From that evening, we held the conference.

While going to conferences, I'm very thankful that though I may be sick, when I hold a conference, I become healed. In my heart, I feel that if I continue to only do conferences, I can live to the age of 150. I have been working for the gospel for 43 years and have a conference almost every week. Even this time, the conference will continue until Saturday evening. I will have service on Sunday morning and Sunday evening; I will go to India and have a conference; then I will return and have service the following Sunday. On Monday, I will leave for Hawaii and have a conference for two weeks; that is how my schedule always is. Over the last 43 years, not once have I been unable to do a conference due to an illness. Recently, as I thought about this, I was truly startled. In my heart, I felt, "Wow, this is the grace of God. God is happy that I am having conferences. If I continue to do conferences, I will not die."

Right then, after the funeral of my grandmother, my body was very exhausted. While having the conference, I completely forgot that I was sick. On Friday, we ended the conference so gracefully, and on Saturday morning my stomach began to hurt. In the morning, I had to go to the missionary school to preach the Word there, but my stomach hurt so badly, I told my wife, "Today, I don't think I can go out." And from the morning, I began to wrestle with my stomach. It hurt so much, I got on my stomach and prayed, "Lord," and I felt okay, but after a little while, my stomach began to hurt again. Later, I learned that this was happening because my intestines were becoming twisted. It hurts when your intestines are twisting, but it hurts less when they are untwisting. The symptoms continued on from 8 o'clock in the morning to 12 o'clock at night. At midnight, I was in so much pain. They say that you and your wife are one body, but actually, you are not one body. Since she was not hurting, she was sleeping and snoring. I hated her so much for that, so I woke her up. "Honey, my stomach hurts so much. I can't take this anymore. Can you call the brothers to send a car? I think I'd better go to the hospital."

They called a car at midnight for me and we departed for the hospital. My stomach was bulging out like a woman who was nine months pregnant. I arrived at the hospital at around 1 o'clock in the morning. The doctors took x-rays and said that I had an intestinal obstruction; my intestines were all twisted. Then the doctor stuck a tube down my nose. As soon as the tube went in, this blue-colored water gushed out all over the doctor's coat. That evening passed by and it became Sunday. In my memory, it was the only time I had not gone to a Sunday service after being born again. Because my intestines were twisted, they said that I had to have surgery. Since my sister-in-law was working at Hanyang University Hospital, she found out who the internal medicine doctors were. Because only doctors in training were there, she recommended that I postpone the surgery. She said that a specialist would arrive the next day and it would be better to have the surgery then.

On Sunday morning, I was lying on the bed and I made eye contact with my wife, who was looking at me worriedly. Then my wife's face became blurry and faded away. My thoughts were clear, but as my wife's face blurred and faded out several times, I thought to myself, "I guess I am dying now. I am dying." I thought that I would have to put things in order before I died. The first thing that came to mind was church. My wife always told me, "You small-hearted stringent man," and she always accused me of nagging too much. As I was dying, there was no need for me to say, "Do this and do that." I felt that the pastors would take care of everything very well. Why would I have to mention anything about this, as I was dying? Before facing death, I had so many things to do and everything was so complicated. But as I thought that I was dying, everything became so simple. Because I was thinking about living, there were so many things to worry about; but as I thought of dying, there was nothing at all for me to worry about. That was so amazing. Before I died, I thought there would be so many things for me to say: "Pastor Kim, take care of this like this and take care of that like that…." But as I actually stood before death, there was nothing for me to say at all. My heart became very simple.

"Okay, the church will be fine, but what about my family?" My wife will live with my children; if not, they would die, but even with my family, it was just useless for me to say, "Honey, when I die, do this." A living person would be much better than someone who is dead. Lastly, I thought about my spirit. What will happen if I die? Right then I remembered October 7, 1962. It was the day I believed that all of my sins were washed as white as snow through the blood of Jesus. It was a day I will never forget. It was early in the morning of October 7, 1962. From that day, whether I knew it or not, Jesus was always with me. And when I thought about how loving Jesus would hold my hand and cross the river of death with me to the riverside where the tree of life is, it was so glorious and it strengthened me. Maybe that's why I survived.

Before, when I thought about death, I thought death would be fearful and painful. But when I thought about the fact that I was actually standing before death, I was not afraid of death at all. "I am just shedding my body. Now I will be living eternally with the Lord. Now I am going to the temple of the Lord." Death was something of great joy. I wanted to go quickly. I wanted to go there and meet the Lord, and the desire to see the Lord's face began to arise inside of me.

Because I was not in church on Sunday, the brothers and sisters prayed continually for me. Maybe it was because they prayed so much for me during the service time that I passed gas that afternoon. I had farted. The doctor said that this was something very precious, so I was told to contact him when I released some. It really was something precious. So I lived without having intestinal surgery.

The funeral yesterday was for a very old woman named Joo-ock Lee. She passed away after having received the forgiveness of sin. While preaching at the funeral, I was so thankful before the Lord. Where would this grandmother be now if Jesus had not been crucified and died to wash away her sins? She would be heading to destruction in the midst of fear and sadness; but this grandmother met Jesus and became freed from sin. She is now resting in heaven. She had received salvation. It was this grandmother who was saved, but it felt as though my own salvation was becoming greater. It felt as though I was receiving more grace.

Can a Roasted Seed Sprout and Bloom with Flowers?

A long time ago, when I used to go to Sunday school, my teacher told me this story: A king of a certain country gathered all of his subjects and spoke to them.

"My loving people, today I will give each one of you a flower seed of the heart. This is a flower seed that sprouts and blooms beautiful flowers if they are planted and raised by kind people. But if they are planted and raised by people who are evil, it will sprout, but flowers will not bloom from them. If the people who plant the seed are even more evil, then it won't even sprout. So if you plant this seed and bring back beautiful flowers, I will look at them and reward the one who has brought back the best flowers.

That day, the king passed out the flower seeds to every person in the country. From that day on, his subjects got out their flowerpots and filled them with soft soil. After planting the seeds, they added fertilizer, watered them, and poured all their hearts into making the flowers bloom. Whenever the people gathered together, they would constantly speak about the flower seeds.

"Mr. Kim. How many sprouts do you have?"

"We have two buds."

"Really? We have three."

People planted the flower seeds and flowers bloomed. A certain family said that a flower had bloomed. Another family said that two flowers had bloomed. Yet another family said that three flowers had bloomed. People were boasting that their flowers had bloomed. About the time that the flowers should be in full bloom, the king announced, "I shall examine your flowers tomorrow. I shall walk along the roadside; so everyone, bring out the flowerpots you have planted your flowers in."

The next day arrived and the time had come. The king came walking along the roadside. The people were all lined up along the roadside. They had all brought out such beautiful flowers. They looked at one another's flowers and said, "That guy's flowers are prettier than mine. Will he receive the reward or will I?" However, the king would not look at the flowers but just passed them by. After the king had walked for a long while, he stopped at a certain spot. There stood a boy named Tom, who didn't even have a flowerpot. He only had an earthen vessel filled with dirt. He was crying and sobbing in front of the vessel. The king asked him, "Child, why are you crying?"

"Your Highness, I'm worthy of death! Because my heart is so evil, the flower didn't even sprout."

As Tom said this, he cried and cried.

"So, how did you plant the seed that a flower didn't even sprout?"

"Well, I watered the seed and I took care of it with all of my heart, but no sprout came from this seed. I know this is because my heart is so evil. Please give me my punishment."

The king smiled and took Tom's hand and said, "Follow me." So Tom took his cracked earthen vessel that was filled with dirt and followed the king. The king stood high above all the people and began to speak, "My loving people."

Everyone became quiet.

"I wanted to know your hearts, so the flower seeds that I had given you had secretly been roasted all night long in a cauldron. So how is it that flowers have come from those roasted seeds?" Because the seeds the king had given the people would not sprout, the people were afraid of being labeled as evil, so they planted different flower seeds and raised flowers. Only Tom had brought a vessel of dirt without a sprout. So who was the good person? Tom was the good person. I didn't know why my Sunday school teacher told us this story, but that story remains vivid in my memory.

Everyone, from the time Adam and Eve sinned, we were planted with the seeds of sin. God says this about us humans. *The heart is deceitful above all things, and desperately wicked. (Jeremiah 17:* 9) In the Bible, God says that nowhere in the heart of man is there any good to be found. That is why we can't do any good. How can a roasted seed sprout or bloom flowers? God said that no good dwells in the heart of man. People make up their own good even though they have none, just as the people planted different seeds and raised flowers and acted as if they had only planted the first seed.

Because we humans have no good in us, no matter how much good we do in front of God: going to church on Sundays, being helpful, and even doing volunteer work, God has no interest whatsoever in any of that. They are just like the flowers that bloomed from the roasted seeds. Because people are planted with seeds of evil, evil things must bloom from us and are borne from us. Today, many churches do not know the Bible well, so they tell their church members to do what is good. Because people are trying so hard to do good things, they are fooled into thinking that they are actually good people. That is why God gave men the law: so that they would sin even more.

The book of Romans says, *Moreover the law entered, that the offence might abound. But where sin abounded, grace did much more abound: (Romans 5:20)* You must commit sin and realize that you are sinners – evil and dirty; then you will give up on what you are doing and the Lord will work. The only righteous seed in the world is Jesus. The only good seed is Jesus alone. The only holy seed is the one and only Jesus. All humans are dirty. We humans are evil and dirty. Everyone, think about this honestly: If you do all the evil things that arise from your heart, all of you would be like animals. Even though such evil things arise in you, trying to be good is hypocritical in the eyes of God. If God is deceived by you and becomes pleased, He would say, "Wow, you are doing great. You shall go to heaven." But would He say that? Never. He will never be that way.

From time to time, when I listen to broadcast sermons, I

hear people boast so much about themselves. It's so funny. What good have they done? They would talk about all the good they have done; how they fasted for forty days and prayed, and all that they have done. In the book of Matthew in the Bible, Jesus said that on the Day of Judgment, many will say, "Lord, Lord. Have we not prophesied in thy name? And in thy name, we have cast out demons. And in thy name we have done many wonderful works." Jesus says that He does not know them. If you have done something, then that is a curse before God, because, by nature, you are a dirty and evil human who can only be cursed. The only thing you can do is throw yourself away. It is denying yourself. Denying yourself is the greatest good you can do for yourself.

Today, many churches teach spiritual life backwards. "Do good things in front of God. Be faithful and do good deeds," is what they say. God, however, is not pleased with that kind of good whatsoever. When you are trying to do good, you can't receive the goodness of God. Because you try to become clean, you can't receive the righteousness of Jesus. Because you are busy trying to exalt your things and you cast away the righteousness of God, He tells us in Roman chapter 10:

For I bear them record that they have a zeal of God, but not according to knowledge. For they being ignorant of God's righteousness, and going about to establish their own righteousness, have not submitted themselves unto the righteousness of God. (Romans 10:2, 3)

If I give much offering and am loyal to the Lord, I can say, "Father God," and be confident. If you fight or do evil and bad things, you feel ashamed before God. That is a person who goes to God with his own works.

When I gave an apple to a certain child, he received it with one hand. When I gave him another one, he stretched out his other hand. When I gave him another apple, the child looked at the two apples in his hands and he let go of the smallest one and received the larger one. Everyone, how can a young child hold two apples in one hand? He must let go of one to hold another one. We, too, must let go of our goodness in order for us to hold the goodness of Jesus. You must throw away your own righteousness to make the righteousness of God yours. However, people hold on to their own righteousness.

Christianity that Has Deviated from the Bible

Once, I spoke with a certain pastor. "Pastor, have you read the Bible?"

"Well, when I was studying abroad in Germany…," he began to show off.

Although he was a pastor, he had nothing to do with Jesus and was a fraudulent pastor. If you have something of yourself to boast about, why would you rely on Jesus? If Pastor Ock Soo Park, who, standing before you, has something to boast of, it is only that he possesses filthy, dirty, evil, deceitful, pitiful, and weak things. If there was something good that I had done, it was not I who did it, but Jesus. There is no good in me.

I met a certain minister at the last Incheon conference. There are many things that he claimed to have received. He said he spoke in tongues and that he received the Holy Spirit. It is funny, isn't it? I heard there are many places today that teach speaking in tongues. I heard that when you go to prayer houses, they say, "Ah- allelujah, allelujah...." If you do that, you can speak in tongues. I have heard that many people in a certain church in Korea speak in tongues, but the funny thing is that the people who go to that church don't even read the Bible. When you read the Bible, in 1 Corinthians chapter 14, in the church, only two, or at the most, three people should speak in tongues. It says that not more than three people should speak in tongues in the church. And even that should be done only when there is interpretation. One person speaks in tongues and the other interprets. Another person speaks in tongues and another interprets. It says it should not be more than two or three people.

How is it then, brethren? when ye come together, every one of you hath a psalm, hath a doctrine, hath a tongue, hath a revelation, hath an interpretation. Let all things be done unto edifying. If any man speak in an unknown tongue, let it be by two, or at the most by three, and that by course; and let one interpret. But if there be no interpreter, let him keep silence in the church; and let him speak to himself, and to God."(1 Corinthians 14:26-28)

The church members in the church mentioned above do not read the Bible, perhaps, but in the church there should only be two, or at most, three people who speak in tongues. There shouldn't be more than three. And they should only speak in tongues when they have an interpreter. But it says that if there is no interpreter, keep your mouth shut at church and do it at home. In some churches, hundreds of people speak in tongues in a single church and it becomes very noisy. How can the Holy Spirit of God not work according to the words of the Bible but work in a way that is different and apart from the Bible? If it is God who wrote the Bible and if it is God who upholds speaking in tongues, then the Holy Spirit works according to the Word of God, and it will never work in a way that is separate from the Word.

There is a certain church in our church. A long time ago, the elder's father faced difficulties in running his business. At the time, a pastor came to him and said, "You must speak in tongues." The entire family spoke in tongues, but the father couldn't speak in tongues. Everyone in his family said, "Gee, Father, you are the problem." The father had difficulty in his thinking, "I can't do it. What am I supposed to do?" Christianity that has nothing to do with the Bible is prevalent in Korea. The large churches are very distant from the Bible.

From time to time, I think about this. Is it because this pastor who leads the church mentioned above doesn't know the Bible that he acts this way? He should know this much. Is a pastor of that caliber ignoring 1 Corinthians and having his church members speak in tongues? 1 Corinthians is the canon of speaking in tongues. These are things that I don't understand.

People become deceived because it says speaking in tongues is a gift. But just as a person's body has eyes, ears, and a nose, some people have the duty of being the nose and others should have the duty of being the mouth. Not everyone should be speaking in tongues.

Have all the gifts of healing? do all speak with tongues? do all interpret? (1 Corinthians 12:30)

They already differ from the Bible. In the Bible, the gifts of born again people are all different. Some people have a gift like that of being the eyes. Some people have a gift like that of being the nose. If a person has no legs or eyes on his body, but only has a mouth, is that a human being?

Is that a person? It's a monster. Everyone, I am not just trying to strike down a church, but churches these days have become very distant from the Word of God. Pastors do not read the Bible, and because human methods and ways are everywhere, they try to live spiritual lives with the ways of man.

You must have your own power to do it with your own ways, but to have faith to believe in God, you must lack in power. When a soldier goes to war, he should clean his gun and load it with ammunition, but he must throw his gun down when he is surrendering. If he says that he surrenders but is wielding a fully loaded machine gun, he can be shot to death at any moment. If one says, "I surrender," while pointing his gun, he will be killed. You must throw your gun away to surrender. Saying, "I surrender. Whether you kill me or spare me, do as you please. I leave myself to you," is surrendering. Spiritual life is not fighting before God but surrendering before God. "God, I cannot do it for all I do are dirty, filthy and evil. Therefore I leave my life to you. Whether I live or die, I leave myself to you. You must wash my sins clean and you must repair me!" This is the beginning of spiritual life. Amen? But people are living their spiritual life backwards. They try to do well themselves. Many pastors teach that you must exert much effort.

About ten years ago, I was invited to give a two hour sermon at a revival called "Move On" at a large stadium in Kenya. Many pastors had come to that revival. The emcee announced that there would be a time of prayer for those who wanted to be healed from AIDS. About seven hundred people raised their hands and stepped forward. A pastor who was praying would shout, "Pokeya!" hit people's heads and they would fall backward and that is how they would receive the Holy Spirit. The organizer of the revival asked me to pray as well, and I stepped from the podium and went down to the field and prayed for a person. That person just fell over. From the beginning, they were prepared to fall over. If the people fell over, I was afraid they would get concussions, so I held on to him. Later on, I saw that there were people behind him supporting him when he fell as I prayed. When the prayer session ended, there were hundreds of people lying on the stadium ground. That was receiving the Holy Spirit for them.

One pastor pushed the head of a young man who had come forward and said, "Pokeya!" The young man was still standing, so again the pastor said, "Pokeya!" and pushed him with much strength, but the young man was still standing upright. The third time, he took a step back and with some momentum pushed him as he said, "Pokeya!" However, this young man was still standing, so the pastor just passed on. I told the organizer, "This is kind of strange. In the Bible, Jesus raised the paralytic and raised the dead. He always raised everyone. Why do you push everyone and make them fall over? Isn't this weird?", but nobody would answer me. They just kept saying, "Pokeya!" and the people kept falling over. The people there called that receiving the Holy Spirit.

Because the people from Africa have simple thoughts, pastors often rip them off. For me to talk about this, I can recall so many heart-wrenching incidents. Most of the people who gathered at the stadium had not worn shoes and could not afford to eat, but I was invited to a meal and was very shocked. At the back of the stadium, there were VIP seats behind the sky box. The pastors were there eating fancy foods that were even rare in America. At times, I, too, get to eat fancy food, but the problem was that from the moment the pastors stood at the podium to the time they finished, their theme or their topic was money. They collected offerings during the service. Later on, they told the people to commit a certain amount of money and they collected that as well. Usually during a service, they give offerings two or three times. Christianity has truly been corrupted.

I was invited to a certain church in Africa and was to give a sermon. The people were dancing and singing and I followed along, but my body is quite uncoordinated. Somebody videotaped me dancing and showed it to my wife who told me, "Your steps are all wrong." At that church, during the service, one by one, people came up to dance, and as they danced, they put money in the offering bin. The whole congregation must come out and dance. They do this so the people have no choice but to give an offering. They did this three times during the service.

Christianity in this world has corrupted so much. I am not going to speak about the churches of Korea because you all know about them even if I don't mention them. People would attend other churches and then start coming to our church. Therefore churches call us heretics because they are losing their church members. There are so many people who were hurt while attending other churches who started coming to our church. That I can allow, but what I can't allow is teaching spiritual life backwards.

How is spiritual life lived? Who would become a beggar in order to eat? You have to be hungry to beg for food. If you have food to eat, you don't ask, "Can I have some food?" You must have no means of your own to be able to rely on

Jesus in spiritual life. You must realize that you cannot do any good by yourself. You cannot do anything righteous. You can only commit sin and be destroyed. A person who thinks he can do things himself, although he says he relies on Jesus, his reliance is only a formality; it can't be true dependence. That is why for us to depend on God, we must throw away all of our own methods. On the other hand, people try to be faithful, pray, and do well on their own. How can they develop the faith to believe in God? They cannot. I hope you will have proper faith and change through that faith. If you stand in true faith, you cannot keep your mouth shut upon seeing the wrongful faith.

"That's not it. That is the wrong faith."

My friend I met in the army came to my house the day before yesterday. He had been the chief of a local police department, but he retired. There are many pastors in the Police Pastor Association. Whenever that friend of mine said that he was a friend of Pastor Ock Soo Park, people would say, "Ah, that church?" They said that I run businesses and I do terrible things. My friend would then explain to them, "I know him very well, and you are wrong about him. I have even slept in the same room as Pastor Ock Soo Park. I also attended the Australia Global Camp. Pastor Park does not run a business. Go find out for yourself. I also know that Pastor Ock Soo Park has sold many copies of his collection of sermons, *The Secret of Forgiveness of Sin and Being Born Again*. However, he didn't take a dime for himself. It seems as if he doesn't care for money."

Many people say different things, such as, "The Good News Mission is a church of heretics. If you go there, you will be ruined." I never want to be like those pastors. I would rather be called a heretic. I don't want to be labeled the same as those pastors. Everything else is okay, but one must know how to teach and demonstrate a proper spiritual life to their church members.

The Chief Butler Who Saw Only the Vine

When Martin Luther began the Religious Reformation, it started with the words, *The just shall live by faith. (Romans 1:17)* Faith is not relying on you, but believing in God. You have to receive the righteousness and holiness of God. Genesis chapter 40, that we read this morning, is precisely about that. On the surface, the chief butler and the chief baker committed sins and were locked up in prison. Each had different dreams, and in accordance with the interpretation of Joseph, the chief butler lived and the chief baker was killed.

In chapter 40, verse 1, it says, *And it came to pass after these things, that the butler of the king of Egypt and his baker had offended their lord the king of Egypt.* Both of them had sinned. But at the end of chapter 40, what happened was, *And he restored the chief butler unto his butlership again; and he gave the cup into Pharaoh's hand: But he hanged the chief baker: as Joseph had interpreted to them. (Genesis 40:21, 22)* In Genesis chapter 40, verse 1, both of them sinned against the pharaoh, but the chapter ends with one person receiving salvation and the other receiving destruction. This is not just any story, but the story of mankind. We (mankind) had sin. But there are those who are saved and there are those who are destroyed. What kind of people are saved? People like the chief butler receive salvation. People like the chief baker are destroyed.

Let us look into the kind of heart the chief butler had that he received salvation, and into the kind of heart the chief baker had that he received destruction. If you see this, you can clearly see the path of how you should live a spiritual life. It is very simple. What did the chief butler do? We will read verse 9 together:

And the chief butler told his dream to Joseph, and said to him, In my dream, behold, a vine was before me;

This is talking about the world of hearts. I was so amazed upon reading verse 9. Why, you ask? If you are the chief butler of the king, then you have a high position and good income. And I think he lived well. One day, however, he did something wrong and ended up in prison. How frustrated he must have been. "How long will I be in prison? Will the king forget me and leave me here for the rest of my life? How many years will I be in prison? How will my children get along while I am in prison? What will my wife eat to live?" He would probably have many complicated thoughts such as these. When the chief butler saw the vine in his dream, he no longer saw any of those things; only the vine.

Behold, a vine was before me;

Everyone, look. It says that there was a vine, so if I hide behind it, can I be seen or not? I cannot be seen. The vine completely covered all his problems. How many problems did the chief butler have? "My wife is ill and has no money. To visit me and to pay for the lawyer, she must have sold the house. I don't know how she is doing. What if she is out on the street in this cold winter? How are my sons doing? I have no idea what they are eating. When will I ever get out of this prison?" He had many troubles and problems, but before him was the vine and those problems were covered.

It is not that a person who lives spiritual life has no problems at all. It's just that Jesus covers thousands and thousands of problems. If Jesus is inside a person, in his spiritual life, thousands or even tens of thousand of problems are taken care of. This is something that's very amazing.

The flowers on the vine bloomed; and the fruit ripened. The Bible is so amazing because the chief butler did not look anywhere else other than the vine. He only looked at the vine. He saw the vine sprouting, flowers blooming, and fruit being borne. This represents Jesus Christ.

In John chapter 8, a woman was taken in the act of adultery. The scribes and Pharisees dragged this woman before Jesus and said, "Master, this woman was taken in the act of adultery and Moses said such a woman should be stoned. What sayest thou?"

Think about the woman taken in adultery. Where does her fate lie? It lies in the actions of Jesus. The only hope for this woman can be found in the words that will proceed from the lips of Jesus. Even though she may have a pretty face, it is useless. Even though she has a lot of money, it is useless. Even though her older brother is a congressman, it is useless. Only what the Lord says will make a difference. A person such as she received salvation. Amen? Amen.

The butler had many complicated issues in his home, but those things were not problems because he had known precisely that there was no other way outside of Jesus. That is why he was only looking at the vine. The vine is growing, flowers are blooming, and fruit are ripening. Our spiritual life doesn't work out because we don't wholly rely on Jesus. "If I fast and pray for 40 days, the Lord will receive me." This is how people give offerings to God. "I took out a mortgage on my house to give this offering." This is what they are holding onto in their hearts. Such people see ways other than Jesus.

I wake up every morning and go jogging. When I had a conference in Ulsan, right next to Ulsan church there is an elementary school. I went jogging at that elementary school every morning. I jogged and ran out of breath and hung on the monkey bars. I was amazed because I used to be very good at pull-ups, but I couldn't do any pull-ups. Have I gotten old? It is true that I have a pot belly and my body is heavier. I pulled with all my might, but I could only go up a little. I couldn't do it.

A long time ago, there was a fire at the Astoria Hotel. All the people went up to the roof to get away from the fire. The Astoria Hotel was just a 100 meters away from Ilshin Elementary School. A helicopter flew in and lowered a rope onto the hotel's roof to move the people to the elementary school. I saw on TV that a person was holding on to the rope. He was holding on to the rope, but could not hold on any longer, let go of the rope, and died. Do you think he wanted to let go of that rope? He died when he let go. I remember the time I had received ranger training in the army. I felt that if they had little knots in the rope, the people could step on to the knots. And even if they hang on to the rope with one hand, they would be okay. It was so heartbreaking. The person was holding on to the rope by the strength in his arms and fell off. Even if you told me to hang on for a while, I think I too would have let it go. I can't hold on because I don't have much strength. A long time ago, when we had to do pull-ups, I was able to manage. I tried to do some a few days ago, but I couldn't.

When you don't have strength, you will let go. In our

spiritual life, if you want to hold on to it, can you? You will meet your limits. It seems that you are good to some extent. But it is a problem that we appear to be good. It is a problem when the net of a sleeper catches fish in the lake. Why? It would be great if the sleeper is a little smart and realizes, "I caught a fish while I was sleeping by accident. How could I catch a fish while I am sleeping?" But if he does not realize this and thinks that he can just catch fish while sleeping, he will end up wasting a lot of time from then on. What kind of fish would get caught by a sleeping man?

It is exactly the same in spiritual life. In spiritual life, there is no other way for you to be saved but through Jesus. It was the same with the woman taken in adultery and the chief butler as well. The story of the chief butler continues as the things in his heart are revealed in his dream. The vine budded, its blossoms shot forth, and it bore fruit. He pressed the grapes and made juice to present to the king. There is no other way for you to be presented to God other than through Jesus who died on the cross.

The Chief Baker Who Placed All Manner of Bakemeats on Top of White Bread

The dream of the chief of baker was different. From verse 16, it talks about the dream of the chief baker:

When the chief baker saw that the interpretation was good, he said unto Joseph, I also was in my dream, and, behold, I had three white baskets on my head: And in the uppermost basket there was of all manner of bakemeats for Pharaoh; and the birds did eat them out of the basket upon my head. (Genesis 40:16, 17)

The white bread in the dream of the chief baker represents Jesus and the wine in the dream of the chief butler represents Jesus as well. During the Holy Communion, don't we eat bread and drink wine to commemorate the Lord's body and blood? All the chief baker needed to do was bring the three baskets of white bread, but on top of that, he added all manner of bakemeats for Pharaoh. Do you know what this represents? It means this was not Jesus alone.

Today, many people say they believe in Jesus, but actually, they do not believe in Jesus. They say Jesus was crucified for their sin on the cross, but they feel as though that alone is not enough. The gesture of the chief butler pressing the grapes to bring the wine before the king, what does that represent? "God, all I have done is commit dirty, evil, and filthy sins. Do not look upon my dirty self, but the blood of Jesus who was crucified and killed on the cross forgave all my sin. Look to that blood and receive me." This is the spiritual life of the chief butler. On the contrary, the chief baker did believe in Jesus, but he thought, "Just like waiting for good luck to roll in, should I just simply wait for Jesus? I have to do what I have to do. There are things that God should do and there are things that I need to do. What I've got to do is what I've got to do. How can I just sit still? Will it be okay to leave everything to Jesus?" That is the kind of spiritual life he had. That is why the chief baker did all kinds of good things. "God, I did it. I fasted and prayed. I helped out the orphans. I witnessed at conferences." Saying that they did this and that for Jesus, people pile the things that they've done on top of Jesus.

Whoever wants true faith to enter them must know that no matter what they do, it is useless and that it cannot be the path to salvation. But Satan deceives us into boasting about the things we have done well.

When I was young, a teacher from my church preached to us about the words, "Do not let your right hand know what your left hand is doing." He then told us a story. One day, this teacher was walking on his way, wearing a coat. There was a beggar shivering in the cold, so he took his coat off, put it on the beggar, and started to run away. This story looked beautiful to me then. I thought that I should do that one time, too. But I didn't have a coat. All I had was a shirt and I couldn't take that off. I had a few crisp bills on me in case of an emergency, and I saw a beggar on the street, gave him the money, and I ran away. I didn't have to run away. The interesting thing is that this happened when I was 17, and even though I am over 60 now, it is still vivid in my memory. I gave money to a beggar and ran away. My righteousness and my goodness, those things remain in my heart as something beautiful, but those beautiful things cover the beauty of Jesus. That is why Jesus cannot become the savior in your heart.

When we see the story of how the woman taken in adultery received salvation, the scribes and Pharisees asked Jesus, "Master, this woman was taken in the act of adultery. Moses commanded such a woman should be stoned, but sir, what sayest thou?" At that moment, because one word from the mouth of Jesus would decide her fate, the woman taken in adultery could only hear the words that Jesus uttered and nothing else. There was no salvation for her outside Jesus. That is how salvation is acquired. People who received true salvation, like the woman taken in the act of adultery, throw away all their methods and ways and their good and bad things. They only rely on the blood of Jesus that was shed on the cross. But since some people are not able to believe in the blood Jesus shed on the cross, and since people can't believe only in the blood, they have to do something on top of everything Jesus did. Because they have such hearts, the definite faith to believe in Jesus can't be clearly established. It can never be established. I hope that you will come to know this well.

A long time ago, people tried to make gold. When they mixed copper and tin, it seemed similar to gold. They thought that if they mixed metals well, they would be able to make gold, so they endlessly tried to make gold. It almost seemed inevitable that they could make gold. Therefore, during the middle ages, alchemists tried to make gold because gold had great value. They sold their entire fortunes trying to mix this and that, but ultimately, they didn't make gold. Later on, they discovered the fact that because gold is an element, they can't make it. Nowadays, no one ever thinks of such a thing as trying to make gold.

During the tenure of President Chung Hee Park, they drilled every corner of our country looking for petroleum. From the East Sea to the West Sea, they drilled the fifth, the sixth, the seventh, and the eighth mine lots. They drilled and drilled. Once, there was news that there was petroleum near Pohang. Because the president wanted to find petroleum so badly, as they were drilling, they accidentally came upon the place where a gas station had been before and something dark came up. They took it to the Blue House, the house of the president. President Chung Hee Park saw this and said, "Petroleum, where have you been? You should have come earlier," and he was happy. So from then on, has our country been supplying its own petroleum, and have we been able to drive around because of that petroleum? No, there is no petroleum. After that incident, there was no more petroleum. Now there is no one in our country who tries to drill for petroleum because we all know that there is none. They had invested a lot of money into looking for petroleum, and because they know that there is none in our country, right now we are drilling in other countries.

There is nothing inside of us that is worthy of making us able to go to heaven. It seems that you are a little good, and from time to time, when you help the poor, you have the heart that you have done something good; that God will be pleased. When you fast and pray all night long, you think that God will be pleased. Satan deceives you into thinking that if you do well like this you will be able to go to heaven. But such people must all go to hell. For us to go to heaven, one thing we must know is that no matter what you do through your effort, it will not work.

When you are going to America, if you learn how to swim and try to swim across the Pacific Ocean to go to America, even if you practice and try to go to America, in your entire lifetime, you will never be able to swim to America. For a person to go to America, he must quit trying to swim. "I can't go to America by swimming. Even if I swim, it can't be done." He must realize this and change his method. He must buy a plane ticket. A native tribal people living in Brazil, South America, ask us where Korea is, and when we tell them Korea is on the other side of the world, they say, "Then why do you buy an airplane ticket? If you keep on digging, wouldn't you get to Korea? As you dig, drink the underground spring water and keep digging." It's because they don't know how big the earth is. They don't have measurement units. They don't know how long a foot is or how long 25,000 miles is. That's why they are saying such things. If they knew about this, they would not say such things.

People who know things precisely, throw away all of the good that they try to do in order to go to heaven. If the good you have done has become a crown in your heart and you keep it, then you can't go to heaven. This morning, throw away all the good things that you have done. You must only hold onto what Jesus has done to go to heaven. Do you believe it? Amen? Amen.

Do You Boast about Jesus or Do You Boast about What You Have Done?

In the story of the chief butler and the chief baker, in Genesis chapter 40, the chief butler had nothing to place his expectations in other than the vine. He plucked some grapes and brought them forward. The grape juice represents the blood of Jesus.

"God, what I have done is dirty, and all I have done can only be destroyed and cursed. Jesus, when you were crucified for my sin, didn't you receive the curse? Therefore, this blood is the proof that my sin is forgiven."

Everyone, from time to time, you have Holy Communion in your church, don't you? You break the bread and drink wine, don't you? Why do we have Holy Communion? As you break the bread, you say, "Just as this bread is broken, the body of Jesus was broken for my sin. You have washed away my sins." As you drink the wine, you say, "To receive the punishment for my sin, Jesus shed His blood and my sins were washed away," and take part in the bread and the wine.

Loving folks, this morning, those of you who pile the things you have done on top of the white bread, like the chief baker, will go to hell. Now, you must throw all of that away. Everyone, throw away everything you have done well before God. You have been deceived by Satan, who wishes to drag you to hell, so those things appear to be good. True good is only inside of Jesus. True righteousness is only within one being, Jesus. Throw away everything you have done well. When you go forward only relying on the blood of Jesus Christ, who was crucified and killed for you, you can go to heaven. Amen?

Loving folks, what kind of spiritual life do you have? Are you satisfied with the things you have done well like the chief baker? You doing something, is that something for you to be proud of or joyful about? Not so. There is nothing for you to boast about. Only the blood that Jesus Christ shed on the cross is what we can boast of. Only that can become our crown. Of course, there may be times when you have helped the poor. There must have been times when you had done something difficult or something good. However, those things should not remain in your heart. Because you can't go to heaven with that, you must rely only on the blood of Jesus, the Son of God.

Then what should we believe in? Just as the chief butler only looked at the vine, we must only look at Jesus. Throw away all that good you have done, and say, "Jesus, all I have done is nothing but evil and sin. I have done nothing but evil. I only have filthiness. But Jesus shed His blood for those sins. You have received all the punishment for my sins. I am cleansed and all my sins have been washed away. Not a single one remains. I come to you, God, relying on that blood." At that very instant, you can have the spiritual life of the chief butler. You will then be able to gain the glorious heavenly kingdom.

7

Thy Sins Be Forgiven Thee

7.
Thy Sins Be Forgiven Thee

Hello everyone. It's nice to see you. Tonight we'll read from the book of Mark. I will read from Mark chapter 2, verse 1.

And again he entered into Capernaum after some days; and it was noised that he was in the house. And straightway many were gathered together, insomuch that there was no room to receive them, no, not so much as about the door: and he preached the word unto them. And they come unto Him, bringing one sick of the palsy, which was borne of four. And when they could not come nigh unto him for the press, they uncovered the roof where he was: and when they had broken it up, they let down the bed wherein the sick of the palsy lay. When Jesus saw their faith, he said unto the sick of the palsy, Son, thy sins be forgiven thee. But there were certain of the scribes sitting there, and reasoning in their hearts, Why doth this man thus speak blasphemies? who can forgive sins but God only? And immediately when Jesus perceived in his spirit that they so reasoned within themselves, he said unto them, Why reason ye these things in your hearts? Whether is it easier to say to the sick of the palsy, Thy sins be forgiven thee; or to say, Arise, and take up thy bed, and walk? But that ye may know that the Son of man hath power on earth to forgive sins, (he saith to the sick of the palsy,) I say unto thee, Arise, and take up thy bed, and go thy way into thine house. And immediately he arose, took up the bed, and went forth before them all; insomuch that they were all amazed, and glorified God, saying, We never saw it on this fashion.

We read up to verse 12.

Skin for Skin and Touch His Bone and His Flesh

This morning, we spoke about the chief butler and chief baker in Genesis chapter 40. When we read the Bible, it's so amazing. The chief butler was in prison. But just a little while ago, he, as the chief butler, had authority, financial power, and was abundant in every way. But because he committed sin, overnight, he was in prison, and I'm sure many thoughts crossed his mind: whether his wife was doing well; whether his children were doing well; what was his family eating; when would he ever get out of prison; and what does the king think of him. Such complicated thoughts could have arisen within him, but the chief butler saw a vine in his dream. He did not see his wife doing well or his children going though hardships; he saw the vine. The vine had sprouted and budded, blossoms shot forth, and fruit was borne.

It really did not work out well for me. When things got difficult for me, I fell into difficulties. When things were sad, I fell into sadness. And when there was suffering, I fell into suffering. This chief butler, however, although he had these many hardships, he did not see any of them in his heart. He saw the vine; he saw Jesus Christ. It means that Jesus Christ had covered all the butler's difficulties that were before him.

Last year, in December, I went to Los Angeles in America for a conference. I went to the conference together with an elder from our church. The elder's daughter had been hospitalized. She is the sister who played the clarinet in the Gracias Choir tonight. When I see such images in my life, I am deeply moved, and just thinking about it brings me to tears. That daughter had a disease called lupus. In our bodies, there is a function that fights against germs when they enter our bodies. But this disease is one where that function is broken, and it cannot distinguish the body from foreign germs. Therefore, the cells that should be fighting against foreign germs end up fighting against your own body. One day it attacks your own heart, your brain is attacked, your stomach is attacked, and your kidneys are attacked. It breaks down the organs of the body. And at the time, the elder's loving daughter caught that disease and she was hospitalized at Samsung Hospital.

While we were in L.A., the elder, who had been sharing the same room with me, received a phone call at about 2 o'clock in the morning. Then he woke me up, saying,

"Pastor! Pastor!" Because of jetlag, in America, it's very difficult to fall asleep, but I had barely fallen asleep though I had tried and tried. He received a phone call from Korea saying that daughter's heart and kidneys were in bad condition and there were problems in five or six other parts of her body. But the most serious thing was that the lupus had attacked her brain and she had a brain infarction. Because the brain could not execute its normal functions, she could not see well and because information was not being delivered to the brain, she was losing her judgment. She fell into a deep coma. The pressure in her brain had gotten very high and there was a chance that she could die. They needed to perform an operation immediately, so in order to ask permission for surgery, they had called her father.

Since the pressure in the brain was so high, the surgery included breaking open the skull and exposing a part of the brain to reduce the pressure. It's a scary surgery, just thinking about it. The elder could not make the decision, so he put me on the phone and I spoke to the doctor for about ten minutes. Unless we decided on this quickly, it was a problem to even reserve an operation room. More than anything, there was a high possibility that the child might die. There was nothing I could decide myself, either. A doctor, from New York, was sharing the same room with us. Since he was a family practice specialist, and I could not make the decision myself, I put the doctor on the phone. The doctor spoke for awhile with the doctor from the other hospital. He said that he would contact them and hung up the phone. It was very difficult for any one of us to decide upon this problem. Nevertheless, we decided to postpone the surgery and I fell asleep. I woke up from my sleep. When I woke up, the elder, who had been lying next to me, was nowhere to be seen.

I thought, “This is the difference between the father and a pastor. The pastor falls asleep because he is tired, but the father does not fall asleep so he goes and prays!”

I felt very guilty in my conscience. I, too, woke up from my sleep, went out to the chapel, knelt down in front of the podium, and prayed. After praying for awhile, I felt my heart being led by the heart of God and God allowed a Bible verse to come to my mind. The words of Job chapter 2, *Skin for skin... and touch his bone and his flesh.* These words clearly came to me.

“What words are these?” I sat and thought quietly about the book of Job. When Satan requested God to give him Job, God said that he would leave Job to Satan, but told Satan not to put a hand on his body. Then Satan killed every one of Job’s sons and killed all of Job’s cattle and livestock. In the end, Job’s wife said to him, “Do you still retain your integrity? Curse God and die.” Job did not curse God. But he said, “You speak as one of the foolish women,” and the story goes on. Afterward, God says to Satan, “Have you considered my servant Job? He still holds fast his integrity, although you move me against him to destroy him without cause.” Right then Satan says, “Skin for skin, and touch his bone and his flesh.” As I thought to that point, a heart came to mind.

“Ah, Satan requested God to strike Job’s flesh and bone. That is why God left Job to Satan, but God told Satan not to touch his life. Ah, then Satan has requested the elder’s daughter. He wanted to strike her skin and bones, but God will not have her life be touched.”

When I had that heart, I was at peace. I thought, "She will live. She will go through hardship because her flesh and bone will be struck, but God will save this child. Her life will not be touched," and fell asleep that day.

Afterwards, we finished the conference and returned to Korea. The elder's daughter was unconscious for four or five days and then she woke up. The amazing thing is, because she had a brain infarction, she couldn't speak or see anything in front of her. However, God worked and she opened her eyes and spoke. Immediately after she regained consciousness, she had no memory and couldn't recognize anyone. If oxygen is not supplied to the brain for just thirty minutes, the brain cannot survive; the brain cells die; and they cannot be restored. However, every part of her brain was completely restored. Within a few days, she completely recovered, and right now, she is attending Ewha Womans University. She is as normal as any other student studying at the school.

Beginning with the daughter's brain, all of her other bodily functions recovered, one by one, but in the end, her kidneys were not good. The kidneys are the part of the body that filter your blood and make urine. The elder's daughter could not urinate at all. The doctors said that her kidneys can never be restored. They said that once her kidneys had broken down, that was it; that was the end of them. Through God's miraculous grace, however, her kidneys got better and better. After a little while, she urinated 80 cc's. Nowadays, she urinates 750 cc's a day.

I'm not speaking about God in theory. One day, I received the heart of God; the Word of God, in my heart. From that time on, the loving God was inside of me. Not once did He ignore the big or small problems that I encountered, but He took care of every single one of those problems. Apostle Paul said:

For I am crucified with Christ, nevertheless I live; yet not I, but Christ liveth in me. (Galatians 2:20)

From the day my sins were washed as white as snow; the day the words of God entered my heart, it was not Ock Soo Park, the man, who was living. But I am just a vessel that is holding Jesus. As I spent 43 years inside of the Lord after receiving forgiveness of sin, there truly were many hardships. There were many difficulties and tribulations, but not once had Jesus ever left me alone. When I went through hardships; when I went through sufferings; when I went through difficulties; those hardships, sufferings, and difficulties were no longer my problems. They became the problems of Jesus Christ. Even if a hundred people fall down before me, and even if a thousand people collapse, it is truly amazing that I am able to stand because of God.

Pastor, There Are No Butterflies in St. Petersburg

Although Korean people are talented, they are a bit short-tempered on the international level. At the 2004 IYF World Camp, I wanted our college students, who were short-tempered and competitive, to hear a lot of music. It is because music softens people's hearts very much. At that time, we invited a very famous Russian opera singer named Larissa to the IYF World Camp.

"It would be so great if you would come to Korea and sing to our students from time to time during the IYF World Camp for one month."

I didn't know she had this kind of a situation, but eight years ago, her son, Alan, got divorced. After the divorce, Alan was in such deep pain that his friend brought him a pistol one day.

"Hey Alan, since you're in so much pain, I came to free you from that pain."

He put the pistol to Alan's head and said, "I want to free you from your pain. If I pull the trigger, you can be freed from this pain, but you are my friend. I need you, so you cannot die!"

He then put away the pistol. Instead, he pulled out a plastic bag from his right pocket and gave him drugs.

"This can also free you from your pain."

From that day on, Alan began to do drugs. He took shots and after a little while, became a drug addict. Now, unless he takes shots of drugs, he will be in so much pain he cannot bear it. Because of that, he sold everything he had in his house. Eventually, there was nothing remaining but the walls.

His mother cried every day.

"Alan! Alan!"

He came to need more money, so he would steal things from his neighbor's house and he stole from his relative's house. His mother was so worn out because of her son. She would go on stage, sing, and come back down with bouquets of flowers in her arms. But when she thought of Alan, she would fall down and cry on the spot. Every single night, without rest, she fought and cried.

One day she thought, "The peace in my family was broken because of Alan. The best way out is to kill him. Since I cannot live after having killed my son, I will die as well. We will die together!"

That was what she had decided in her heart. She then went to the most famous fortune teller in St. Petersburg. She wanted to find out about her son before dying. But this was what the fortune teller said:

"I see something cloudy. Your son; Alan's head; there is an evil spirit. Your son is in pain because of that evil spirit."

"How can I get rid of that evil spirit?"

"There is a person who can cast out that evil spirit. He is a person with grey hair. You must meet him."

"Where is that man with the grey hair?"

"He is in a place where there are lots of pine trees."

"There are lots of pine trees in Finland. Is he there?"

"I don't know about that, but you will find him in a place where there are lots of pine trees."

Then Larissa was invited by us in late June of 2004 and she came to Korea. When she came to Gangnam Church, she was completely startled. There are lots of pine trees at Gangnam Church. In Young-yang, Gangwon Province, they were doing road construction, so they had to dig up the pine trees from the mountains. A single, tall, beautiful pine tree would be carried on a trailer, and one by one, they were all brought over and planted in front of our church. The amazing thing was that we planted them however we wanted, and these pine trees, which have difficulty surviving, all lived. Larissa came to Gangnam Church, and she was completely startled by the pine trees. She came to our house and was startled for a second time that day because I have grey hair.

After I preached the sermon that evening, Larissa said, "Pastor Park, there is something I need to talk to you about." That day I was so busy that I said, "I apologize, but I'm a bit busy right now. Let's talk in a few days." After a few days, through the translation of a missionary from Russia, I preached the gospel to Larissa. Larissa received salvation that day. There were lots of worries inside Larissa's heart, but she began to rejoice and her face became bright. As the World Camp continued, she brought her son, Alan, and asked me to pray for him, so I prayed for Alan. Afterwards, through having fellowship with someone else, Alan received salvation. I can never forget this incident. This is what Alan said after receiving salvation:

"Pastor, in St. Petersburg, where I live, there are no butterflies. I've only seen specimen butterflies on display. But it's my first time seeing real butterflies actually flying. The butterflies flying around are so beautiful. Pastor, it's my first time seeing dragonflies flying around. We don't have dragonflies in my country. Korea is so beautiful."

I came to tears as I listened to those words. Why? Drug addicts cannot feel the beauty of flowers. They do not have enough room in their hearts to feel beauty. They have no space in their hearts to taste beauty. Drug addicts think, "Drugs, drugs, drugs." They think of nothing else besides that. I was able to know that Alan was freed from drugs. As they returned to Russia, I cannot forget how Larissa and her son had cried, holding each other's hands.

Everyone, people live spiritual life backwards: they try to pray hard and work hard. They are determined to quit drinking, doing drugs, and try to live a good spiritual life. Then what is there for Jesus to do? Spiritual life is not you doing things for yourself, but leaving things up to Jesus Christ to do the work, and accepting His words.

As the pastor of Gangnam Church, for me to minister the

best, do you know what I need to do? It is not that I should lead early morning services and zealously go around visiting and preaching the Word. It is for me to step back and allow Jesus the opportunity to work in our church. Every time I have faced difficulties in my life, and whenever I have collided against those difficulties with my own works, I have always failed ten out of ten, a hundred out of a hundred times. But when I stepped back and Jesus stepped forward, there was not a single thing that did not work out. It is not that Pastor Park is great, or smart, or good at ministering, but our church brothers and sisters see so clearly that God is living and working in the midst of our church.

A few years ago, while giving a sermon in Tacoma in the United States, I said, "I have never once seen a division in our church. I have never seen one conflict in our church." After the sermon, a middle-aged woman came to see me, and said, "Pastor I have a question."

"What is it?"

"Pastor, honestly, has there truly never been a division or conflict in your church?"

I thought about it for a while. "When has there ever been a division or conflict in our church? I don't have a single memory of that."

So I said, "There was none."

"Pastor, is that really true?"

"Yes."

"Pastor, is there really a church like that on this earth?"

"Come and see."

Everyone, if Jesus lives and works inside of you, instead of yourself, He will give you rest. Spiritual life is not something tiring and difficult. The fact that you feel spiritual life is tiring and difficult means that it is you who are doing everything. You cannot live a spiritual life, but it is done by Jesus, because believing in Jesus is spiritual life. Your spiritual life being tiring, difficult, and confusing is because your spiritual life is wrong. It is so peaceful when you live a true spiritual life. You have joy; you have comfort; and you have rest.

Cherry Tree, How Could You Make Such Clean, White Flower Petals?

This evening, we read Mark chapter 2. When I read these words, I feel this Bible is so amazing. If it weren't for God, these words could not have been written this way. He uses the same words and letters that we use, and arranges them like this…

And again he entered into Capernaum after some days; and it was noised that he was in the house. And straitway many were gathered together, insomuch that there was no room to receive them, no, not so much as about the door: and he preached the word unto them. And they come unto him, bringing one sick of the palsy, which was borne of four. And when they could not come nigh unto him for the press, they uncovered the roof where he was: and when they had broken it up, they let down the bed wherein the sick of the palsy lay. (Mark 2:1-4)

This is a story we know very well. What did Jesus say to the paralytic?

When Jesus saw their faith, he said unto the sick of the palsy, Son, thy sins be forgiven thee.

Who is this Jesus? He is God. When He said, "Let there be

light," there was light. When He said, "Let the waters divide above the firmament and below the firmament," the waters were divided.

Let the earth bring forth grass, the herb yielding seed, and the fruit tree yielding fruit after his kind, whose seed is in itself, upon the earth: and it was so. (Genesis 1:11)

The words of God are different from our words, in that, within the words of God, the power to achieve those words are included. They go together to fulfill the Word. The Word of God said, "Let the earth bring forth grass, the herb yielding seed, the fruit tree yielding fruit after his kind, whose seed is in itself upon the earth." Even though the earth had no condition to fulfill these words, because the Word, itself, has the conditions to achieve them, from the earth, buds began to sprout, flowers bloomed, and fruit was borne. That is why He is God. What kind of God would He be if He couldn't do this?

Once I was going to Namhae, and I was driving my car across the Namhae Bridge. Because it was summertime, the cherry blossoms were in full bloom and were so beautiful. As I saw the cherry blossoms, I asked the cherry tree a question.

"Hey cherry tree, how did you make such white and clean flower pedals? Where did you get that white coloring?"

It's so amazing. So, let's ask the red rose.

"Rose, where did you get the red color? At which paint store did you buy the color to dye your petals?"

"I don't know."

Dig the ground. No matter how much you dig, there is no red color. But where did the red rose get its red color? Where did the cherry blossoms get their white color to beautifully decorate the tree?

For us to make cars, we have to select the factory site and build a factory. We have to bring in power and have to bring in materials to make engines. Then we assemble the parts that are made this way, to make the car and sell it. No matter how good the car factory is, if you don't have the needed materials, cars cannot be made. Without iron you cannot make cars. God, where did you get the white color for the cherry blossoms?

Our Gangnam Church is located on the side of Mt. Woomyeon. I'm sorry to say this, but in our bathroom, we have a small window. If you look out to the left from the window, you can see the freeway. If you look to the right, you can see the woods. If you look through the window to Mt. Woomyeon for a year; for all 52 weeks, there has not been a time when there was no change. Every winter, only the black tree branches stand tall, but when it becomes spring, the blue-green leaves begin to show, and it changes every single week. Last week, I had a conference at the Ulsan KBS Hall, and I came back late at night and slept. When I went to the bathroom the next morning, I was completely amazed. Over one week, the leaves were in their fall foliage. It was so wonderful.

"Hey, how could you so evenly make all those leaves yellow?"

There is a sister named, Mi-kyung Kim, from Paraguay, who speaks Spanish well. I called her to our church to translate my sermons into Spanish. Now, she has gone and married. That sister stayed at our church for two or three years. Not once had this sister seen fall foliage. One day, the sister was completely amazed. The ginkgo trees that a week before were green, were completely yellow.

"Wow, that ginkgo tree! Who painted these ginkgo tree leaves?"

She was so amazed that she couldn't get a hold of herself. That was nothing. The day it snowed, she was so excited. She didn't know what to do because she had never once seen snow.

Where do such beautiful colors come from? For us to do construction, we need materials. And no matter what, we have to have the conditions met. However, inside the Word of God, the power to accomplish all of this work is included and it is done according to the Word.

In Genesis chapter 1, it says, *In the beginning God created the heaven and the earth. And the earth was without form, and void; and darkness was upon the face of the deep. And the spirit of God moved upon the face of the waters.* Within the condition of being without form, void, and in deep darkness, maybe tens of millions of years, or maybe hundreds of millions of years, or maybe even billions of years had passed. One day, on this earth there was no life and there was no hope. Nowhere on this earth were there any flowers blooming, and nowhere on this earth was there any beauty. But as the Word of God entered, the light began to shine, plants sprouted, flowers bloomed, fruit was borne, and the earth changed into a beautiful garden, overflowing with hope. It's because the love that was inside the Word of God made the earth into a beautiful world of love.

One day, as I was reading Genesis chapter one, I was completely astonished.

"What in the world? This is talking about my heart!"

I started going to church when I was still very immature. I was born again at the age of nineteen, but I had gone to church before then. My heart was dark. Although I went to church, there was no hope in my heart. Although I went to church, I had no light in my heart. Although I went to church, I had no faith in my heart. I was confused and in emptiness, so I wanted to kill myself. But one day, one Word of God entered inside of me.

"Let there be light."

Everyone, now I feel flowers blooming in my heart. The fruit of love is being borne in my heart. I have experienced peace in my heart, hope in my heart, and joy in my heart. The Word of God accomplished this work.

The Conversation Between God and Man

Jesus said to the paralytic, "Son thy sins be forgiven thee." This is the Word of God, but the fearful thing is, *But there were certain of the scribes sitting there, and reasoning in their hearts, Why doth this man speak blasphemies, who can forgive sins but God only?* They were saying this and judging the Word of God. It was man, daring to judge God.

Think about yourself as an individual. Without knowing anything, you are born into this world. From that day on, you see with your eyes, hear with your ears, and feel with your hands. As you learn your own philosophy is developed, your own perspectives are formed, and the thoughts of the person, called, "You," are formed. From then on, whenever you accept anything, you match it against the perspective that's already fixed inside of you, and you accept the things that fit your experience and knowledge, or otherwise you refuse them. From then on, Satan has ruled over man from the time of Adam and Eve and led the heart of man to the side of refusing the Word of God. That is why, although a person hears the Word of God, they follow after their own thoughts. The history of mankind is telling us that they follow after their own thoughts and refuse the Word of God.

At the time of Noah's flood, God told Noah, "The wickedness of man is great in the earth; therefore, I will destroy the earth with water. Make an ark." There were many people who heard these words. But other than the eight family members of Noah, no one entered the ark. Why? Because certain thoughts inside of their hearts made them refuse the Word of God.

"What flood? There'll be some rain and that'll be it. Because God loves us, He will not kill us. He will not destroy us."

Such thoughts arose and made them refuse the Word of God that there would be a flood, and made them unable to accept those words. That is why, at the time of Noah's flood, those who were destroyed were not destroyed because they committed theft, adultery, or murder. They were destroyed because they refused the Word of God. No matter what time period it is, God destroys those who refuse the Word of God. It is not that we commit theft, adultery, or murder that we go to hell. People go to hell because they refuse the Word of God.

At the end of the book of Matthew, it talks about the people who refuse the Word of God. There is much written about people who refuse the Word of God. They follow their own thoughts to refuse the Word of God. Even today, you think you believe in the Word of God, but Satan has worked inside of the many experiences and thoughts you've had until now. He has made it so that when you're actually about to receive the Word of God, you refuse.That is why, unless you throw away the thoughts that you have had, you can never please God, and you can never follow God.

Jesus said, "Whosoever shall follow me, will deny himself." Isaiah chapter 55 says, *Seek ye the LORD while he may be found, call ye upon while He is near: Let the wicked forsake his way, and the unrighteous man his thoughts: and let him return unto the LORD.* Your thoughts may appear to be right, proper, and definite in your eyes, and it may seem that you are following the Word of God. But ultimately, Satan has made you able to only refuse the Word of God, and that is how Satan has worked inside of your heart. When you live spiritual life with that heart, you may understand some parts of the Bible, but there are some aspects that you cannot accept. Therefore there are many parts you cannot accept. So at that decisive point, Satan has made it so that you will refuse the Word of God, and be cursed.

I have talked about this story many times, but a father and a son walked in the desert and they got lost. They ran out of water, and both the father and the son were exhausted. The problem was that in the father's heart, there was hope, but in the son's heart, there was no hope. As they're going through the desert, the father's thoughts and the son's thoughts were completely different. Finally, the son complained.

"Father, you have gone through the desert many times. Why did you lose your way? Now we will die. I am so thirsty. I cannot take one more step."

But the father's thoughts were completely different from his son's.

"Son, why will we die? We're not going to die. I don't know if you know this, but because the sand hills are constantly moving in the desert, I have lost my way. This isn't the only time, but right now, I am sure that the direction we're going right now is to the East. I can tell by the sun. We have almost reached the eastern edge of this desert. Now if we go a little more, we'll come to a village. Then we can drink water. We are not going to die."

"Father, you said that yesterday, and the day before yesterday, but did we really reach the edge? Father, you're deceiving me. What do you mean we're not going to die? We're going to die. I don't believe you. I cannot walk anymore."

"No, Son, I've been through this desert many times. We're not going to die. We have almost arrived at the edge of the desert."

They were walking the same direction, but the father, who had hope, and the son, who was without hope, were completely different. The son had lost strength in his heart because they were already dead in his heart.

"Hey, Son, let's walk."

"Father, what's the point of walking? We're going to die anyway. Father, I cannot walk anymore. Father, we're going to die."

"No, get up and walk. We have almost reached the edge. We will not die. Why would we die?"

"Father, think about it. How long has it been since we last had water? Father, do you think that I can walk? I cannot walk. I am exhausted. Now I can only die. I'm going to die!"

"Son, you're not going to die. Let's walk."

The father had hope, but the son had no hope. The father wanted to put hope into his son's heart. If the son has hope, he can gain strength and walk. But the son believed in his own thoughts and would not believe his father's words.

"Son, we're heading east. We'll reach the eastern edge of this desert. I don't know exactly when, but we have almost reached the edge."

"Father, we have not had water for days. Do you think that we can walk further? Even if I do walk, it's useless. We're going to die. Father, you've been saying this for days."

The son kept on thinking that his own thoughts were right and refused his father's words. The father talked about the last time he had lost his way in the desert but survived. He constantly spoke words of encouragement to put hope into his son's heart.

"Son, let's walk just a little more."

"Father, you go. I'm going to stay here and die."

"How can you say that? Let's get up and walk."

The father comforted the son, and little by little, they walked. After walking a little while, all of a sudden, the son let out a deep sigh of despair.

"Father, look over there! Now we're dead!"

The father looked where the son was pointing, and it was a grave. It was a tomb.

"Father, look at that tomb! That person was lost, just like us, and he struggled and died of thirst. We, too, are going to die like that. That person could not find an oasis, and he died. That's going to happen to us, too!"

The father smiled and spoke.

"Son, we have made it! This is the edge of the desert!"

"Father, what are you talking about? You always say that it's the edge of the desert."

"Son, listen carefully to what I have to say. Suppose the person in that tomb did get lost and died of thirst like you said. Do you think he would dig his tomb, go in, and die? There must have been somebody to bury him. The fact that there is a tomb here means that there is a village nearby. Now we're almost to the village. Now we've made it!"

Although they are looking at the same tomb, the thoughts of the son and the thoughts of the father were completely different. Only then did the father's heart enter the son.

"That's right, even if a person did get lost and die of thirst, he could not have entered the tomb himself and somebody must have buried him. That's right, if there is a tomb here it means…," thought the son.

"That's right! Father, you are right! Civilization is nearby! Father, let's walk fast!"

And soon after, they arrived at a village, and survived.

When we read the Bible, every one of the 66 books of the Old and New Testaments have one thing in common. There are many scenes in the Bible of the conversations between God and man; the conversations between God and Abraham; the conversations between God and Moses; and the conversations between Jesus and people. In those conversations, the thoughts of man and the thoughts of God were always different. Therefore, God is laboring sorrowfully to put the heart of God inside of man. On the other hand, because the heart of God does not fit the heart of man, we see the images of man refusing and betraying God. No matter where we read in the Bible, we see those images.

Because the father knows the desert well, and he knows that the edge of the desert is near, not once did he think in his heart that he would die. That was the father's heart. But in the son's heart, there was despair and death, and he had no hope. The father wanted to deliver the hope and the heart that they would live to his son. However, the son did not try to accept it because he had his own thoughts.

"Father is only saying that to comfort me. We're dead. Father has said that we have reached the edge of the desert days ago, but we still haven't come to the edge of the desert. I have no more strength, how can I walk? Father is just saying that, but we're going to die."

The son had his own thoughts.

God said to Noah, "I will send a flood to this earth and destroy the world with water." The people at that time all heard these words, but they believed in their own thoughts. They did not believe in the Word of God.

"God's not going to send the flood. What flood? He's just saying that because we commit too many sins and He wants us to be good. Now all we have to do is just be good. It's just going to rain a little, and that'll be the end of it."

Following after their own thoughts, they did not enter the ark. These kinds of works exist in mankind's history from beginning to end. Inside the heart of man, and as man followed after their own thoughts, they all flowed towards destruction.

This evening I cannot meet and speak with all of you individually. But if I were to, I can feel that inside of you, your own experiences, opinions, and thoughts are standing strong rather than the Word of God. This is so althuogh you believe in God. Those things only make you refuse the Word of God, such that the Word of God cannot enter and live inside of you as it is.

The Word of God is God. In John chapter 1, it says, *In the beginning was the Word, and the Word was with God, and the Word was God. The same was in the beginning with*

God. All things were made by him; and without him there was not anything made that was made. In him was life; and the life was the light of men. (John 1:1-4) The Word is God. However, Satan puts thoughts inside of us that are different from the Word and has fixated our thoughts on other thoughts so that we are unable to receive the Word into our hearts. That is why, of the words of God, you accept those that fit your heart, but because you do not accept the things that do not fit your heart, God cannot work inside of you. If you acknowledge God and acknowledge His words, there is not one person among you who cannot be changed this evening. To keep you from doing that, Satan blocks your hearts with your own thoughts and has made it so that the Word of God cannot come in.

Mark chapter 2 is telling us so clearly about that. Jesus said, "Son, thy sins be forgiven thee." Everyone, this is the Word of God. "Ah, Jesus, is that so? Are my sins forgiven?" Shouldn't they have accepted it like that? But instead, the Jews said, "Blasphemy! Who does he think he is to say that sins are forgiven?" They said this and refused the words of Jesus with their experiences and thoughts.

In the 66 books of the Bible, man was cursed and destroyed not because they committed theft, adultery, or murder, but because they refused the Word of God. In addition, when we look at the history of Christianity, no matter what time period it was, there were many multitudes claiming they believed in God, but they refused the Word of God. At the time of the flood, the people did not say that they did not believe in God. Although they said that they believed in God, they all refused the Word of God. That's how it always was. Even during Jesus' time, all the Jews said that they believed in God, but they ended up refusing Jesus.

It is exactly the same today. Satan, who, according to the history of mankind, works inside of the hearts of man, has captured the hearts of you, who are the descendants of Adam. He has fixated your thoughts, which are different from the truth of God, inside of your hearts and has made you unable to receive the Word of God. Due to that, people do not look deeply into the Bible, but simply think, "All I have to do is be good. All I have to do is keep the law." In that way, they only live after their own thoughts and they do not receive the Word of God into their hearts. That is what is evil. That is the thought of Satan. Who did God curse? God cursed and destroyed all those who did not accept the Word of God.

You Don't Have Sins, If I Say You Don't Have Sins

Jesus spoke to the man who was sick from palsy.

"Son, thy sins be forgiven thee."

If Jesus said this, then have sins been forgiven, or have they not been forgiven?

When President Syngman Rhee was alive, he met a private at his villa. He saw that the private was cleaning fervently, and he asked him a question.

"Did you clean this place?"

"Sir, yes, sir! It is an honor to receive the command to clean this place for you, Mr. President, sir."

"It wasn't tiring? It wasn't difficult?"

"Sir, no, sir. For you, Mr. President, nothing I could do would be tiring."

The President was deeply touched.

"The rank that you have on you, what is it?"

"Sir, I'm a private, sir."

"What is above that?"

"Sir, a corporal, sir."

"What is above that?"

"Sir, it's a sergeant, sir."

"Above that?"

"Sir, staff sergeant, sir."

"Above that?"

"Sir, sergeant first class, sir."

"Above that?"

The private froze and said, "Sir, there is no other rank higher, sir."

Then the President said, "Be that."

The President was telling him to be a master sergeant, which is the rank above sergeant first class. The secretary who was standing next to the private asked him, "Your regiment, military I.D. number, and your rank." Then he called the army headquarters.

"This is the President's secretary's office. Special orders from the President: promote private so-and-so to master sergeant."

From that point on, is this soldier a master sergeant or a private? He is a master sergeant.

"What? You are a master sergeant? You've only been in the army for just a few months."

"But I'm still a master sergeant. This insignia is not a toy."

The late Chairman Ju-yung Chung (founder of Hyundai) once visited the Ulsan Hyundai Motor Factory. A person heard that Chairman Ju-yung Chung was coming, so with a broom, he was fervently sweeping the grounds. As he was cleaning, Chairman Chung saw his name tag and said, "Hey, Supervisor Lee, good work." Then the person said, "Mr. Chairman, I have not become a supervisor yet." Right then, Chairman Jung said, "If I say that you're a supervisor, then you are a supervisor." From that day on, he became a supervisor. Is he a supervisor? Yes, he is a supervisor. If the chairman of the Hyundai Group says that he is a supervisor, then he is a supervisor.

The words of the president and even words of the chairman of a company are this way. Then how would it be with the words of God? However, man has gone against the Word of God with his own thoughts.

"If I say that you have no sins, then you don't."

"Yes, I do. I am a sinner."

"If I say that you have no sins, then you don't have sins."

"Yes, I do, Lord. I'm a sinner. Forgive me, please."

One day, I was reading Romans and was completely stunned while reading Romans chapter 3. In Romans chapter 3, it says, "There is none righteous, no not one. There is none that doeth good, none that seek after God. Their throat is an open sepulchre, with their tongues they have used deceit. The poison of asps is under their lips whose mouth is full of cursing and bitterness, their feet is swift to shed blood." The verses go on about this, but in verse 23, there are these words, *For all have sinned, and come short of the glory of God.* While reading this, the parable of the prodigal son in the book of Luke came to mind.

The result of the prodigal son working hard was eating with the pigs in a pigpen and living like that until he starved to death. However, when the father worked, although his son did not do anything, his son was wearing the best robe, had a ring on his hand, shoes on his feet, and had eaten the fatted calf. He had changed so much. The result of him working himself was that no matter how hard he tried, he could not be freed from the pigpen. But in Romans chapter 3, it says, "The work we humans have done is all dirty, filthy, and evil, and thus there shall be no flesh justified in his sight by the deeds of the law." In Romans chapter 3, verse 23 it says, *For all have sinned, and come short of the glory of God.* This is the result of the work that man has done.

Yet, in verse 24, it shows not the work of man, but the work that God has done. The result of the work that man has done was, *For all have sinned, and come short of the glory of God.* But when God worked in verse 24, it says, *Being justified freely by his grace through the redemption that is in Christ Jesus.* The work that the son did was to eat with the pigs, sleep with the pigs, smell like the pigs, and he become like the pigs inside the pigpen. However, he had become glorious when the father worked.

Even tonight, the work that we have done is dirty, and we have done things worthy of being cursed and destroyed. But the work that God has done has made us justified, clean, glorious, and blessed. Then, everyone, we believe in the work that we have done; the sins that we have committed, but we must believe that God has cleansed us as well. Amen? Do you believe?

> *For all have sinned, and come short of the glory of God; Being justified freely by his grace through the redemption that is in Christ Jesus.*

People have fallen deeply into their own thoughts, so they do not believe this.

"Lord, I'm a sinner. God, forgive me."

"No, you have been made righteous."

"But I'm a sinner."

"No, you have been cleansed. I washed your sins whiter than snow."

"No, I'm a sinner."

With their own thoughts, they do not accept the Word of God.

God, Let Me Hear Your Voice

In Mark chapter 2, Jesus spoke to the man sick with palsy.

Son, thy sins be forgiven thee.

Now, everyone, what is the name of this man sick with palsy? Raise your hand if you know the name of this man, sick with palsy. There is no one? Then let me ask you something. Although we do not know the name of the man who was sick with palsy, do you think he had a name or not? He probably had one. Who doesn't have a name? If he had no name we would give him a name like Tom, Dick, or Harry. If you go to Ghana, Africa, because it is complicated to give names, they name the child according to the day he's born. My grandson is born on a Wednesday. Boys that are born on Wednesdays are called, "Kwaku." Ghanaians kept looking at my grandson and kept calling him, "Kwaku, Kwaku." I asked them why they called my grandson, "Kwaku," and this is what they told me. Giving names is complicated, and they hate complicated things, that they had done this to everyone. Therefore, when you listen to the names of Ghanaians, you can tell what day their birthday is on.

They at least do this when they want to give names. Do you think this man sick with palsy had a name? He had a name. But the Bible does not say his name. He's just known as the man sick with palsy. Why? Because when Jesus said to this man sick with palsy, "Son, thy sins be forgiven thee," these words, not only applied to the man sick with palsy, but these words applied to all mankind. If you were to use the name of the person sick with palsy, then you would have to put in the names of all mankind.

"Ock Soo Park, thy sins be forgiven thee."

"Joseph Park, thy sins be forgiven thee."

"Terry Henderson, thy sins be forgiven thee."

If you were to write in all of these names and include them in this manner, then it would take many, many trucks to carry the book of Mark around. These words are for all mankind. As the representative, I believe He spoke these words to the man sick with palsy. He said, "Son, thy sins be forgiven thee." There is no reason Jesus, who said that, is not saying to me, "Thy sins be forgiven thee." Why would Jesus, who forgave the man sick with palsy, not forgive my sins? But when Jesus said to the man sick with palsy, "Thy sins be forgiven thee," the man sick with palsy said, "Amen," and accepted it. The scribes and Pharisees cried out, "Blasphemy!" and they refused the words of Jesus, using their own experiences and knowledge.

This evening, everything you have learned, experienced, and all the knowledge you have gained in this world through education have made you refuse the Word of God until now. It makes you refuse the Word of God at decisive moments. That is why, although Jesus is saying, "Thy sins be forgiven thee," you don't accept it, but say, "God, I'm a sinner, forgive me." These people are not people who believe in God.

One day, in John chapter 8, I read about the woman taken in the act of adultery. While reading those words, a thought popped up. There was no difference between this woman's image and my own image. I'm sorry to talk about such a thing, but if I could commit adultery and not get caught, I, too, would have committed more than adultery. I was just afraid of getting caught in the act of adultery, which was why I couldn't do it. But inside of me, I truly had such a heart many times. I was not different from this woman whatsoever. The only difference was that this woman had a little more courage to actually do it, while I did not.

That day, as I read John chapter 8, I felt, "This woman is just like me. She is exactly like me." But the amazing thing is that Jesus said unto this woman, "Neither do I condemn thee."

"That's right," I thought. "I'm a person exactly like this woman. The words Jesus said to this woman, He said to me as well. The words that said He does not condemn her, He is saying to me. Amen."

That was how I came to look at it.

Everyone, let me ask you a question. Would you believe the Word of God is speaking to you only when God writes your name in the Bible, saying, "So-and-so, thy sins be forgive thee"? That is not how it should be. Everyone, these words of the Bible apply, not only to the woman taken in the act of adultery or the man sick with palsy, but I believe that these words apply to all mankind. Amen? If so, everyone, is there a reason when Jesus said to the man sick with palsy, "Son, thy sins be forgiven thee," that He could not say that to me? Is there or isn't there? Did Jesus forgive only the sins of the man sick with palsy on the cross? Did He not forgive your sins? If He had forgiven my sins and said, "Ock Soo Park, thy sins be forgiven thee," then my sins are forgiven.

A long time ago, I did not know the Bible, so I wanted to hear the voice of God. After confessing my sins, repenting and begging for forgiveness, I could not tell whether my sins were forgiven or not. So I prayed, saying, "God, if you did forgive my sins, let me hear your voice. Let me hear it just once." I heard no voice whatsoever. I sat up in the chapel by myself and waited for the answer of God. Because God would not answer, I guess the rats in the ceiling thought that they needed to answer me. All I could hear were the sounds of the rats running around. These words of the Bible are the words of God, but without believing the words of God, I just wanted to hear the voice of God.

After becoming born again, I believed one by one that these words were the words of God. He was speaking to me. Therefore, there is nothing for me to be responsible for. God took the responsibility. God said that He washed my sins away. Suppose I felt safe and went to heaven. But if God says that I cannot enter, then God has to take that responsibility. There's no way God would do that. I believe these words of promise.

Your Thoughts and the Word – Which One Will You Believe?

A lot of time has passed, so I will speak just a little while longer.

The man sick with palsy accepted the words, "Thy sins be forgiven thee," and again, Jesus said unto him, "Arise, take up thy bed, and go thy way to thine house." The man sick with palsy is also human, so why would he not have any thoughts? Can this person walk or not?

"He surely knows that I cannot walk. Jesus, I cannot walk. If I could walk, then I would have walked here. Why would I be carried here on a bed? Do you know how much it broke my heart to see my friends tearing the roof open? If I could walk, then why would they have to tear up the roof and carry me down on a bed? I would just walk in. I cannot walk. It seems that you do not know about this, Jesus, but I cannot walk. I have strained to walk, but I cannot. My legs are stiff, like wooden logs. They are completely dry, I cannot walk."

These are the words that came forth from the man sick with palsy. The man with palsy, in a short moment, thought about it.

"The sounds from my own heart tell me that I cannot walk, but Jesus is telling me to walk. Will I listen to the sounds of my heart, or will I listen to the words of Jesus?"

The man sick with palsy had to decide on this. From the sounds of his heart, he said, "I cannot walk. When I think about this with my own experience and my own logic, I cannot walk. I had tried to walk, but it did not work." Until now, the man sick with palsy had listened to that voice, but he decided to no longer listen to the sounds of his own heart.

"That's right. As a result of listening to my own voice I was nothing more than a man sick of the palsy, correct? I will no longer listen to my own voice. I will no longer believe in my own heart. I will not believe in myself. I will believe in Jesus. Even though my own voice tells me I cannot walk, I will not listen to the sound of that voice, but will listen to the words that Jesus tells me. I will rise up and walk!"

The man sick with palsy rose up and picked up his bed.

This is so with us. If we listen to our own voice, we say, "How could I dare say that I do not have sin? How could I dare say that I am righteous? Is there anyone who is as dirty and filthy as I am? I am such an evil human being, so I cannot say such a thing. I can only say that I am a sinner. I'm a sinner! I'm a dirty human being! I am evil! Then how can I say that I am righteous? No, not me!" This is the sound of your own voice. The voice of Jesus says, "Son, thy sins be forgiven thee."

Everyone, whose sound will you adhere to? Until now, we have foolishly believed in our own thoughts. We have followed our own thoughts. That is why spiritual life did not work out. This evening, there is something that you must truly repent of. You should not repent of the fact that you have committed theft, adultery, or murder. But having believed in you; having followed your own voice; and having believed in your own thoughts; repent of that. "No longer will I live by my own thoughts, but by the thoughts of Jesus. If you say that I am righteous, then I am righteous! If you say that I have received forgiveness of sins, then I have received forgiveness! If you tell me to walk, then even though my legs are withered and twisted, I will walk!" I believe that this is true spiritual life. Do you believe it? Amen?

Loving folks, those of you who believe that the words spoken to the man sick with palsy apply to you as well, say, "Amen," and raise your hands. Everyone, how pleased God must be. Until now, we have lived by our own thoughts, not the Word of God. Now, therefore, put your thoughts away and believe in the Word of God. I know that God will be pleased.

Everyone, if you believe Jesus is saying, "Thy sins be

forgiven thee," to you, then your sins are washed as white as snow just like the man sick with palsy. All of your sins have been washed away through the blood of the cross! You have been made clean, and you have no sin! You are righteous! If you believe this, then raise your right hands. Amen! Hallelujah! I praise God.

For a long time, Satan had deceived us and made us live believing in our own thoughts. Tonight, throw your thoughts away, and believe simply one word; this one word spoken to you by God. A certain pastor criticized the book I wrote, *The Secret of Forgiveness of Sin and Being Born Again*. He also wrote an article stating, "Until the day of my death, I declare that I am a sinner." He spoke of his own thoughts, but he did not include the Word of God whatsoever. Through the blood of His son, Jesus, God washed our sins away.

He'll forgive your transgressions,
And remember them no more;
He'll forgive your transgressions,
And remember them no more;
"Look unto me, ye people,"
Saith the Lord your God;
He'll forgive your transgressions,
He'll forgive your transgressions,
And remember them no more,
And remember them no more.

In the Word of God, it says that God has erased the memory of all our sins! He has completely blotted out your record of sins in heaven. Now, nowhere in heaven is there a record of our sin, and there is no record of our sin in the heart of God. The only thing is that in your hearts you remember the sins that you have committed. However, those sins are already washed away. According to the Word of God, when you believe that your sins have been washed away, that is a person who believes in God.

Many people today believe in Christianity backwards. They do not believe that Jesus has forgiven their sins, and with their own zeal, they try to have their sins washed away. With what talent could you wash away the sins that Jesus could not wash away? I cannot wash my sins away. Jesus is the only one who can wash sins away. You must accept that He has washed them away by faith. Sins cannot be washed away no matter what you do with your efforts. If the blood of Jesus on the cross cannot wash your sins away, you must know that you are people who can only receive destruction. It is because there is no other way to wash sins away other than the blood of Jesus on the cross. But we believe that Jesus has forgiven our sins with His blood. Whiter than snow, whiter than snow! Let us sing just one verse of the hymnal, "I Can Sing Now the Song," together.

I can sing now the song Of the blood-ransomed throng
In my soul there is peace, rest and calm;
I am free from all doubt, And I join in the shout,
I'm redeemed by the blood of the Lamb.
I'm redeemed, I'm redeemed,
Jesus saves me and keeps me just now, Hallelujah,
And I join with the throng round the throne In the song,
I'm redeemed by the blood of the Lamb.

8

Abraham's Faith

8.
Abraham's Faith

Hello everyone. Please open to the Old Testament, Genesis chapter 17. I will read from Genesis chapter 17, verse 15.

And God said unto Abraham, As for Sarai thy wife, thou shalt not call her name Sarai, but Sarah shall her name be. And I will bless her, and give thee a son also of her: yea, I will bless her, and she shall be a mother of nations; kings of people shall be of her. Then Abraham fell upon his face, and laughed, and said in his heart, Shall a child be born unto him that is an hundred years old? and shall Sarah, that is ninety years old, bear? And Abraham said unto God, O that Ishmael might live before thee! And God said, Sarah thy wife shall bear thee a son indeed; and thou shalt call his name Isaac: and I will establish my covenant with him for an everlasting covenant, and with his seed after him. And as for Ishmael, I have heard thee: Behold, I have blessed him, and will make him fruitful, and will multiply him exceedingly; twelve princes shall he beget, and I will make him a great nation. But my covenant will I establish with Isaac, which Sarah shall bear unto thee at this set time in the next year. And he left off talking with him, and God went up from Abraham.

I have read up to verse 22.

One Must Discover the Heart of God Hidden Inside of the Bible

There was a couple in which the wife had to go stay with her relatives. She had prepared kimchee and Doenjang stew so her husband could eat at home by himself while she was at her relatives' house. And just in case all the side dishes would run out, she had written a note about how to cook certain foods, telling him that if he ran out of food, cook like this, and eat. The husband saw the note his wife had left behind, showing him how to make Doenjang stew, kimchee soup, and even how to make kimchee. Because she had done this, he was so thankful. After his wife left, he spent several days with the side dishes she had prepared, but he ran out of the side dishes one day, so he opened the note that showed how to cook Doenjang stew. He made the Doenjang stew exactly as it was written on the note, but when he ate it, it tasted very bad.

"Gee, why doesn't she teach me how to make delicious soup? Why does she cook it deliciously and write the recipe like this?"

He turned to the next page and made everything exactly as it was written on the recipe that his wife had written, but this one was a mess as well, and he got angry.

"She said that she had prepared this with all of her heart, but she taught me how to cook what tastes disgusting!"

Later on, when his wife returned, the husband was angry.

"What's wrong with you? Why didn't you write instructions on how to cook delicious food, but instead, wrote recipes for making terrible tasting food!?"

"Why honey, what's wrong? You said that the food I make is delicious, didn't you?"

"Yes I did."

"I wrote it down exactly how I cook it."

"What are you talking about? I did everything exactly as it was written on the notes and it tasted terrible."

"Then shall I do it?"

"Fine, try it."

The wife opened the notes and cooked the Doenjang stew exactly as it was written on the note. The Doenjang stew made by the husband tasted so terrible, but the Doenjang stew cooked by the wife was so delicious. The husband had nothing to say.

If you could cook well just because you make it exactly as it's written, then all you would need is one cookbook to become a world class chef. What else would you need? When housewives cook Doenjang stew, they have different methods and they all have their own know-how.

Everyone, just because you read the Bible precisely and live spiritual life as it's written, it doesn't mean that all of your spiritual lives are the same. When you read the Bible in the state where all of your own thoughts are emptied out, after reading for a while, you're not just reading the Bible, but you see the heart of God hidden inside the Bible. When you discover the heart of God hidden inside the Bible and become one with that heart, it is such a blessing. I have found the heart of God inside the Bible as I have lived the past few decades after receiving salvation. When I united my heart with the heart of God, whenever I felt, "This is the heart of God. That is why this was done by God," every single thing that was impossible, I see all them being accomplished. Everyone, when we see the heart of God flowing inside the Bible, there's no need for us to worry about how to live life, because God accomplishes everything.

From this Sunday evening, I will be going to a place called, Orissa, India, and I am scheduled to hold a conference there. Missionary Soo-yeon Kim, of our mission, is there preaching the gospel in the deepest, most remote areas of the country. It is a region where Hindus recently surrounded a car that a missionary was driving and set it on fire, killing the missionary's family. I received a phone call from Orissa this morning. Missionary Kim told me that Hindus were organizing to obstruct our conference. He said he received such information from the police, so he called me and said, "Pastor, pray for us."

Everyone, one thing I know for sure is that my going to Orissa, India and having a conference is a work God is pleased with and I believe that God will accomplish this. As I have traveled throughout Africa, South America, and Europe, I have caught malaria and have contracted many diseases. Because I am within the will of God, I will never die of malaria or some other disease. When God calls me, then I can die of malaria, die of typhoid, or die in the jungle.

I am so thankful for the single fact that I am within the will of God.

Abraham, Who Has Sinned, Is Righteous?

Today, I would like to speak to you about Abraham. Abraham is the father of faith. When we read the words in the Bible about Abraham, it is interesting. First we'll look at chapter 15 which is before chapter 17 that we read earlier.

Chapter 15, verse 4.

And, behold, the word of the LORD came unto him, saying, This shall not be thine heir; but he that shall come forth out of thine own bowels shall be thine heir.

Chapter 15, verse 5.

And he brought him forth abroad, and said, Look now toward heaven, and tell the stars, if thou be able to number them: and he said unto him, So shall thy seed be.

Everyone, if you have your Bible with you, let's read Genesis chapter 15, verse 6 out loud together.

And he believed in the LORD; and he counted it to him for righteousness.

Everyone, what does it mean to be righteous? What is righteousness? Righteousness is the opposite of sin. So if you have sin, you're a sinner, but if you have no sin whatsoever, then you are righteous. But in our perceptions, we think that for us to become righteous we have to do good things, not commit sins, keep the Ten Commandments, and live according to the Word of God. That is why you labor to not commit sins, don't you? And don't you also try to live as a good person? You try hard, don't you? According to our perceptions, we must repent in front of God to have our sins washed away because we are sinners. Afterwards, we must not commit sins and live as good people for us to become righteous. However, there is not a single righteous person who has lived like that.

What about Abraham? One day, God said to Abraham, "Abraham, let's go outside," and He took Abraham outside. Back then, there were no electronic lamps and there was no city, so the night sky must have been so dark. That dark night was filled with stars that dotted the entire sky. God then spoke to Abraham.

"Abraham, look to the stars in the sky."

"Yes, God, the stars are beautiful."

"Yes, the stars are beautiful aren't they? Can you count them?"

"No, I cannot, God."

When I was young, in the countryside, we would lay out a mat in the yard, lie down, and count the stars in the sky. "One star, two stars, three stars, four stars, five stars, six stars, seven stars, eight stars, nine stars, ten stars," and when I reached that number, I didn't know how far I could count. There were so many stars in the sky that I could not count them all. One, two…

God told Abraham to look to the stars in the sky and asked if he could count them.

"I cannot count them."

"So shall thy children be."

Abraham simply believed those words. "Ah, so that is how my children will be." Abraham never thought that he would ever have as many children as the stars in the sky, but he heard God say that He would make them that numerous. Abraham simply believed those words exactly as they were and his believing those words meant that he accepted those words.

The amazing thing is that the Word of God is different from our words. The Word of God is alive. The Word of God is power. Like we spoke about yesterday, the book of John says, *In the beginning was the Word, and the Word was with God, and the Word was,* what? *The word was God. The same was in the beginning with God. All things were made by him; and without Him was not anything made that was made. In him was life and the life was the light of men.*

In John chapter 1, verse 14 it says, *And the Word was made flesh, and dwelt among us, (and we beheld his glory, the glory as the only begotten of the Father,) full of grace and truth.*

The one, who was the Word who had come to earth in the flesh is named Jesus. Amen? Everyone, because the Word of God is God, refusing the Word of God is refusing God, and accepting the Word of God is accepting God. That is why, when our sins are washed away, they are not washed away through our crying, begging, praying for a hundred days, holding on to the roots of pine trees crying out, "Lord!", speaking in tongues, prophesying, shedding tears, weeping, or wailing. Our sins are washed away when we accept the Word of God into our hearts. That is when our sins are washed away. Amen? Amen!

Yesterday, we spoke about how Jesus said to the man sick with palsy, "Son, thy sins be forgiven thee." When I think that the Bible is saying those words to me, it is so touching. In reality, those words are meant for me. Long ago, I did not know this, and I asked God to allow me to hear one voice telling me that God had forgiven my sins. The Bible is the

Word of God, and the Word says, "Thy sins be forgiven thee." What other voice do I need? I don't need any other proof. This word, alone, is more than enough.

Suppose one day, my son comes and asks of me, "Father, buy me a car."

"Sure, do you need a car? I will buy you one."

"Father, give me proof that you will buy me a car."

"Proof? What proof? If I tell you that I'm going to buy you one, then I'm going to buy you one."

"But still, give me proof that I can believe in."

"My word is proof that I will buy it for you."

"But still, give me proof that I can trust."

This is not believing in me. If he believes me, then the words, "I will buy you one," alone, are more than enough.

"Mother, Father said that he would buy me a car, so I have a new car."

That is believing me. No other proof is necessary. You need proof when you don't have faith.

The greatest, most definite proof that our sins have been forgiven is found in the 66 books of the Bible. In those words, Jesus, who does not lie, says, "Son, thy sins be forgiven thee." It is your freedom of choice to believe or not believe. You are free to not believe and go to hell, or to believe and go to heaven. Jesus forgave sins and tells us that they have been forgiven, but even so, if you don't believe, there's nothing you can do.

God saw that Abraham believed in the Word of God and called him righteous. Isn't it in verse 6? Let's read it out loud together.

And he believed in the LORD; and he counted it to him for righteousness.

Let me ask you a question. Did Abraham sin or not? Please answer me out loud. He did sin. People who live in Seoul live among many people, and they try hard not to make mistakes. That is why when children speak, they do not give clear answers.

"Son, which direction is it to the South Gate?"

"If you go this way, you'll probably find it."

Instead of clearly explaining it this way, "The South Gate is this way," they say, "You'll probably find it." They do not want to make any mistakes because they live amongst so many people; therefore, they say, "That's probably so. That may be right. I guess that's right." People from Seoul cannot give a straight answer saying, "That's it!" Perhaps you feel that way a little as well. You may think, "What if I answer and get it wrong?" But you are no longer people of Seoul, but people of God. You are people of heaven. Understand?

When God said to Abraham, "Your children will be like the stars in the sky," Abraham believed it. Abraham, believing in that, and the man sick with palsy, believing in the words of Jesus, "Son, thy sins be forgiven thee," are both believing the Word of God.

But everyone, did Abraham commit sin or not? Did he lie or not? He lied very well. He deceived people, saying that his wife was his sister. Not only that, but he took another woman and had a son through her because he wanted a son. Think about it. You see Abraham in a good light because he is mentioned in the Bible, and that's why you just pass it by. But if Pastor Ock Soo Park was said to have taken another woman to bear a son because his wife could not bear a son, then wouldn't you say, "The world has gone mad"?

Suppose the assistant pastor of our church, Pastor Sung-hoon Kim, went somewhere one day and came home with another woman. And let's say that he also brought a child back with her.

"Who is this?"

"Pastor, this is my son."

"What? Pastor Kim, you had a son?"

"Yes, I wanted to have another son, so I took a pretty woman, slept with her one night, and now I have a son."

What should he do? Should he live with them now?

"Oh, no. What are we going to do? What are we going to do? This cannot be."

If our church members found out about this, then everyone would gossip, gossip, gossip, gossip. Such gossip would spread so fast. People have cellular phones nowadays, and through text messages, the whole church congregation would find out about this.

"Pastor Sung-hoon Kim and this other woman had a son together! And he brought them here. He's just a little kid, but he has really round, twinkling eyes."

"Oh no! Our church is ruined, ruined! It has been corrupted, corrupted!"

However, you look at Abraham in such a good light. Even though Abraham did such a thing, you just pass it by softly, don't you? Actually, that is quite unfair. When you're in a good mood, you just simply let it slip, but when you are in a bad mood, you become very picky. Of course, you must be this way because you are human. If you were perfect, then you'd be a machine.

Everyone, did Abraham sin or not? He deceived people saying his wife was his sister and he took his wife's handmaid and had a son by her. However, Abraham believed in the Word of God that said, "Your children shall be like the stars in the sky." That is why God says, "You are righteous! You are a righteous person!" without discretion. Because you live in the here and now you are accepting, but if you lived at that time and were living next door to Abraham, you would have said, "God, that's nonsense! How could Abraham be righteous? He made his handmaid his concubine and had a son by her! What's so righteous about that? He also lied. I don't know why God said that!" Isn't that what you would have said? If you were living next door to him, surely you would have gossiped and gossiped about this.

Therefore, the standard of righteousness that we know, and the standard of righteousness that God knows are different. Repeat after me.

For my thoughts are not your thoughts... saith the Lord.

Is there anyone among you who has the same thoughts as God? Raise your hand. God said that His thoughts are not as your thoughts. The standard of righteousness is different as well. There's only one who is righteous in the eyes of God and that is Jesus who is God. One day, when the lawyer said to Jesus, "Good Master, what should I do that I may inherit eternal life?" Jesus answered, "Why callest thou me good? There is no one good except God alone."

We are truly dirty and filthy humans, but we accepted the Word. That Word is God; that Word is Jesus. Abraham accepted the words that said, "You shall have children like the stars of the sky." Because the Word is God, God had entered and remained in Abraham's heart. When we receive the Word of God, God remains in our hearts. God is righteous; therefore, would I be righteous or unrighteous? God is holy, so would I be holy or unholy? I would be holy. I am holy!

Everyone, how does a woman have a child? Does she make a child out of clay and say, "Be a beautiful child. Be my baby." Is that how it is done? Babies are not made beautifully out of clay. No matter what kind of woman she is, if she receives the seed of a man, then her stomach will begin to bulge and she can have a son or a daughter. It's exactly the same. It is about us receiving the seed of the Word of God into our hearts.

There are two kinds of people. There are those who accept the seed of the Word of God, and when God says, "Son, thy sins be forgiven thee," are people who throw away their own thoughts. They say, "Ah, then my sins are forgiven," and they accept it like that; they are righteous. However, people who say, "What forgiveness of sin have I received? I have many sins. I am still a sinner. Lord, forgive me of my sins," do not accept the Word of God, but are people who hold on to their own thoughts. This person is evil, dirty, and should be cursed and destroyed for that.

A person is not destroyed because he committed murder, adultery, or theft. He is destroyed because he refuses the Word of God. On the other hand, people who receive the Word of God, not only accept the Word, but they accept Jesus Christ who is inside the Word. He enters you with the Word. The reason this person is righteous is because Jesus is righteous. Amen?

The Faithless Father of Faith

Now let us talk about the Bible. God spoke to Abraham in Genesis chapter 15, and the years passed by. The words we read today are in Genesis 17. One day, God appeared to

Abraham and said to him:

As for Sarai thy wife, thou shalt not call her name Sarai, but Sarah shall her name be. And I will bless her, and give thee a son also of her: yea, I will bless her, and she shall be a mother of nations; kings of people shall be of her.

Abraham heard this when he was 99 years old, and because Sarah was ten years younger than Abraham, she heard this when she was 89. Abraham was now very old. How old he must have been at 99. Sarah was very old as well. The two of them would sit down every day and talk about how old they had become.

"Ah, old man, why do I feel such a cold wind in my legs? Oh, my back. I'm out of breath. Now, we're both so old, aren't we, old man?"

"Ugh, grandma, you lost another tooth today, eh?"

They are so old. However, God appeared and said, "Now thou shalt not call her name Sarai but Sarah shall her name be, and she shall give unto you a son." Now this became a conflict.

Everyone, do you know what conflict is in Korean characters? It is *kal-deung*. Kal means arrow root. When arrow root vines wrap around something, they always wrap around to the left. Deung means wisteria. Wisteria vines, however, always wrap around to the right. When these two vines meet, they never wrap around things in the same direction but always in the opposite direction. In the same way, whenever there are two situations that do not fit one another at all, that is called a conflict, or *kal-deung*.

It would not be a conflict if Abraham's thoughts fit perfectly with the thoughts of God. If it's an arrow root, then it's an arrow root. If it's a wisteria, then it's a wisteria. When

God is turning to the right and Abraham is turning to the left, that's when there is a conflict. Everyone, if God says to you, "The sun will rise tomorrow," you would say, "Yes, God, thank you." If He says, "It will be cold in the winter," you would say, "Yes." Who would not be able to accept those things? But the things God does cannot be the same as what man does.

After I wrote the manuscript for the book, *The Secret of Forgiveness of Sin and Being Born Again*, I asked Pastor Han-gyu Lee, a Korean language teacher and literature scholar, to do the final revision. This pastor had revised the manuscript and brought it to me. He had fixed it so much with his red pen that the papers were all red. I looked carefully and they were no longer my words, but had become the words of Pastor Han-gyu Lee. "What should I do?" I felt a conflict. Upon much thought, I said, "Pastor Lee, this is not a Korean dictionary nor is this a Korean grammar book. It's okay to have some grammatical mistakes, so let's make a book that expresses my words, exactly as they are." In doing so, we did not repair the manuscript, but published it exactly as it was and printed the book, *The Secret of Forgiveness of Sin and Being Born Again*, part I. After the book came out, there was no one who said that the wording was wrong or that the grammar was wrong.

Actually, if you look at the book, there are many sentences that are grammatically incorrect. Even the sermons I give are not all grammatically correct. As I have given sermons with the Bible, I lack proper grammar. That is why I often make up phrases that are not grammatically correct. Once I said, "Living spiritual life is very difficult, but it is not difficult." I said that it was very difficult, but not difficult, and that made no sense, but that's exactly how it is in reality. Therefore, this cannot be expressed through the proper use of grammar.

It is also this way with the works of God. Because the works of God are beyond the scope of our understanding, there are so many things we do not understand. That is why we should not try to understand it with our thoughts. In the past, you needed a telephone wire to make a phone call. If you had to carry the phone around with you, you also had to carry the phone wires with you. But nowadays, you don't need telephone wires to use cellular phones. If a person who lived 50 years ago comes here and sees the children of today in the streets carrying around something small and laughing and talking by themselves, they would say, "They are crazy." Because they wouldn't understand, they would say, "What is he doing?" Everyone, people make things now that could never have been imagined at that time. A long time ago, I heard that Japan was making a camera that does not use film. So I thought, "How is that possible? That's nonsense." Later on, I found out, it was the digital camera that does not use film. Back then I couldn't understand, but now I understand it.

Because God is almighty, we cannot understand all the work He does. Therefore, people who know their weaknesses accept the Word of God, regarding it to be correct, even though they don't understand it. That is the position of faith! You cannot experience the world of God when you only accept the words that fit your own thoughts and are not able to accept those that do not fit your thoughts, saying things like, "How could that be? That's nonsense." Just like I said yesterday evening, when Jesus tells the man sick with palsy, "Rise, take up your bed, and go your way," and he answers,

"Jesus, if I could take up my bed and walk, would I be crazy enough to be lying here? Stop this nonsense, please. How can I pick my bed up and go? I can't walk," he cannot walk. "It shall be done according to your faith." Everyone, how could the woman who had an issue of blood for twelve years be healed simply by touching the cloak of Jesus? She should be taking medication. However, it works when you have faith. You are healed.

God told Abraham, "Your wife, Sarah, will have a son," and Abraham laughed. "How could a person 100 years old have a child? Sarah is 90." That is the heart of man. You too accept things when they fit and make sense to your eyes, but cannot accept things that do not fit your thoughts. "How could I have a child? I cannot do that!"

Let's look at verse 17.

Then Abraham fell upon his face, and laughed, and said in his heart, Shall a child be born unto him that is an hundred years old? and shall Sarah, that is ninety years old, bear?

That's right. How can a 100 year-old man have a child? The wife was 90 years old. This is something I always say. Even when young people have children, they say that they are becoming exhausted and going to die. I would be afraid if a 90 year-old grandmother got pregnant. Is that so or not? That is right.

When I was in Daejon, a sister in our church had gotten married when she was 40 and became pregnant. On a Sunday morning, I had to ask this sister about something, so I phoned her. While speaking to her on the phone, since I was busy, I told the sister, "I am busy right now, but you're going to come to church, right? I will speak to you at church." Right then, the sister said, "Pastor, I cannot go to church today."

"Why not?"

"Because I'm having morning sickness; I cannot move."

And I yelled at her.

"Sister, how old are you this year?"

"I am 42."

"You're over the age of 40, and this is your first birth. Do you think you can have the child without the grace of God? If you don't want to receive the grace of God, come or don't come, whatever. But if you want to receive the grace of God, come, even if you have to crawl. You need faith!"

Right then, the sister probably thought,

"The pastor of our church is so coldhearted! I bet there's not a drop of blood in him. Has he ever been pregnant? Has he ever had morning sickness? What does he know about my situation, that he just yells and tells me to come?"

It is obvious that she probably complained like that even though she said nothing. I just left her to complain and complain. Why? Because after the complaining she has to decide, "Shall I go, or not go?" This sister thought, "This is my first child and I am already past the age of 40. Can I truly have the child without the grace of God? What my pastor says is right. For me to receive the grace of God, even if I die, I should crawl and go." She made up her mind. She came to church and she was absolutely fine. The sister was completely amazed. "What's wrong with my body?" After the service, I spoke with that sister.

"I thought you couldn't come because you had morning sickness. How did you come here?"

"Pastor, I am completely healed! I have some business to take care of, so I'm going to drive my car to Cheongju."

"You can't even come to church. How can you go to Cheongju?"

"Pastor, I am completely healed."

"Yes, Sister, that's what faith is."

Faith is not only looking at the circumstances, but thinking, "When I am in this kind of situation, what would happen if God helps me?" and living life following that. When I saw this sister have a healthy son and run around holding him, I had the heart, "That's how you should live, not falling into circumstances."

If you don't have God, you will be caught by even the smallest of circumstances. When you get a disease, you will just be sick. And when hardships come, you will fall into the hardships. When debts come, you will fall into those debts. However, God is not bound by anything. God is not bound by traffic lights, nor is He caught by the nets in the sea. Live together with that God. How free it is! But for you to live together with that God, you must unite your heart with Him.

Abraham thought, humanistically, "Gee, God, how can a person 100 years old have a child? Sarah is 90 years old. This is nonsense." That was the heart that he had.

And Abraham said unto God, O that Ishmael might live before thee! (Genesis 17:18)

And God said, Sarah thy wife shall bear thee a son indeed; and thou shalt call his name Isaac: and I will establish my covenant with him for an everlasting covenant, and with his seed after him.(Genesis 17:19)

Abraham's heart changed as he listened to the Word of God once again.

"That's right. If God says that we will have a child, then we will have a child. It is God who can raise the dead and who makes man from the dust of the earth. What does it matter if someone is a hundred, a thousand, or ten thousand years old? We will have a son!"

The Bible is so great. Abraham was a person without faith in the beginning, but the process by which he entered into faith is written here. Do you know why it was written here? The process is the same with you. In the beginning, nobody has faith. When God speaks, people say, "Oh, that can't be. How could that be?" But when you listen to the voice of God afterwards and think about it again, you are able to have faith. Amen? If you could believe at once when you hear the Word, then such scriptures would not need to be written. Why would they have been written? They are saying, "Abraham was like that too, so don't be too disappointed in yourself. In the beginning, Abraham, who is the father of faith, also didn't have faith, so he had humanistic thoughts." God looks upon us, who have humanistic thoughts, sparingly. But if you continue to not believe all the way until the end, He will not look upon you sparingly. Understood?

Then I Will Have a Son!

In chapter 18, God appears to Sarah. Let's look at Genesis chapter 18 briefly. Chapter 18, verse 10.

And he said, I will certainly return unto thee according to the time of life; and, lo, Sarah thy wife shall have a son. And Sarah heard it in the tent door, which was behind him. Now Abraham and Sarah were old and well stricken in age; and it ceased to be with Sarah after the manner of women. Therefore Sarah laughed within herself, saying, After I am waxed old shall I have pleasure, my lord being old also? (Genesis 18:10-12)

Even in her own eyes, Sarah had become too old. It had already been fifteen years and she had no son. She gave her handmaid as a concubine unto Abraham to have a son and because she thought that she could not have one, right? If Sarah could bear a son herself, would she be crazy enough to send another woman into her husband's bedroom?

"I did that fifteen years ago because I could not have a son. Now fifteen years have passed; what son could I have at the age of 90?"

Everyone, this is not a story about Sarah, but a story about you. You are exactly like Abraham and Sarah. If it just ends here like this, then Sarah is a person who has no faith. But if she has faith here, then she becomes the forbearer of faith! Amen? Amen!

Everyone, look at this. You have your own thoughts when I say your sins are forgiven. "What sins are forgiven? I sin every day. I have no faith. I have to lie in order to run my business. Later on, when my sons get married, and I don't have to run this business anymore, then maybe I'll start believing. But I have to lie all the time right now. No, not me."

"Thy sins be forgiven thee."

"Sure, my sins are forgiven, but at my young age, I had to make money. I had three abortions. I don't think those sins were forgiven."

People have their own thoughts.

"Thy sins be forgiven thee."

"They all are forgiven, but my sin of stealing the church hoe, that seems to still remain."

Everyone, aren't these the thoughts of man? What human

does not have thoughts? In Abraham's thoughts, does he think he can have a son or not? There's no reason for you to curse Abraham if you put yourself in that kind of circumstance. Take the old grandmother sitting here in the front. It seems to me that you're not 80 yet. If God says to you, "Grandmother, you will have a son," wouldn't you say, "Oh my God"? This is not just about someone else, but put yourself in that kind of a situation. Take that grey-haired grandfather sitting in the back. If God says, "You will have a son," you would say, "Ha! Ha! God's pretty funny. That was funny. Does God crack jokes sometimes?"

However, God spoke.

And the LORD said unto Abraham, Wherefore did Sarah laugh, saying, Shall I of a surety bear a child, which am old? Is anything too hard for the LORD? (Genesis 18:13, 14)

Right then, Sarah was able to sense it.

"That's right! If God does it then it can be done!"

Everyone, if God says that your sins have been washed as white as snow, many of your thoughts come out and you say, "Oh, I have no faith. That makes no sense. I didn't do anything, so how can my sins be washed away? No, not me. My sins still remain. I don't think my sin of stealing the church hoe is forgiven. I don't think my sin of stealing is forgiven." Right then, God speaks.

"Is anything too hard for the Lord? If God washes it, He will wash it clean. God sent his son, Jesus Christ, and washed all your sins away."

"Amen! That's how it is, if God washes it. Jesus has washed it; how could my sins remain?"

Having that faith is having the same faith Abraham had

when he believed. Amen?

Everyone, have you become like Abraham? Abraham is the father of faith. Abraham was not able to have faith because he flew around on the clouds. He is exactly like us. He lied. He had a son through a concubine. Abraham was a human just like us. However, he had faith.

"You shall have a son."

"That makes no sense!"

"Is anything too hard for the Lord? Will it not be done even if God does it?"

"Oh yeah, that's right. Then, I will have a son!"

He believed it. Amen? That is how he became the father of faith. It is exactly the same with you.

"Everyone, all of your sins have been washed away and you do not have sin."

"But I still think that my sins remain."

Do your thoughts come forth or not?

"Son, thy sins be forgiven thee."

"How nice that would be, but I don't think it's like that with me."

Those thoughts of man well up within you.

"I remember your sins no more."

"Why wouldn't God remember my sins? He remembers them all."

That is how our thoughts are constantly. They are different from the heart of God. However, God asks us, "Is anything too hard for the Lord?" Everyone, is there anything that is too hard for God? Is there? Is there anything that is too hard for the Lord or not? There is nothing!

Every one of you sitting here this morning has committed many, many sins. Suppose you are people who have committed many, many sins. And ever since you were young, like Nolbu, who is one of the biggest villains of Korean fables, you did many terrible things. You ran horses over other people's pepper fields, nailed stakes into other people's pumpkins, kissed women who were carrying pots of water on their heads from the well, and kicked pregnant women in their stomachs. And let's suppose that has been that way for you ever since you were young and you were the biggest villain in this world. And let's say that all of the biggest villains of Seoul were gathered here at this one place. All of the most evil women and men are here. And let's suppose that in the village where you live, the people thought, "If only he weren't here, we could live. We would be so comfortable if he would just leave this place." Understand? This is just an example. Everyone, you are all villains. Okay? You have committed the most sins in the world. You have killed people like you would kill ants. Apart from your wife, you have fifteen other women you live with. You have done drugs, stolen, committed robbery, and have done everything there was to do out there.

Sin is boiling inside of you as we speak, but if God wanted to wash you, could He wash you or not? "How can I be washed? I can only be washed if I have a little bit of sin. I have so many." Just like those thoughts, would God say, "I don't think I could wash away your sins. I think you must go to hell"? Even if you are just a pile of sin, God is able to wash you as white as snow in a blink of an eye. There is nothing that God cannot do, but it is because we look with our thoughts, we are unable to believe.

In the beginning, Abraham had his own thoughts as well.

"How can I have a son? I cannot have a son. I am too

old. And my wife, look at her; she has an old crooked back, she has so many wrinkles, her hair is all grey, she has no strength, and she even runs out of breath when she walks a little bit. How can we have a son? Is having a son easy?"

Abraham and Sarah had such thoughts; just like us.

"Is anything too hard for the Lord?"

"That's right. If God does it, it can be done!"

And they believed. That is how Abraham became the father of faith. You are all the descendants of Abraham who believed. By believing in what? Believing, by faith, that Jesus has forgiven your sins. In your thoughts, you say, "I am a sinner. I have many sins I can't even mention. I am dirty." But if God makes you clean, why would you not be clean? If you have your own thoughts, you cannot accept the Word of God. Having the faith to believe in God is throwing your thoughts away and saying, "If the almighty God does it, then it can be done!" Amen?

Sarah, the Grandmother Who Received the Strength to Conceive

In Hebrews chapter 11, verse 11, it says that Sarah when she was past age received strength to conceive through faith. When God told Sarah, "You will have a son," inside, she said, "I am old and my master is old also. How can I have a son?" and she spoke her own thoughts. But when God said, "Sarah, why are you laughing? Is anything too hard for the Lord?" She was startled. "Ah, that's right! If God does it, I will have a son although I am old!" She believed. At first, she refused the Word according to her own thoughts, but with the faith to believe that she will have a son, the Word had entered inside of her. And the Word is God, isn't it? Therefore, because God entered inside of her, she began to receive the strength. *Sara herself received strength to conceive seed...*

"Old man, shall we go hiking? Do you want to play a game of tennis?"

"Is this granny crazy?"

"Crazy? I'm healthy like this because God protects me."

Everyone, my body used to be very weak. My heart was also weak. About three years ago, I didn't know how much longer I would be able to do conferences. I accepted almost every invitation I was given for conferences, and for one year I continually held conferences without rest. God gave me the strength. God gave me a healthy heart and a healthy body. And when this conference ends, I will be going to India. India is far away. My destination is in the hills and valleys, so after I get off the airplane, I have to ride in a car for many hours. I even heard that tigers appear there sometimes.

Everyone, truly there is nothing God cannot do. Do you think there is a single sin of yours God cannot clean? He cleans them all! Because God loves you, He was concerned that even one sin might remain, so He accomplished eternal redemption without leaving even a single sin remaining. He said, "Son, thy sins be forgiven thee." Faith is simply accepting those words. People who go to a cave and fast for 40 days and pray for 100 days are not people of faith. People of faith must eat food, put on clothes, and sleep as well. It's just that you must believe the Word of God rather than your thoughts, although it may not fit your heart. In your eyes, it surely seems that you cannot have a son. It ceased to be with Sarah after the manner of women, but she had a child through faith in the Word of God. Hallelujah! I praise the Lord.

A pastor's wife of our church had a lump on her womb. There was a large lump, so they needed to perform surgery and had to cut out her womb. The doctor almost removed her womb completely, but left just a little edge remaining on one side. She had not had a child during the first two years of her marriage. However, after receiving that surgery, eight years had passed, but she was still unable to bear a child. There are many people who cannot have children even though they have healthy wombs. She was a woman who had almost her whole womb removed and there was just a little piece remaining. How could she have a child? This pastor's wife one day was holding another sister's baby, when that sister said, "You have never had a child, so how could you know how to hold a baby?" And she snatched the baby away from her. She felt so wronged, and she was very upset.

"How could she do that? I am a pastor's wife. How could she do that to me?"

She groaned with pain inside and was very upset. Then another sister said something to her.

"You have never had a baby, so you don't know about these kinds of things," and she felt so mortified. So she knelt down before God and prayed.

"God, allow me to have a child as well."

She heard my sermon at the retreat about, "It ceased to be with the manner of women, with Abraham's wife, Sarah, but she had a child." Then faith entered her. "If that is true, then will God allow me have a child as well?" One day, she came to me after service and said, "Pastor, I have faith now. Please do the laying-on-of-hands prayer for me. I, too, will have a child. I believe that God will give me a child." So I did a laying-on-of-hands prayer for her. Amazingly, she did become pregnant. The child was growing in her womb, but there was a problem. When she received surgery before, in order to remove all the lumps, the doctor had to remove almost the entire womb. However, he had no choice but to leave a little of the womb remaining as well as a little of the lump. So in her womb, the child was growing and the lump was growing. It was such a difficult situation. But this pastor's wife had faith in her heart even during this time. "Ah, God allowed me to become pregnant. Then He will have me give birth to this child. God will protect me." She was ministering in Nonsan, and one day, she called me.

"Pastor, today I'm going to deliver."

I thought, "The minister is not too well off. I wonder if they have enough for the hospital delivery fees," so I asked them to stop by my house before they went. However, the minister said, "Pastor, we are busy, so we're just going to go." I told them to go, but after a couple of days, they came to see me with their son. I asked them, "You don't have any money. How did you pay the hospital fees?" When her in-laws heard that she had a son through the ways of God, although she originally could not have a child, they all gathered. Her sister, her sisters-in-law, her brothers-in-law, and her uncles-in-law all came together and said, "Alright, you pay for this. You pay for the hospital. You take care of this." They all brought one large package each.

Everyone, if God works, even a grandmother who is 80 years old can have a son. If God does it, can your sins not be washed clean? The fact that your sins remain means that you are committing the sin of despising God. The sin of despising the power of God!

"Even though He said so, God couldn't have washed my sins away."

It is because you despise God.

In the beginning, Abraham did not receive the Word of God and had his own thoughts. But afterwards, he accepted the Word. That is righteousness. That is the righteousness of Abraham! "How could I be righteous? I have sin." That is your own thought. In the Bible, God says, "I will remember your sins and iniquities no more. They are all washed away. They are washed whiter than snow." Now, like Abraham, you will say, "That's right. If God says that they are washed away, then they are washed away. I cannot see whether they have been washed away or not. But if God says that they are washed away then they are washed away," and accept it into your heart by believing in this.

Everyone, when you accept the Word, because the Word is Jesus, Jesus enters you and becomes your strength and your power. When Abraham's wife, Sarah, accepted the Word of God, the Word became the strength and power that allowed her to become pregnant and bear the child. Then that son had a son, and that son had a son, and they became the country of Israel today. And the words of God, "Your children shall be like the stars in the sky," were achieved.

It is the same with you. We have many sins and we are dirty, but God can wash our sins as white as snow, and He did wash them. If God did not wash our sins away, for the sake of saving face, He could have just said that He washed them away. But then God would be a liar, and He would never allow such a thing. At first, Abraham did not believe in the words that said, "Your children shall be like the stars in the sky." But when he quietly thought about it, he believed in those words because they are correct, and he became the father of faith. In the same way, in the beginning, you may say, "Are my sins washed away? Um, they are not washed away. I think my sins remain." Even though you may have that heart, but when you accept that the blood of Jesus clearly washed your sins away, by faith, you become people of faith. Because the Word is God, when you accept the Word, you become righteous and holy, and the power of God lives and works inside of you.

I Believed in One Word, and That Word Was God

When I was nineteen, I was always suffering because of sin. One day, I came to know that the blood of Jesus washed all of my sins away. I was able to believe that on the cross of Jesus, all of my sins were forgiven. I just believed that one thing, and Jesus, who was living within the Word, entered me. From that day on, my life began to change.

What a wonderful change in my life has been wrought
Since Jesus came into my heart

Jesus came into me. Not because I said, "God, I believe you! Please come into me!" but I just accepted the Word. "My sins are forgiven! I am clean! Amen. Thank you!" From then on, no matter where I went, Jesus was always with me, when I went into the army; when I went abroad; and when I was in Korea. This is a secret, but I once had a conference in China at a place called Jiang-Jia Dian. In China, even if you just give one sermon, they arrest you. And because I had a retreat scheduled for one week in the countryside, it was the same thing as saying, "Come and arrest me." Because I went to China, the missionaries in China said they were having a retreat. I couldn't say, "I'm scared. I'm not going to do it." Could I do such a thing? Since the answer was no, we had the retreat.

We made a brother stand lookout at the other end of the chapel. He was to give us a sign when the Chinese police came. I would then quickly cease preaching the sermon and hide, and a Chinese brother wearing a suit, would stand and act as if he was giving the sermon. So we had everything scripted to do this. While giving the sermon, I constantly looked at the brother who was standing lookout. If the brother moved just a little bit, I would get scared all of a sudden. After one hour, I would say, "God, we have finished one hour. Continue to help us." That is how we spent an entire week. It was the hour for the last sermon of the last day. I prayed after the sermon and after singing a hymn. I said, "In the name of Jesus, I pray. Amen." When I said, "Amen," and opened my eyes, there were hundreds of people still on their stomachs, not getting up. They were all crying. My heart was deeply moved.

We went to our quarters and one of the pastors said, "Pastor, there's a favor I need to ask of you. One hour from here, there's a place called San-Yuan Pu. There are many saints there waiting for you, Pastor. Could you go there and preach for just on hour?" In China, just because there is a retreat, it does not mean that just anyone could come. Because they must come secretly, thc headquarters assign how many people may attend. From this church, this number of people, and from that church, this number of people.... So only those, who had overcome those great odds were selected to come. Even if the people come, they don't even know where they're going. When they get on the bus, only one leader knows the destination and they continue to go in circles, when, all of a sudden, they get off. That is the site of the retreat.

Hundreds of people who were not able to attend the retreat gathered at San-Yuan Pu. They said, "It would be great if Pastor Park could stop by just once, and preach the Word." And they were waiting for me. "Really? Then let's go." It was a cold morning and they brought over a truck. I got in that truck and we went to San-Yuan Pu. When you leave from the chapel at Jiang-Jia Dian, there is a large T-intersection. At the entrance, there is a police post, and to the right, it leads to San-Yuan Pu. If you go to the left, it leads to the village and the driver was turning left. I asked the driver, "Why are you turning left?" and he said, "I apologize, but there was something I had to tell my younger brother today, but I forgot to tell him. It will just take five minutes, so I will tell him the message and then we will go." So we went to the village, turned back around, and headed towards San-Yuan Pu.

When we were at San-Yuan Pu, people came up to me and said, "Pastor, hurry up and hide! The police are coming after you!" And without looking back once, we got into a car and went to a place called, Maihwagu, entered a Chinese restaurant, and ordered food. Then I called to see what was going on. That morning, the police chief said, "Arrest Pastor Ock Soo Park," and he had given that command to every policeman. How? All of the cars coming out of the chapel were to be stopped. But because it was so cold that morning, the windshield was covered with frost, so they couldn't really see who was inside. And because the truck that I was on came down from the chapel and turned to the left and not to the right, the police thought, "That car is from this village. It's not coming from the chapel. It was just coming from that way for its own reasons." So, they let our car through. Afterwards, even though they stopped every car coming from the direction of the chapel, they could not find Pastor Ock Soo Park. Right then, I realized how serious this was. "God made me avoid this!" If I had tried to avoid this, I could not have done it. It is not just once or twice that God had me avoid dangers like this. There were many times that I had to go through these kinds of fatally dangerous situations.

I just accepted that one word that Jesus forgave my sins. However, that word was God. And because that God is inside of me, I am righteous. Through that God, I am holy. I have power. Today, since there are many people who come to our church, the common churches call us heretics and say all kinds of lies. But over the last 40 years, God was always with me, and He has protected me.

Everyone, don't do good things yourself. If the electricity comes into your house, that electricity runs the refrigerator, runs the washing machine, allows the TV to turn on, allows lights to turn on, and runs the air conditioner. Without electricity, you cannot do anything. Just as electricity does all of that work, if Jesus enters you, from then on, Jesus gives you a holy life, joy, protects your life, and washes your sins away to lead you to heaven. Jesus does everything.

Now, how can we accept Jesus? People who don't know how, pray, "God, I am a sinner! God, come into my heart!" But that is not how you accept Jesus. The Word is God. It is accepting the Word. By accepting the Word, Abraham became the father of faith. Just as Abraham did not accept the Word in the beginning, you, too, may refuse the Word with your thoughts in the beginning. But today, at this time, receive the Word! Then God will live and work powerfully within you. God will help and protect you, and He will never leave you your entire life.

9

Joseph's Tears

9.
Joseph's Tears

Good evening everyone. It is such a joyful and blessed evening. I have never seen you with this much joy. Today, the music of the Gracias Choir made us praise God from the center of our hearts, and I am so thankful. Tonight, I will read Genesis chapter 45. We will read from Genesis chapter 45, verse 1.

Then Joseph could not refrain himself before all them that stood by him; and he cried, Cause every man to go out from me. And there stood no man with him, while Joseph made himself known unto his brethren. And he wept aloud: and the Egyptians and the house of Pharaoh heard. And Joseph said unto his brethren, I am Joseph; doth my father yet live? And his brethren could not answer him; for they were troubled at his presence. And Joseph said unto his brethren, Come near to me, I pray you. And they came near. And he said, I am Joseph your brother, whom ye sold into Egypt. Now therefore be not grieved, nor angry with yourselves, that ye sold me hither: for God did send me before you to preserve life. For these two years hath the famine been in the land: and yet there are five years, in the which there shall neither be earing nor harvest. And God sent me before you to preserve you a posterity in the earth, and to save your lives by a great deliverance. So now it was not you that sent me hither, but God: and he hath made me a father to Pharaoh, and lord of all his house, and a ruler throughout all the land of Egypt. Haste ye, and go up to my father, and say unto him, Thus saith thy son Joseph, God hath made me lord of all Egypt: come down unto me, tarry not: And thou shalt dwell in the land of Goshen, and thou shalt be near unto me, thou, and thy children, and thy children's children, and thy flocks, and thy herds, and all that thou hast: And there will I nourish thee; for yet there are five years of famine; lest thou, and thy household, and all that thou hast, come to poverty. And, behold, your eyes see, and the eyes of my brother Benjamin, that it is my mouth that speaketh unto you. And ye shall tell my father of all my glory in Egypt, and of all that ye have seen; and ye shall haste and bring down my father hither. And he fell upon his brother Benjamin's neck, and wept; and Benjamin wept upon his neck. Moreover he kissed all his brethren, and wept upon them: and after that his brethren talked with him.

We read up to verse 15.

Make the Straw Rope Thin and Tight

Although I had gone to church, I lived wandering inside of sin. One day, I received the amazing grace of God and discovered myself. Before then, I thought that I was good, that I believed in God well, and that I was smart. But when I saw myself through the eyes of God, I discovered how filthy, dirty, and evil a human being I was. When I no longer trusted myself, denied myself, and could no longer believe in myself, I was strangely able to believe in God. The words of the Bible began to enter my heart by faith, and I was able to believe my sins were forgiven.

From then on, I read the Bible. The amazing thing was that no matter where I read, the Bible was about me, and I have come to know that all my sins were forgiven eternally. The Bible was so amazing, and as it began to work and live inside my heart, God began to work inside my heart. I am not a person who can stand here in such a place, but I know God has made me stand here. It is so amazing that God opened the way for me and I was able to boldly preach the words of God among the people who spoke ill of me and went against me. There would be no end if I were to talk about these things.

When I was able to preach the words of God this week, I didn't know which words to preach. There were so many things that I wanted to preach about. I selected a few of those things and began to lead the sermons and preach with true repentance and faith as the topic.

When we don't know what true repentance is, we repent for sins that appear outwardly, such as: stealing, committing adultery, and murder. We had disregarded that we are clusters of sin; humans who have sins constantly springing up. We had only said, "I have committed theft, adultery, and I have lied." Because sins are continually springing up inside of us, all we are able to do is continually repeat sinning and repenting, sinning and repenting. One day, I came to discover that the scariest thing was not that I was lying, stealing, or committing some other sins. But it was the sin continually springing up inside of me. This was the problem. After I recognized all my sins were resolved on the cross, infinite peace came upon me. Afterwards, I began to preach the gospel to many people. I saw many people truly becoming renewed and changed. I can't tell you how amazing it was.

This evening, we read about Joseph. The amazing thing about the story of Joseph is that, God reveals exactly the things that are in our hearts because He looks upon the heart.

A long time ago, there was a rich elderly man who lived in a lavish house. There were many servants living at that house. During the winter of a certain year, the term of servitude had ended and the day for them to return home had arrived.

"Tomorrow, I will be going home! I am going to go back to my house and meet my children. My life as a servant is over. This is great!"

The servants were sitting in their room, thinking about home, and sharing dreamy words about it. After dinner, the old man, who was the owner of the house, came to that room.

"Ahem! You are all here."

"What brings you down here, sir? Please, come in."

"You have done a very good job as you served in my house. Thank you. Because you are returning home tomorrow, I want you to rest tonight. But there is one thing that I forgot to mention. There is just one more thing that you must do."

"Sir, what is it? Please tell us. We'll be on it right away."

The old man brought a handful of straw and began to make straw ropes. After making the straw ropes for a while, he spoke to them.

"Make me thin, tough, and long straw ropes like this," he said, demonstrating how to make straw ropes.

"Yes, sir. We will do it."

"Then, I will be on my way."

After the old man left the room, the servants began to complain.

"This old man is too much! We are leaving tomorrow, and he is going to make us work till the last day? Can't he ever give us a break? Gee, that old man!"

"But what can we do? Let's make the ropes."

When you make straw ropes, you have to spit on your hands and pull hard to make them tight and thin. You can't make them very quickly if you make them thin.

"This is our last assignment. He is not going to say anything to us for making them a bit thick."

They took handfuls of straw, rubbed them together, and twisted them together. They quickly finished their bundle of straw and filled the place with ropes, although they were quite thick. Among the servants, there was a servant named, Tim. He was a servant who believed in God. This is a story I heard when I was in Sunday school. Tim followed the words of the master and made the ropes tight and thin.

"Hey Tim, do you think he is going to reward you for this? Forget it. We are leaving tomorrow. He is not going to say anything. Just make them like this. We have a long way to go tomorrow. Let's go to sleep."

"Hey, I don't know what the master will use these straw ropes for, but this is the last assignment from him. Since it is our last assignment, let's do it well. Make the ropes thin."

"Okay, go ahead. You do it."

The other servants heartlessly made the ropes together and tied them at the end. "Wow! We have made a lot," and they slept on the ropes. But all night long, Tim made the straw ropes tight and thin. It then became the next morning and the old man came down.

"Did you sleep well?"

"Yes, sir. Master, you have come."

"You worked hard last night as you made the straw ropes, didn't you?"

"No, not at all."

"Bring those straw ropes and follow me."

"What's he doing?"

The master went forward and the servants followed behind with the straw ropes they made. The master took them to the shack. Because the only one who could enter the shack was the master, and no one else was allowed in, it was a place the servants had never been to. From his waist, the master took out a key and clicked open the door of the shack and went in. The inside of the shack was dark, so he turned on the lamp and the shack became bright. "Follow me," said the master. Inside the shack, there was another door. With a key he opened it, and behind the door there were mountanis of brass coins. "Wow!" The servants were completely awed.

"This is all money, isn't it? These are all brass coins!"

"That's right."

"We didn't know you had this much money in your house!"

"I was able to make this much money because of your help. I am an old man. How much longer do I have to live? So I thought of giving this money to you. Now bring me the straw ropes that you made. These coins have holes in the middle of them. Stick your ropes through as many coins as you can."

Tim was able to run his long rope through many, many coins. He had one, two, three straw ropes full of coins and he was piling up more and more straw ropes full of coins. He threaded so many, and they were so heavy, that he couldn't pick them up. The master saw this and said, "I don't think you can carry all that. Put them in a wheelbarrow." He piled up all the coins he threaded with his straw ropes until the wheelbarrow was completely full.

"Tim, good work. Buy a farm, some fields, have lots of children, and live well."

"Master, thank you! Thank you!"

Tim struggled to push the wheelbarrow home.

The other servants made thick ropes, so would the coins fit? They didn't fit. They had to undo the ropes and remake their straw ropes. Even if they do remake some straw ropes, how many could they make? They made a small number of ropes and on those, they threaded only a few coins.

"Take that at least."

"Yes, Master."

That is how the story goes.

Everyone, the servants did not know the master's heart. If they knew that the master told them to make straw ropes because he had the heart to give them coins since he was getting old, they would have made straw ropes with tears in their eyes. They would have said, "Because the master loves us, he is telling us to make straw ropes so that we can thread them through the coins. Thank you. If had I known he would do this, I would have treated the master much better. I have been so wrong! Thank you!" But since they didn't know his heart, they said, "Gee, our master is too much. That old scrooge. We will be traveling very far tomorrow. Why can't he give us a day off? To make us work to the very last day; telling us to make straw ropes! Let's make them thick or however they turn out." Because the servants did not know the master's heart, he felt so disappointed. Although Tim took many coins with him, the master didn't hate him for it, but instead, was happy about it. Although it may have been a financial gain to the master because the other servants took fewer coins, the master was not happy about that at all.

After I received the forgiveness of sin and threw my thoughts away, the amazing thing was that I could see the heart of God, little by little, in the Bible. "Ah, this is the heart of God!" When I started this church, there were so many Presbyterian, Methodist, and Lutheran churches in Korea. It would have been very convenient for me to follow along with those churches. However, as I followed the guidance of the Word of God, I couldn't follow them. The churches were so corrupt, and they only lived within the power of the church. In Daegu, there is a place called Pa-dong. We started our church on the second floor of a Chinese restaurant called Hwashin Banjum in Pa-dong. Although we were few in number, the people who came to our church became free from sin and were born again, one by one. I was so thankful that God was working and living in my life.

Through the guidance of God, I was able to preach this gospel all over the world. However, people said all kinds of evil things about us like, "They are heretics. They are the Five Oceans Cult. They have service completely naked." I did witness while I was completely naked at a bathhouse before, but I never had a church service completely naked. It is too cold, so how could I do that? However, people don't listen to good things, but those kinds of things really attract their ears. So I was often persecuted, went through unspeakable suffering, and I was cursed at by many people. There were many sisters who were beaten by their husbands for attending our church. There were some sisters who were beaten and had their legs broken. I can't express all this in words. However, God was still together with us. That is why it is so glorious that I can speak about the forgiveness of sin in front of you. Because God is pleased with this, He is leading the hearts of those who are listening to the Word through the Holy Spirit. I am very thankful about that.

"Joseph Is Only Human, So One Day, He Will Take Revenge"

Joseph's brothers spoke among themselves.

"Now we are in big trouble. We sold Joseph!"

"Joseph said he will not seek revenge on us for our sin. Joseph is different from us, isn't he?"

"He said that, but will Joseph really not seek revenge on us? We said we wanted to kill Joseph. We threw Joseph into a waterless pit because we wanted to kill him. We sold Joseph, and he worked as a slave. He went to prison, and went through so many hardships and sufferings. Although

Joseph said that he wouldn't, but if he gets mad one day, he may take revenge on us! You go to Joseph's house and treat him well. Okay? Don't ever get on his nerves. When you see things, don't touch them. When you go to Joseph's house, don't even act like you like the things that are there. You have to keep Joseph in a good mood!"

The servants did not know the heart of their master since their hearts were different. In the same way, when we read the Bible, the thoughts of God and our thoughts are always different.

Once, our church brothers and sisters gathered money to send to the mission field. At the time, our church was small and I would count the money myself. Then I would give it to the brothers and tell them to do this and that. My son was in the first grade of elementary school at the time, and he saw me carefully counting the money. When I gave it to the brothers, he said, "Dad, I don't understand you."

"Son, what do you mean you don't understand me? What don't you understand?"

"Dad, I don't understand why you have so much money, but you don't buy yourself any ice cream."

"That is the difference between Daddy and you!"

Fathers are different from sons. What would happen if I was just like my son?

"Hey, Yeong Kook, I have money! Let's go get some ice cream!"

I would buy a box of ice cream and put it in the freezer. And if I eat some after breakfast and eat some after lunch, then what kind of a father would I be?

As I live with my wife, at times, we have differences of opinion.

"Honey, your thoughts and mine are different. That's why I am the husband. If you and I were exactly the same, who's the husband and who's the wife? Since you are the wife and I am the husband, and since the husband is the head of the household, our thoughts are different. All you have to do is follow me."

From time to time, what our church members are thinking and what I am thinking are different. A shepherd was taking his sheep home and it became evening. It was becoming dark and they were going up the hill. The sheep were getting tired and said they could not go any further.

"Let's sleep here and then go."

"No, you little rascals, if we sleep here, the wolves are going to come out, and we are going to die."

"I can't go. I'd rather have wolves come out and bite me and kill me. There are not going to be any wolves here."

"No, little ones, let's go!"

If they are hit with sticks, the sheep are not going to understand. The thoughts of the shepherd and the thoughts of the sheep are different. The thoughts of the church members and the thoughts of the pastor are all different. If the thoughts of the church members and the thoughts of the pastor are the same, what kind of a pastor would he be? What would happen if the thoughts of a father and the thoughts of a son were the same? The father would play video games all day with his son, go eat ice cream, and play around. What kind of a father is that? The thoughts of a pastor should be different from the thoughts of the church members. If they are the same, he is not qualified to be a pastor. A father should not have the same thoughts as his son. His thoughts should be ahead of his son's, and he should be able to look ahead.

Everyone, if the thoughts of the Lord are the same as ours, what kind of God would He be? God has thoughts that are different from ours. When you search the Bible to figure out the problems in your spiritual life, you will see that every problem in every chapter and every verse of the Bible arise because of the difference between our thoughts and God's thoughts. That is why repentance is absolutely necessary before you have faith. This repentance is not asking for forgiveness, saying, "I have stolen. I have committed adultery." Even though you may think that your thoughts are right, but because your thoughts are different from the thoughts of God, you must throw your thoughts away. We must feel out the heart of God and receive the heart of God into our heart. That is faith.

Joseph's brothers sold Joseph, and he was dragged to Egypt to become a slave. I don't know why the brothers hated their younger brother so much and were so eager to kill him, even though Joseph was their brother. Joseph was sold, tied to the back of a camel, and was dragged along into Egypt. The weather was hot and he was thirsty. Even when his shoe laces become undone, how could he tie them? He barely hung on to his shoes that were falling off and carried them in his hands. Then his feet were torn, he was exhausted, and he was in so much pain.

"Brothers, why did you hate me? Why have you sold me?"

Inside of Joseph's heart, he was filled with hatred and bitterness against his brothers. How agonizing it must have been to serve as a slave in Egypt. However, he received the grace of God, and in the house of Potiphar, he was recognized and became the ruler of the house. His life was getting a little better. But one day, Potiphar's wife began to seduce him. When he refused the temptation, she conspired against him, and sent him to prison. So he had to serve some time in prison.

"Brothers! You sold me, didn't you? I hope you are still alive! One day, I will have my vengeance!"

Such a heart began to boil inside of Joseph.

One day, however, Joseph became the governor. Even after having become the governor, Joseph's rage against his brothers wasn't resolved. After becoming the governor, he got married, and his wife became pregnant. One day, his wife asked him a question.

"Honey, when our child is born, what should we name him?"

"I'm not sure. What should we name him?"

At that moment, Joseph thought about his family.

"Is my father well? I wonder how my brothers are doing since they sold me."

He remembered the dream he had a long time ago. When Joseph had his sheaf, his sheaf stood up and his brothers' sheaves bowed down to his sheaf. The sun, the moon, and the eleven stars in the sky bowed down to him. Upon remembering these dreams, he was completely stunned.

"I am the governor. Those dreams have come true! I have become the governor according to those dreams. Exactly! According to those dreams, my brothers will come to me and bow down to me! The stars, the sun, and the whole world will come to me and bow down to me! That's right. Because my father loves me and would not have sent me to Egypt, God made my brothers hate me to send me here to make me the governor. It was not that my brothers hated me, but it was the will of God! I blamed my brothers because I didn't know!"

Upon knowing the will of God, the heart of bitterness and hatred toward his brothers disappeared from Joseph's heart.

Joseph's wife asked him once again.

"Honey, have you thought about a name for our son?"

"Let's name him Manasseh."

"What's Manasseh?"

"Manasseh means, 'to forget.'"

"Why would you name our son 'Forget,' or Manasseh?"

"I have forgotten all the hatred that I had against my brothers. I hated my brothers because I didn't know why they had sold me, but now I no longer have hatred against my brothers. I have no heart of revenge. I love my brothers! I have now forgotten everything! His name is Manasseh. Forget! Hey, Manasseh, hey, Forget!"

In Joseph's heart, he no longer remembers the evil sin of his brothers selling him, and he had forgotten it. So he named his son Manasseh. He named his son Forget.

The famine continued. And after seven years of prosperity, Egypt and the surrounding countries were out of food. Also in the land of Israel, Joseph's father, Jacob, and brothers were hungry. They heard that there was food in Egypt and they came to Egypt to buy food. Joseph was the governor, but was he selling the food because he had nothing to do? However, Joseph was there selling food. So the people working under him would continually ask:

"Governor, wouldn't it be okay for us to do this? Governor, why don't you go and rest?"

"Don't worry about it! I will be the one selling the food to foreigners."

Why did he do that? He surely knew that his brothers would come to buy food, so he looked carefully as he sold food.

"Treat them well, okay? Where did you people come from to buy food?"

"We are from Canaan."

"Is the famine severe in Canaan? Tell me about it."

"We have no food, whatsoever."

"Really? Then buy a lot of food here."

"Yes, Governor."

And people from Canaan would come and buy food.

"Then my brothers will come also!"

One day, he saw his brothers coming to buy food.

"My brothers! My brothers have come to buy food!"

I can't tell you everything that happened. But after so many things happened, he revealed himself to his brothers.

"Brothers, I am Joseph! I am Joseph, whom you sold to Egypt! Look at me."

His brothers were stunned, and when they looked at the governor, it really was Joseph.

"Oh! Governor!"

They thought, "Oh, no, we are all dead! We hated Joseph and tried to kill him, but now we are standing before Joseph! If we are killed, who will bring food back to our children?"

However, Joseph spoke.

"Therefore be not grieved, nor angry with yourselves, that ye sold me hither."

There are so many interesting things in the Bible. Now open the Bible. I will read from chapter 45, verse 5.

Now therefore be not grieved, nor angry with yourselves, that ye sold me hither: for God did send me before you to preserve life. For these two years hath the famine been in the land: and yet there are five years, in the which there shall neither be earing nor harvest. And God sent me before you to preserve you a posterity in the earth, and to save your lives by a great deliverance. So now it was not you that sent me hither, but God: and he hath made me a father to Pharaoh, and lord of all his house, and a ruler throughout all the land of Egypt. (Genesis 45:5-8)

Joseph spoke.

Therefore be not grieved, nor angry with yourselves, that ye sold me hither: for God did send me before you to preserve life.

Joseph knew the reason why his brothers had to sell him.

"The heart to hate and kill me arose in the hearts of my brothers to protect us in the time of famine. God had to make me the governor of Egypt, and in order to do that, He had to send me to Egypt. God knew my father would not send me because he loves me too much. Therefore, God put hatred in my brothers' hearts in order for them to sell me to Egypt."

Because Joseph knew that this was all the providence of God and that it was not his brothers who sold him, Joseph did not hate or have a heart of vengeance at all against his brothers. His heart was completely clean. Joseph stated his heart to his brothers. Let's read verse 5 together.

Now therefore be not grieved, nor angry with yourselves, that ye sold me hither: for God did send me before you to preserve life.

He explained it in detail like this, and said, "Now, brothers, I will not seek vengeance against you, and I will not be angry at you." He had said more than enough to resolve the hearts of his brothers. This is not just Joseph's lips, but it was his heart. It was his heart! Even if the brothers had accepted these words, they would not have addressed him as the younger brother of the past, saying, "Hey, little brother!"

But this is how they would have spoken.

"Brother, upon hearing your words, you are right. At the time, we didn't understand why we hated you so much. God did it to make you the governor. Now we know. Still, we do apologize, and we do feel bad."

"Brothers, now do you get it? Don't worry. I will never try to take revenge. I have no such things in my heart any more."

"Good. Good. We are brothers, brothers!"

"Now let us live happily together!"

How great that would have been. It would have been good if the brothers listened to Joseph's words and simply accepted them. However, they had their own thoughts. Why? Even though Joseph has the heart to forgive his brothers, in their hearts, if they were in Joseph's situation, they didn't think they could forgive. They saw it with their own thoughts. Therefore, they thought, "Joseph is a nice guy, but still, one day he will have his revenge. He is also a human, and we did try to kill him." That was the heart they had. So when they go to Joseph's house for his birthday party, they would argue with each other.

"Be good to Joseph! What if you make Joseph angry and he kills us? He is only human, you know. What are you going to do if he gets mad? Don't ever act impolitely to Joseph. What are you doing? Are you trying to get us killed?"

Joseph did not have that heart whatsoever, but they just fought among themselves.

God Has Forgotten All of Our Sins

Time passed, and Joseph's father, Jacob, passed away all of

a sudden. When the father passed away, the brothers began to worry.

"Joseph wanted to have revenge on us, but he held back, because if he killed us in front of Father, then Father would have been sad. Now that Father is dead, he might have his revenge on us. Oh, no, we are in big trouble!"

That was their thought.

Let me ask you a question. Did Joseph have a heart to seek revenge on his brothers even a little? Inside the heart of Joseph, the brothers' wrongdoings had been completely forgotten and erased and not even the least bit remained. So Joseph hoped to share that great amount of food he had and live happily together. However, Joseph's brothers didn't accept Joseph's heart, but followed their own thoughts instead and said, "Joseph might take his revenge and kill us." They fell into their own thoughts.

Lastly, we will look at one place in the Bible, Genesis chapter 50, starting from verse 15:

And when Joseph's brethren saw that their father was dead, they said, Joseph will peradventure hate us, and will certainly requite us all the evil which we did unto him. And they sent a messenger unto Joseph, saying, Thy father did command before he died, saying, So shall ye say unto Joseph, Forgive, I pray thee now, the trespass of thy brethren, and their sin; for they did unto thee evil: and now, we pray thee, forgive the trespass of the servants of the God of thy father. And Joseph wept when they spake unto him. (Genesis 50: 15-17)

Joseph was extremely sad and thought:

"I told my brothers that I would forgive them, but they have yet to receive my words. My brothers are still afraid of me.

They didn't believe me. I sincerely spoke to them, but they didn't believe my words."

"Brothers, why don't you believe my words? Brothers!"

Joseph cried.

"Brothers, didn't I tell you? You sold me, but it wasn't you who sold me, but God wanted to preserve our lives and to make me the governor. It was God who did this! Brothers, I will never seek revenge on you. How can I take the place of God? Brothers, I will take care of you and raise your children. Don't worry!"

As I read Genesis, I often thought a lot about these words.

"Why did God record these words? Why did God want us to hear these words?"

Joseph forgave all of his brothers' sins, but since the brothers didn't believe Joseph's words, they thought that their sins still remained. God has illustrated the heart of people in this world today. God sent Jesus Christ, His son, to this earth. When He was crucified, all of your sins were crucified along with Him. That's why Manasseh was born in the heart of God. Manasseh! Forget! All the sins that humans have committed and all of our wrongdoings have been erased and have ended in the heart of God. In the heart of God!

In the heart of Joseph, his brothers' sins were forgiven, and he told them that he remembered those sins no more. However, the brothers didn't accept Joseph's heart but thought with their own hearts, "Joseph will seek vengeance upon us. While Father was alive, he was unable to have his revenge, but since Father has passed away, he may kill us. Then what are we going to do?" They always said these words in fear, and they lived with the guilt of the sin. Joseph was so heartbroken.

"Brothers, I told you so sincerely. Brothers, why don't you believe me, and think that I will seek revenge on you? I am so heartbroken. Heartbroken!"

Joseph wept.

Everyone, if we do not believe in Jesus and have our own thoughts, we make the Lord sad. Because the Lord loved us, He forgave all of our sins on the cross. We humans have sinned not because we lack determination and will; it is because Adam and Eve had sinned, and the characteristics of sin entered inside of us. Because of that, Jesus was crucified and He forgave all of our sins. Now God tells us, "Your sins are forgiven. I have purified you. I do not remember your sins. I have forgotten them." This is what He says. However, according to our thoughts, we humans say, "I have so many sins. How can I not have sin? I am a sinner, God!"

I once went to the Mt. Juam prayer house in the city of Daegu. Since it was on April 5th, which is a holiday, many people had come to pray. In the mountain valley, people were crying and saying, "God! Forgive me!" I was getting the chills, and it made me shiver. They were doing it with all their hearts. However, God would be saying the same thing Joseph said.

"I told you I forgave you. I told you I don't remember your sins. Why don't you accept my words, and why do you only think with your own thoughts?"

When you read the Bible, there are so many people who do not think with the heart of God but act according to their own heart in every verse. If they think that they have sin in their own thoughts, they don't think about what God may think, but they say they have sin and break the heart of God. And there are so many people who make the death of Jesus

Christ on the cross vain.

Loving folks, though you may have been this way until now, throw away your thoughts now. No matter how your thoughts may be, do not believe your own hearts but believe in the heart of God and receive the words of Jesus.

"You have sold me to Egypt. Do not be grieved nor angry with yourselves that you sold me to Egypt. God sent me before you to preserve life. Therefore, it is not you who have sent me here, but God."

If that is what Joseph says, no matter how they are, they can say, "Brother, is that so? You mean you do not have a heart to hate us? Thank you, Brother. Thank you!"

How great it would have been if Joseph's brothers had lived with reconciled hearts with Joseph. Though they lived in one house and though they lived together in the land of Egypt, the brothers thought, "Joseph may seek revenge on us. Joseph might kill us." They always had that heart. How tormented Joseph must have been! How saddened he must have been!

Everyone, as I read this Bible, what I feel is that the foolish heart Joseph's brothers had is the same heart churchgoers all over the world have. This is something that saddens God. Let's turn our hearts around! Let's change our hearts so that God will be pleased! In the eyes of his brothers, Joseph would seek revenge, yet they should not have believed in that heart; they had to receive Joseph's words. Although it seems that you have sin and although you may feel that your sins are not forgiven, ignore your thoughts and believe what the living words of God say. Let us accept that!

From now on, let us not live according to our own

thoughts, but by the heart of God and by the Word of God. No matter if it may seem that you have sin, if the Word says that you do not have any, then you do not. No matter how evil you may be, if God says that He doesn't remember your sins, then He doesn't remember them. Do not believe in yourselves or your thoughts, but believe in the words of God. That is what pleases God.

The Word Says that My Sins Are Washed Away

Recently through a program called the Good News Corps, we gathered college students to send them as missionaries all over the world. We had basic training and 650 students participated. We recruited candidates among college students and received 2,100 applications. At the end of this year, we will select 700 people and train them to be sent out as missionaries in 2006. In order to do that, we held an orientation on October 3rd, and from October 27th to the 30th, we held a workshop and trained the students for four days.

The students changed so much in four days. This afternoon we had a meeting here with those students. The students performed a skit of the life of a student who was in the process of earning a doctorate. Ever since she was young, she heard that she was ugly. She was scolded by her father and mother for not being very smart, and she was always rejected by her classmates. This student, who lived like that, gave a testimony about how she had changed through attending the Good News Corps and receiving the training for four days. When I saw that student, she was so beautiful. People speak of their own greatness and their intelligence, but they hide their dirty and bad things. But this student spoke in detail about how she was despised and put down.

"How could this be?"

At the conference in Ulsan, the Good News Corps students from the Youngnam region gathered at the Ulsan KBS Hall and we had a meeting. There, we saw a skit about a different female student. That student also attended the Good News Corps, and over the four days of training, she received change and was born again. We all cried as we saw this student's life. I can't tell you how tearful I was.

During the Good News Corps training, students often ask me, "Pastor, how are we going to change in four days?"

"Until now, as you went to church, you tried to listen to the Word of God and tried to change yourself. That's why it didn't work. Now, don't try to change yourself, but empty your heart and receive the heart of Jesus. When the heart of Jesus enters, you will automatically change. You will change."

Yesterday, after the sermon, a few people came to speak with me.

"Pastor, I am a pastor, but I have become born again during this conference."

"I am an elder, but I received forgiveness of my sins now."

Everyone, this is not something that Pastor Ock Soo Park is doing. Instead, it is the Holy Spirit working inside of us.

Everyone, until now, you didn't believe others, but you only believed in your thoughts. You just lived according to whatever thoughts you had. The greatest people are people who know how to throw away their thoughts and those who know how to defeat their own thoughts. When you look at your own thoughts, these are the thoughts you have: "How could I have no sin? I still have sin." Although Joseph's brothers fell into those thoughts, if you do not accept those thoughts, you can throw them away and say, "That is how my thoughts are, but God says that my sins are washed away."

What path will you follow, everyone? Will you take the path the Christianity of the world is taking, or take the path the Word of God is taking? Although all of Christianity in this world says, "You are sinners," I really believe that you will not follow that way, but stand on the side of the Word of God!

The story of Joseph and the relationship between he and his brothers that we spoke about tonight illustrate the relationship between God and us. Joseph told his brothers, "Brothers, your sin has been erased from my heart. I will not hate you, brothers." Then, they should simply have accepted those words. However, the brothers said, "No. Joseph will have his revenge. There is no way that Joseph will not take revenge. We have committed such a terrible sin. We have treated Joseph very badly," and had their own thoughts. That was what tormented Joseph. Today, you also have your thoughts, and if you think, "I still have sin. I have many sins," then you are tormenting the Lord. Throw away your thoughts from this time forward. Although Joseph's brothers did not believe the words of Joseph, let us believe in the words of God. Amen?

In the words that we talked about yesterday, Jesus said, "Son, thy sins be forgiven thee." These are words that He has spoken to us. Let's read one more Bible verse. Romans chapter 8, verse 30.

Moreover whom he did predestinate, them he also called:

and whom he called, them he also justified: and whom he justified, them he also glorified.

God said that He has called us and justified us. Why? The blood of Jesus washed away all our sins. I don't know how it may seem in your eyes, but in the eyes of God, all your sins have been washed away. Are the eyes of God more accurate or are your thoughts more accurate? The eyes of God are more accurate. That is why we believe in the Word of God, and not in our thoughts.

Verse 33:

Who shall lay any thing to the charge of God's elect? It is God that justifieth.

Who shall lay anything to the charge of God's elect? This is such a thankful thing. When I used to go to church a long time ago, I committed sins every day. I thought my sins would never be washed away my entire life. That was just my own thought. These words say that God has washed my sins away and I am righteous. I decided to throw my thoughts away and believed in these words. Throw everything away as well, and believe in the words of God that you are righteous! Do you believe? Those of you who believe say amen. Amen! Hallelujah!

Everyone, what would please God? God will be pleased if you are loyal and give offerings, but there is nothing that pleases God more than you believing that your sins have been washed as white as snow. If you don't believe in that fact, you make God sad. Now, everyone, no matter who says what, don't listen to anything else. Don't listen to your thoughts, but believe in the words of God exactly as they are.

"God said that I am justified. God said that He doesn't remember my sins. Jesus washed away my sins as white as snow. Sure, I have committed many sins, but I am not a sinner anymore!"

God will be most satisfied when you have this kind of faith, not your own thoughts. Jesus would say, "I am glad I was crucified on the cross. That's how this multitude of people were freed from their sins!" I believe Jesus would say that and become truly happy. Now let us not worry God. Everyone, do not worry the Holy Spirit. I hope that you will throw all of your thoughts away and stand in the midst of the faith to believe in the promise of God.